24.00

The Soviet Invasion
of Afghanistan

The Soviet Invasion of Afghanistan

A Study in the Use of Force in Soviet Foreign Policy

Joseph J. Collins
U.S. Army

Lexington Books
D.C. Heath and Company/Lexington, Massachusetts/Toronto

Library of Congress Cataloging-in-Publication Data

Collins, Joseph J.
  The Soviet Invasion of Afghanistan.

  Bibliography: p.
  Includes index.
  1. Afghanistan—History—Soviet occupation,
1979–   . 2. Soviet Union—Military policy.
I. Title.
DS371.2.C65   1985   958'.1044   85–45167
ISBN 0–669–11259–3 (alk. paper)

Copyright © 1986 by D.C. Heath and Company

All rights reserved. No part of this publication may be reproduced or transmitted in any form or by any means, electronic or mechanical, including photocopy, recording, or any information storage or retrieval system, without permission in writing from the publisher.

Published simultaneously in Canada
Printed in the United States of America
Casebound International Standard Book Number: 0–669–11259–3
Library of Congress Catalog Card Number: 85–45167

The paper used in this publication meets the minimum requirements of American National Standard for Information Sciences—Permanence of Paper for Printed Library Materials, ANSI Z39.48–1984.

*To Anita,
whose patient love
sustains us.*

Contents

List of Tables ix

Acknowledgments xi

Introduction xiii

1. Russian/Soviet-Afghan Relations, 1838–1945 1

   Land, People, Culture 1
   Historical Summary: 1838–1918 4
   1919–1945 8

2. Soviet-Afghan Relations, 1945–1973 17

   1945–1963 17
   1963–1973 26
   Evolution of the People's Democratic Party of Afghanistan 28
   Summary 29

3. Soviet-Afghan Relations, 1973–1978:
   From Revolution to Revolution 33

   The Daoud Coup 33
   The Changing International Environment 35
   Soviet-Afghan Relations, 1973–1975 36
   Pursuing Nonalignment: Afghan Initiatives, Soviet Reactions 37
   Soviet-Afghan Relations, 1975–1978 38
   PDPA Activities 41

4. The Saur Revolution: April 1978–August 1979 47

   The Coup 48
   Soviet-Afghan Relations After the Coup 52
   The New Government 54
   The U.S. Reaction 56
   The Death of Ambassador Dubs 58
   The Herat Massacre and Beyond 59

5. **From Revolution to Disintegration, August–December 1979   65**

   Prelude to Invasion   65
   The Soviet Estimate of the Situation in Afghanistan   69
   Amin's Final Days   71

6. **Invasion, Consolidation, and Reaction   77**

   Invasion   77
   The Karmal Government   83
   International Reaction   85
   Consolidation and Damage Limitation, January–July 1980   89

7. **Soviet Motives for the Invasion of Afghanistan: The Background Factors   99**

   Spurious and Unsupported Explanations   99
   Background Factors   108

8. **Soviet Motives for the Invasion of Afghanistan: The Immediate Factors   123**

   The Pressure of Events   123
   Soviet Security Concerns and Commitments   124
   Absence of Constraints   133

9. **The Use of Force in Afghanistan, June 1980–December 1984   139**

   The Domestic Political Situation in Afghanistan   139
   Current Military Operations   144
   Soviet Foreign Policy   152

10. **Conclusions   165**

References   177

Index   191

About the Author   197

Tables

2–1. Volume of Soviet-Afghan Trade   24
3–1. Soviet-Afghan Trade, 1975–1977   40
4–1. Alignment of Forces by Unit, April 27   50
7–1. Ranges of Selected Soviet Aircraft   104
7–2. Soviet Build-up in Nuclear and Conventional Forces, 1964–1980   112
9–1. Number of Registered Afghan Refugees in Pakistan   143

Acknowledgments

This study, although it bears only the author's name, could not have been completed without the generous assistance of many teachers, colleagues, and friends. Prof. George E. Hudson of Wittenberg University read the initial draft and made significant comments on both style and content. At Columbia University, Marshall D. Shulman and Zalmay Khalilzad guided my research efforts and set a high example of scholarly excellence. Many of my colleagues in the Department of Social Sciences, U.S. Military Academy provided useful comments on various parts of the study. I owe an especially great debt to Colonels Lee D. Olvey and James Golden. I must also express my appreciation to Mr. Henry Bradsher and Dr. Louis Dupree who generously lent me a large number of documents which they had used in their own research. Ms. Robin Gee and Ms. Vicky Lilos patiently and expertly typed the numerous drafts.

My family undoubtedly gave the most to this cause. Were it not for the love and encouragement of Joseph Jr., Jude, and my wife, Anita, this project would never have come to fruition.

Finally, despite the help of those mentioned above, any mistakes or omissions in this book are my sole responsibility. It must also be stated at the outset that the material which follows does not purport to represent the policy or the interpretation of the Department of Defense, the Department of the Army, or any other government agency.

Introduction

The Soviet invasion of Afghanistan was an event of unusual significance for many aspects of postwar international politics. It was the first time since the end of World War II that Soviet ground forces engaged in combat outside the Warsaw Pact area. No longer limited to advisers and proxies, the Soviet military became directly involved in an internal Third World conflict. The invasion adversely affected Soviet relations with the developing world and added to Western fears concerning the future course of Soviet foreign policy in the Middle East and South Asia. Even more ominously, the Soviet invasion appeared to some analysts as the meeting place between growing Soviet military power and the more aggressive tenets of Marxist-Leninist doctrine. Finally, the Soviet invasion again brought into question the value and the future of a superpower detente. As one Soviet analyst told Robert Legvold, "We broke the rules and we know it. In Angola the rules were ambiguous. Not in Afghanistan."[1]

While the invasion of Afghanistan appeared at the time to be yet another dramatic extension of Soviet influence, with the same promise of success already achieved by proxy in Angola and Ethiopia, today, more than five years later, Soviet forces are still fighting from insecure base areas to maintain their hold on the cities and their ground lines of communication back to the USSR. Soviet efforts to rebuild the Afghan regime have generally failed, and, if anything, the resistance now exercises de facto control over more of the countryside than it did in 1980. The vaunted Soviet Army—terror tactics aside—has shown itself to be operationally impotent in Afghanistan. Having built an army for World War III on the plains of Europe, the Soviets are finding that it is not performing well in an unpopular counterinsurgency in the mountains of South Asia.

The work which follows will analyze the Soviet use of force in Afghanistan. More specifically, this work—subject to the limitations imposed by the available, unclassified sources—will attempt to answer the following questions:

1. What were the Soviet motives for invading Afghanistan? What role was played by conditions internal to Afghanistan, and what role was played by exogenous factors, such as Soviet-U.S. relations?

2. How was the invasion conducted and how have subsequent military operations been prosecuted? What is the relationship between the methods chosen and the Soviet motives for the initial invasion?
3. How does the Soviet invasion of Afghanistan fit the commonly accepted propositions that describe how and under what conditions the Soviets have previously used force in support of their foreign policy? How can one explain the aspects of this case that do not fit the theoretical propositions?
4. What conclusions may be drawn from the Soviet invasion of Afghanistan regarding changing trends in Soviet foreign policy?

The first three chapters will analyze Russian/Soviet-Afghan relations up to 1978. Chapters 4 and 5 will cover Afghanistan under the Marxist regime of the People's Democratic Party and the start of the insurgency there. Chapter 6 will describe in detail the Soviet invasion and subsequent Soviet policy up to June 1980. Chapters 7 and 8 will analyze Soviet motives for the invasion and Chapter 9 will look at Soviet policy towards Afghanistan from June 1980 to December 1984.

A word about sources is in order. Since much of this work concerns the Soviet perspective on events, Soviet materials, particularly the official statements of the Soviet and Afghan leadership, will serve as the principal sources for this work. These materials will be reinforced where necessary by U.S. government documents, interviews, and many of the excellent secondary works that have appeared since the invasion.

In spite of the tremendous volume of all of these materials, it is clear that not all of the data that one would wish for are available. Both the Soviets and the Afghan resistance have concealed pertinent information for their own purposes. The primitive nature of the communication systems within Afghanistan and the decentralized nature of the war also make accurate analysis very difficult. Moreover, some of the materials relevant to this work deal with coups or covert operations which, by necessity, are secretive activities. Unfortunately, many of the principals in these activities are now dead.

The analyst's job is made tougher by the fact that there is no commonly agreed upon theory on the nature of Soviet foreign policy in general and on some aspects of its use of force in particular. Some analysts, like Harvard's Richard Pipes, see an aggressive Soviet Union following an indirect but deliberate plan aimed at separating Western Europe and Japan from the United States. Others, like Robert Legvold of the Harriman Institute at Columbia University, see the Soviet Union as "gardener" not "architect," exploiting opportunities that it had little role in creating. Brookings' Raymond Garthoff emphasizes the deterrent role of Soviet military power as its "principal" function.[2] An analyst firmly wedded to any of these beliefs will, of course, tend to evaluate the events in Afghanistan through his or her own conceptual lens.

Finally, the existing information is in itself a problem. Any author who attempts to decode Soviet sources faces an uphill struggle complicated by the nature of propaganda and by his or her own analytical biases. In that respect, I can only hope that my interpretations in this study will sharpen the analytical focus of other scholars who will deal with these issues in the future with better information and more objectivity.

Notes

1. Legvold, "Containment Without Confrontation," p. 81.
2. Richard Pipes, "Soviet Global Strategy," *Commentary,* April 1980, pp. 31–39; Robert Legvold, "The Nature of Soviet Power," *Foreign Affairs* 56 (October 1977), p. 60; and Raymond Garthoff, "Mutual Deterrence and Strategic Arms Limitation in Soviet Policy," *Strategic Review* (Fall 1982), p. 37.

1
Russian/Soviet-Afghan Relations, 1838–1945

To gain a complete picture of contemporary Soviet-Afghan relations, it is instructive to look at the relations between the two countries in the nineteenth and twentieth centuries, in order to observe the role that each state played in the relationship and in the international system as a whole. More specifically, one must determine whether Soviet policy toward Afghanistan changed in the postwar era and again after the communist coup in 1978, or whether the communist coup and the subsequent invasion were the logical consequences of an Imperial Russian and/or an expansionist Soviet foreign policy. Before directly addressing these issues, however, it will be necessary to examine the geographic and demographic characteristics of Afghanistan which have, to a large extent, shaped its role in international affairs.

Land, People, Culture

Afghanistan is a landlocked, mountainous country which is bordered on the north by the Soviet Union (1500 miles), on the west by Iran (550 miles), on the south and east by Pakistan (1500 miles), and on the extreme northeast by the People's Republic of China (50 miles). About 260,000 square miles, roughly equivalent in size to the state of Texas, the country is sliced from the northeast to the southwest by the Pamir Mountains and the Hindu Kush. The former are a narrow chain of mountains covering the Wakhan Corridor which connects Afghanistan with the People's Republic of China. The Pamirs run to 7,500 meters in height. The Hindu Kush, which covers nearly half of Afghanistan, contains peaks as high as 5,000 meters. More than 80 percent of Afghanistan can be classified as desert or semidesert. The climate features hot, dry summers and cold winters.[1]

Economically, Afghanistan can be considered underdeveloped by any standard. In 1978, per capita income was only $168 per year. Literacy is estimated at only 10 percent of a population whose life expectancy is currently 40 years. Subsistence agriculture and herding are the principal occupations of the nearly 90 percent of the population who live in rural areas. Only 12 percent of the land is suitable for farming, and only half of this expanse is cultivated. Natural gas (after 1967), fruits, nuts, and karakul (Persian Lamb) pelts are the nation's principal exports.

The major population centers are the cities of Kabul (population 800,000 in 1978), Kandahar (230,000), Herat (150,000) and Mazar-i-Sharif (100,000). Travel and transport are difficult because of the terrain and the virtual absence of railroads. The main hard-surfaced road system, depicted on map 1–1, is a circular network which connects the major cities. Two-thirds of this system was constructed with Soviet aid. The crown jewel of this network is the more than mile-long Salang Tunnel, constructed by the Soviets in the early 1960s, which breaches the Hindu Kush and connects Kabul to the northern portion of the country and the Soviet Union.

There are no scientific estimates of Afghanistan's population. A 1979 Afghan government estimate put the population at 15.54 million.[2] The country is ethnically and linguistically mixed. The largest and politically the most dominant group are the Pushtuns, at least 6 million of whom reside full-time in Afghanistan with, before the war, another 3–4.5 million living in Pakistan. Up to the mid-1960s, as many as 300,000 Pushtuns may have moved nomadically between the two countries. The next largest groups are Tajiks (3 million), Uzbeks (1.5 million), and the Baluch (100,000).[3] Although Pushtu speakers outnumber all others, the lingua franca is Dari (Afghan Persian).

As one might expect, imposing national unity on such a patchwork of groups has been a perennial problem. To this day, the essential social dynamic is clan or tribal loyalty. Although before 1978 nearly 42 percent of the land was held in units of twenty hectares or more, landlord-tenant relations were governed by a tradition which rarely infringed on an Afghan's "pride in his dignity and worth as an individual." One noted authority summed up the Pushtun character as one of a "warlike nature . . . a fanatical disposition and a passionate love of freedom."[4] Louis Dupree, perhaps the world's foremost expert on Afghan culture and society, characterized Afghan culture as seen through Afghan folklore and music as follows:

> [T]heir suspicion of outsiders is modified by a traditional code of hospitality; they believe but seldom worship; they are ruggedly irreligious unless an outsider challenges their beliefs; their brutality is tempered with the love of beauty; dynamic when work is to be done, they are easily swayed to indolence; their avarice is combined with impetuous generosity; they have an anarchistic love of individual freedom softened by the accepted rule of their aristocratic khans; their masculine supe-

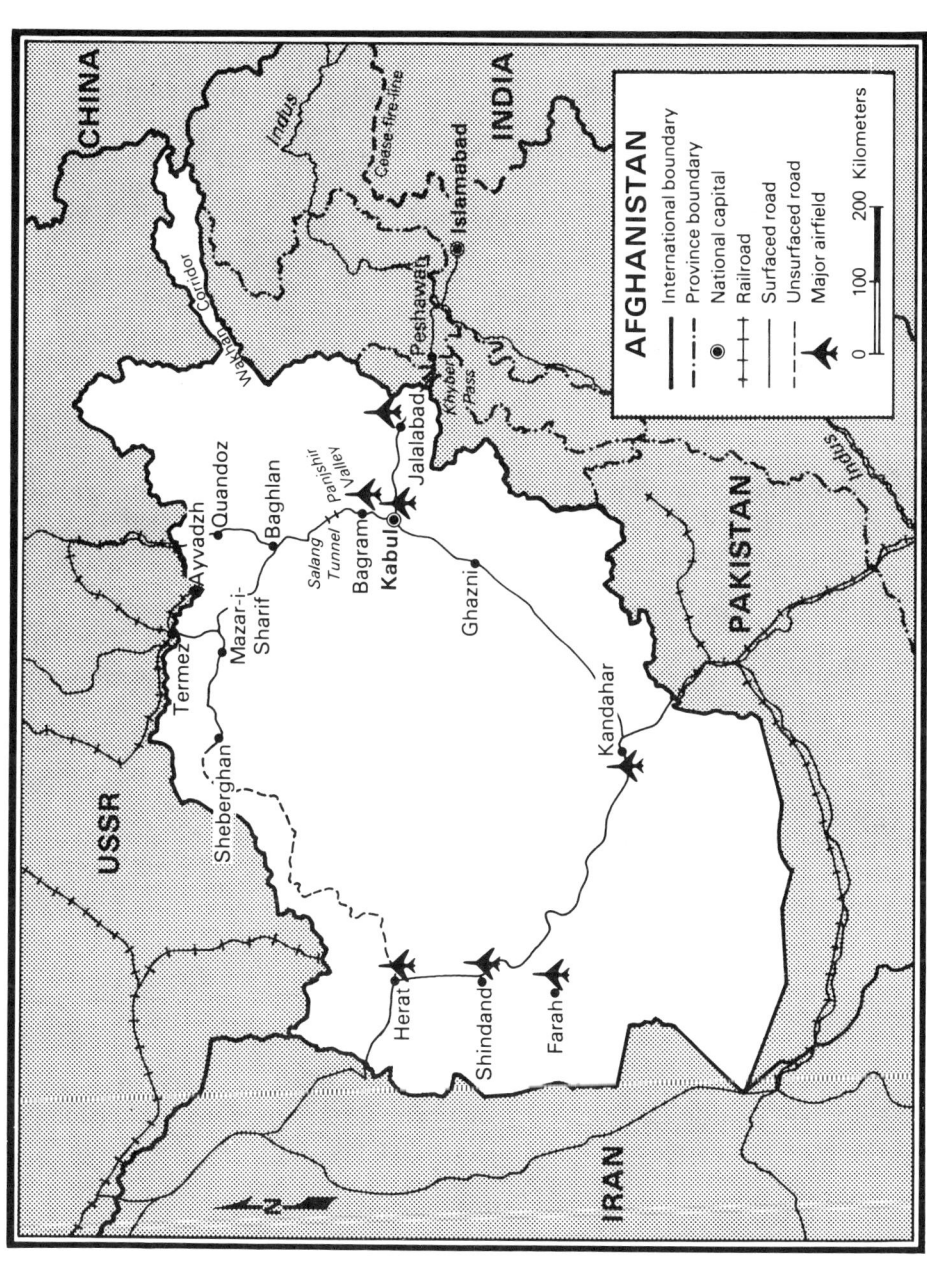

Source: Joseph J. Collins, "The Soviet Afghan War: The First Four Years," *Parameters* 14 (Summer 1984):50.

Map 1–1. Afghanistan

4 • *The Soviet Invasion of Afghanistan*

riority complex tacitly recognizes women's rights; their love of isolation is overlaid by curiosity about the outside world.[5]

In short, cultural contradictions typify the Afghan way of life.

Though the various ethnic groups in Afghanistan agree on little except their devotion to Islam (approximately 90 percent Sunni sect) and resistance to foreign domination, the rural populations generally live by strict codes of conduct which control intergroup and intragroup behavior. One such code, the *Pushtunwali,* is illustrative of the rules by which many Afghans live:

> To avenge blood.
> To fight to the death for a person who has taken refuge with me . . .
> To be hospitable and provide for the safety . . . of guests.
> To refrain from killing a woman, a Hindu, a minstrel, or a boy not yet circumcised . . .
> To punish all adulterers with death.
> To refrain from killing a man who has entered a mosque or the shrine of a holy man . . . also to spare a man in battle who begs for quarter.[6]

Historical Summary: 1838–1918

Russian-Afghan relations during the period 1838–1918 reflect the interacting interests of Tsarist Russian, Afghanistan, and Great Britain.

For its part, Afghanistan's interests were simple. The maintenance of independence, territorial integrity, and the security of the throne dominated Afghan concerns. The essential problem of Afghanistan's foreign relations was summarized by Abdur Rahman Khan, who ruled Afghanistan from 1880 to 1901:

> How can a small power like Afghanistan, which is like a goat between these lions [Britain and Tsarist Russia], or a grain of wheat between two strong millstones of the grinding mill, stand in the midway of the stones without being ground to dust?[7]

Tsarist Russia was interested in balancing British moves in South and Central Asia and, even more importantly, interested in establishing and securing its own frontiers. This latter interest entailed expansion. Prince A.M. Gorchakov, the Russian Imperial Chancellor, at the behest of the Tsar, summed up the rationale for Russian policy in 1864:

> The position of Russia in Central Asia is that of all civilized states which come into contact with half-savage, wandering tribes possessing no fixed

social organization. It invariably happens in such cases that the interests of security on the frontier, and of commercial relations, compel the more civilized state to exercise a certain ascendancy over neighbors whose turbulence and nomad instincts render them difficult to live with. First, we have incursions and pillage to repress. In order to stop these we are compelled to reduce the tribes on our frontier to a more or less complete submission. Once this result is attained they become less troublesome, but in their turn they are exposed to the aggression of more distant tribes. The state is obliged to defend them against these depredations, and chastise those who commit them. . . . If we content ourselves with chastizing the freebooters and then retire, the lesson is soon forgotten. Retreat is ascribed to weakness, for Asiatics respect only visible and palpable force; that arising from the exercise of reason and a regard for the interests of civilization has as yet no hold on them.[8]

Gorchakov's program was simple: link the Russian frontier "stretching from China to Lake Issik-kul" with the other frontier from "the Sea of Aral along the lower course of the Sir Darya" through a "chain of strongholds," each mutually supporting and settled in fertile areas. Later operations would take Russian forces into the Khanates of Kokand and Bukhara, putting Russian friends or forces south of Gorchakov's line and along the present-day northern boundary of Afghanistan. Even more ominously, from a British perspective, "as each region was conquered, the Russians brought in logistical support, built roads and railroads, and organized themselves in such a way as to facilitate their going on to conquer the next adjoining territory."[9] Indeed, as Prince Gorchakov himself noted, "the greatest difficulty [was] in knowing where to stop."

For its part, Great Britain was from the mid-nineteenth to the mid-twentieth century Russia's rival and the ruler of India. Britain was primarily interested in maintaining both European and Asian power balances, and secondarily in protecting its interests in India from both direct Russian moves and from the threat of revolution, maintaining its favorable trade position in the Middle East and South Asia, and securing its sea lines of communication with India and Southeast Asia. The contest between British democracy and Russian autocracy also became a bone of contention between the two great powers. As David Fromkin has noted, "Britons in ever greater numbers came to object to Russia not merely for what she did but for what she was. The Russophobia soon outgrew the particular political differences between the two countries."[10]

Afghanistan was one of the boards upon which the "Great Game" was played.[11] Twice in the latter two-thirds of the ninteenth century, Britain and Afghanistan went to war, ostensibly over the relationship between Russia and Afghanistan. Britain wanted a stable, nonaligned or pro-British regime in Kabul. Twice Britain found it necessary to fight to obtain this end. Twice it was at least partially victorious but at a price so high that the cost undoubtedly exceeded the benefit in both cases.

The First Anglo-Afghan War, 1838–1842, was a particularly telling experience. In the first phase, the British entered Kabul from the northwest frontier and installed their puppet, Shah Shura, on the Afghan throne to shore up what appeared to be a tottering regime against Russian and Persian encroachments. By October 1841, a local revolt, coupled with the counterattacks from relatives of the deposed Dost Mohammed, made the situation untenable for the British, especially after their political leader, Sir William Macnaghten, was found hanging headless in the Kabul bazaar. The ensuing winter retreat of 1842 saw the total destruction of the Kabul expeditionary force which at one time numbered 4,500 troops and 12,000 camp followers. Only a medical officer arrived in Jalalabad to tell the tale, although subsequent operations disclosed the existence of hundreds of prisoners or deserters from the original force.[12] In the autumn of 1842 a British punitive expedition entered and destroyed Kabul, Charikar, and Jalalabad but soon left, leaving Dost Mohammed again in control of Afghanistan, and more than 15,000 British and Indian soldiers in their graves. Afghan casualties were estimated at 70,000. The Afghan fiasco also caused the fall of the Lord Melbourne's government in England.

In the late 1870s, renewed tension between Russian and Great Britain again involved Afghanistan in the Great Game. In 1873, Russian forces took Khiva. In 1876, the Russians squashed a revolt in Kokand and added it to the province of Turkestan. On another front, Turkey went to war with Russia. Britain responded by threatening war with Russia. In July 1878, Russia dispatched emissaries to the Afghan ruler, Sher Ali. Kabul's failure to provide a timely answer to a British ultimatum created a pretext for the November 1878 invasion. Though Russian aid was sought, none was provided in spite of the fact that Sher Ali had, at least in British eyes, actually "concluded a treaty of close alliance with Russia which would have given the Russians virtual control of Afghanistan."[13] Sher Ali abdicated and the new Amir, Yaqub Khan, quickly established peace with Britain (The Treaty of Gandamak) which gave the British control over Afghan foreign policy. The war did not end there, however. In September 1879, the British regent, Sir Louis Cavagnari, was killed in a local revolt and British forces had to fight to retake Kabul. Afghanistan was in fact ruled by a British general until February 1880 when Abdur Rahman crossed the Amu Darya ending his twelve-year exile in Russia. In July, a conference of tribal chieftans proclaimed him Amir. The British, tired of the game, supported his claim in spite of the fact that Abdur Rahman's forces were obviously supported and equipped by the Russians. The British reasoned that, in all probability, the Iron

Amir was a nationalist and would not become either a British or a Russian puppet.[14]

In retrospect, it is clear that in both wars the British overreacted and that the Russians never posed a significant threat to India.[15] To take such a view, however, requires one to possess the clear vision of a modern historian. In fairness to the British, one must add that Russian pressure on India and its Afghan buffer appeared quite real in the second half of the nineteenth century. Although the dream of taking India was never turned into a realistic plan, the Russians knew that pressures on Britain in Central Asia could produce positive effects in Europe. Russia, aided by its ambitious generals, went far beyond Gorchakov's 1864 line and Britain continued to perceive a threat even after the second Anglo-Afghan war.

In March 1885, Afghan and Russian soldiers fought over the control of an oasis 100 miles south of Merv in what has become known as the Panjdeh Incident. Fearing that the ultimate Russian objective was Herat, Britain mobilized. Only a successful arbitration by Denmark avoided a war where Britain and Afghanistan might have fought as allies. As a result of this incident and one in the Pamirs in 1895, however, the present-day Afghan-Soviet boundary began to take shape. In 1893, the British, consolidating their rule over northwest India, forced Abdur Rahman to agree to the Durand Line which, temporarily in Afghan eyes and permanently in some British eyes, separated the eastern Pushtuns from their Afghan brothers, thus laying the groundwork for future conflicts after the British had retired from the subcontinent in 1947.[16]

The end of the nineteenth century and the beginning of the twentieth saw the end of the Great Game. Both Britain and Russia feared a reinvigorated post-Bismarck Germany. Russia was chastened by its defeat in the Russo-Japanese war of 1905 and more than preoccupied by the Revolution of 1905. Greater fears and other tasks brought an end to direct competition in Central Asia. In 1905, the new king, Amir Habibullah, insecure on his throne, offered the British control over Afghan foreign affairs in return for a subsidy of 160,000 British pounds and access to military supplies.[17] Moreover, without the concurrence of Afghanistan, Russia and Britain entered into the Anglo-Russian Convention of 1907. By this agreement, Tibet was neutralized, Persia was divided into spheres of influence, and Russia acquiesced in British control over Afghan foreign affairs, reinforcing the "Gentlemen's Agreement" of 1873 in which Russia had agreed that Afghanistan was outside its sphere of influence. For its part, Britain agreed not to invade or occupy Afghanistan and Russia was granted equality of commercial opportunity in Afghanistan.[18]

In World War I, despite concerted efforts by the Turks and the Germans, Afghanistan remained neutral. Amir Habibullah, at the war's end, tried to parlay his loyal neutrality into recognition by the Paris Peace Conference of Afghanistan's "absolute liberty, freedom of action, and perpetual independence,"[19] but India and Britain demurred, granting only an increase in the Amir's subsidy. Habibullah and the Afghan elite were disappointed. On February 20, 1919, an unknown assailant killed the Amir, bringing to power his son Amanullah, whose first task was to restore the independence of Afghanistan, a task which would bring him into close contact with the newly victorious Bolsheviks in Soviet Russia.

1919–1945

Afghanistan and Soviet Russia were natural allies at this point. Amanullah needed at least the appearance of Soviet aid to exert leverage on the British, while the Soviets needed the goodwill of Turkey, Persia, and Afghanistan to offset British strength in South and Central Asia.

Prior to 1921, there is no doubt that the Bolsheviks overestimated the revolutionary potential of the peoples of the East. Furthermore, there is little reason to doubt their immediate objective was to tie down the British in Afghanistan, Persia, and elsewhere, and thus make them unable to threaten the Soviet Union. The "Manifesto to the Peoples of the East," published after the First (and only) Congress of the Peoples of the East in August 1920, called for a holy war against Britain:

> Peoples of the East! Many times you have heard from your governments the summons to a holy war, you marched under the green banner of the prophet; but all these holy wars were deceitful and false, and served the interests of your selfish rulers. . . .
> Now we summon you to the first genuine Holy War under the red banner of the Communist International.
> England, the last mighty imperialist robber remaining in Europe, spreads over the Muslim countries of the East her black wings, trying to reduce the peoples of the East to her slaves and her prey. . . .
> Rise, all of you, as one man, for a Holy War against the English conquerors!
> Arise, India, exhausted by starvation and heavy slave labor!
> Arise, Anatolian peasant, crushed by taxes and usurers!
> Arise, Persian *rayah*, choked by the *mulkadar* . . .
> Arise, Arabs and Afghans, lost in the sandy deserts and cut off by the English from the entire world!
> Arise, all of you for the struggle against the common enemy—imperialist England![20]

The congress was a failure. Less than a third of 1,891 delegates were from abroad and any prospective gains were cancelled by Gregoriy Zinoviev's uncautious attack on Islam, both in his congress speech and in the manifesto cited above.[21] Having been defeated on the revolutionary front in South and Central Asia, the Soviets increasingly turned to patient, pragmatic, and somewhat reactive diplomatic efforts to further their interests in the area.

For his part, Amanullah was determined not to repeat his father's errors and declared war on Britain in May 1919. Although his armies lost most of the battles of the three-week war, Britain granted independence. With unrest in Ireland and India, and war-weariness at home, a protracted war with Afghanistan or a costly occupation had to be avoided at all costs. To salute the Afghan victory and to further relations, a scant three days after the termination of hostilities Lenin suggested diplomatic exchanges, which began between June and September 1919. In November, he wrote to "His Majesty the Emir of Afghanistan," and stated, in contradiction to his later views against Pan-Islamism, that "at present, flourishing Afghanistan is the only independent Moslem state in the world, and fate sends the Afghan people the great historic task of uniting about itself the enslaved Mohammedan peoples and leading them on the road to freedom and independence."[22]

In September 1920, the USSR obligated itself to a one million gold ruble subsidy per year for the Amir. Several aircraft and 5,000 rifles were thrown in for good measure.[23] In February 1921, the Bolsheviks, matching their actions toward Persia and Turkey, signed a friendship treaty with Afghanistan in which both sides pledged "to refrain from entering into a military or political agreement with a third power to the detriment of the other signatory nation."[24]

From 1921 to 24, Soviet-Afghan relations suffered from a serious problem: the revolt of the *basmachi,* anti-Bolshevik Central Asian rebels. The basmachi problem was complicated by the Soviet promise to Afghanistan in their friendship treaty to respect the "independence and freedom" of Khiva and Bukhara "in whatever form that agreed with the wishes of the people"[25] and by Amanullah's Pan-Islamic attitudes which would, in his dream, produce a single Central Asian confederation with Kabul as its capital.

The first phase of the basmachi movement lasted from 1918 to 1920 and was sparked by the turbulence of the Civil War and the general breakdown of law and order.[26] The disorders ended with the seizure by the Bolsheviks of Khiva, renamed the People's Republic of Khorezm, in February 1920, and in response to a "call for assistance"—a common Soviet ploy used to justify nearly all of their twentieth century interventions—from the Young Bukharans, the seizure of Bukhara in September 1920. The Amir of Bukhara, Said Alim Khan, escaped to Afghanistan and left Ibrahim Beg to conduct guerrilla operations against the Bolsheviks.

The second phase of basmachi movement took place when the Soviets introduced conscription in Central Asia. In the fall of 1921, a Bolshevik guest, Enver Pasha, a former co-ruler of Turkey and a fugitive from his rival, Kemal Ataturk, arrived in Bukhara "to hunt" and promptly defected to the basmachi. Allied with Ibrahim Beg, his followers seized Dushanbe in 1922 but a dispute with Ibrahim Beg generated disunity and soon rendered the movement impotent. Enver Pasha fell victim to the fortunes of war in August 1922 in a chance contact with a routine Red Army patrol. Ibrahim Beg soon fled to Afghanistan where he remained until 1930, when collectivization initiated a third and final phase to basmachi revolt.

Although for short periods of time the basmachi were able to control the Ferghana valley and to seize various cities, their weaknesses far outweighed their zeal. As Richard Pipes has pointed out, the problems of the basmachi were similar in some ways to those of the contemporary Afghan rebels:

> The principal weakness of the basmachi movement was its lack of unity. The various detachments operated independently of each other under the leadership of ambitious and jealous chieftains, who refused to coordinate their activities and at times engaged in internecine wars. Not infrequently, in critical situations, basmachi units went over to the Reds. Basmachestvo represented essentially a number of unconnected tribal revolts and exhibited all the shortcomings of such forms of resistance. It never attained its ultimate purpose—the overthrow of Russian rule in Turkestan—because the Russians were infinitely better organized, controlled the cities and the lines of communication, and had at their disposal a more numerous and more experienced armed force.[27]

Throughout the first two phases of basmachi revolt, Amanullah supported the rebels. General (later King) Nadir Khan, a hero of the Third Anglo-Afghan war, was appointed commander in the north and directed to aid the rebels without involving his own country.[28] The death of Enver, coupled with a stiff Soviet protest, indicated to Amanullah that his dreams of empire were unrealistic. Amir Said Alim and many of his followers emigrated from Bukhara and took up life in northern Afghanistan.

Amanullah's foreign policy from 1924 to 29 was designed to prevent either Britain or the USSR from gaining undue influence in Afghanistan. To the greatest extent possible, Amanullah tried to pursue modernization with the help of nationals from other than the two rival countries or by playing one giant off against the other. Balancing actions were the rule.

For example, the February 1921 treaty with the Soviet Union was offset later in the year by a treaty of "neighborly relations" between Afghanistan and Britain, a remarkable feat since Amanullah was an avowed Anglophobe. At other times, Britain and the Soviet Union directly competed for Afghan favors, each no doubt overestimating the degree of influence which the other exerted.

In the summer of 1924, a rebellion broke out in Khost against Amanullah. He appealed first to the British to send airplanes which, not to offend traditional sensibilities, would be flown by Germans. Not to be outdone, in October 1924 the Soviets also began delivery of eleven airplanes, as well as pilots and mechanics. A British official around this same time offered the following evaluation of the Afghan air force: "The so-called Afghan Air Force is to all intents and purposes a Russian Service and may indeed be regarded as a Russian advanced base. . . . In the event . . . of a serious rebellion which threatened the capital, it is doubtful whether the Russian aviators would support the Central Government."[29]

Although some would later refer to Amanullah as "the Socialist King," Soviet military aid, trade, or assistance did not prevent Amanullah from pursuing and protecting his country's interests. Contrary to the British evaluation, the Russian air detachment never threatened Amanullah's government. In 1925, when Soviet troops occupied a disputed Afghan island in the Amu Darya, apparently to keep some of the remaining basmachi from using it as a base, the two nations nearly went to war. Soviet advisers were suspended from their duties and only quick, successful negotiation prevented a more severe split in Afghan-Soviet relations. The Soviets ultimately ceded the island to Afghanistan.

In 1928, Amanullah toured Europe, stopping off in London, Rome, Ankara, and Moscow. Although his trip netted few substantive gains for Afghanistan, he came back further imbued with the spirit of reform in the tradition of his hero, Kemal Ataturk. Arriving in Kabul at the wheel of a Rolls Royce automobile, Amanullah soon called for a *Loya Jirga*, or council of tribal elders, at which he announced a number of reforms. They included: removing the veil from women, opening coeducational schools, and forcing all Afghans to wear Western clothes inside the capital. To conservative Afghans, Amanullah appeared irreligious, Westernized, and hopelessly out of step with his own countrymen.

A revolt began late in 1928 and Amanullah was forced to abdicate, though this was to be a temporary move. After a three-day rule by his brother Inayatullah, the throne was captured by a Tarjik brigand, Bacha Saqqao, the son of a water carrier (also known as Habibullah), who ruled a chaotic Afghanistan for only nine months until he too was deposed by Nadir Shah.[30]

Early in 1929, Ghulam Nabi, who had been the Afghan ambassador in Moscow, came to the aid of Amanullah and, with obvious Soviet complicity, raised an army of 800–1,000 Kirghiz soldiers, crossed the Amu Darya and conducted military operations. Although he was able to seize Mazar-i-Sharif in April, he quickly became bogged down and quit the field in June 1929 when Amanullah abdicated for the second time.[31]

In the meantime, Nadir Khan, the former Afghan ambassador in Paris, had returned from living in France and entered Afghanistan through India with little apparent help from the British. After raising an army, he routed the forces of the Tajik "pretender" and executed Bacha. On October 15, 1929, he was named king. *Izvestiia,* the Soviet government newspaper, pronounced what may be seen as a typical Marxist-Leninist conclusion on the entire affair by recommending that the new government stand up to clerical reactionaries, take care of the needs of the peasants, guarantee minority rights and pursue an independent foreign policy.[32]

Nadir Shah quickly returned the country to customary Islamic law and abjured any discussion of Amanullah-type reforms. Through his patient, moderate leadership, he developed a new constitution which lasted until the early 1960s.

In foreign affairs, although Nadir Shah was more pro-British than Amanullah, relations between Kabul and Moscow remained cordial. The Soviet Union was the first to recognize the new government as it had with Amanullah, and would later with Daoud and Taraki as well. Although Nadir accepted 10,000 rifles and a de facto subsidy (180,000 pounds sterling) from Britain, and reduced the Soviet presence in the air force, the Soviets made no apparent protest.

Soviet-Afghan relations were, however, complicated by an old Soviet nemesis: the basmachi. In 1930, basmachi raids, apparently in reaction to collectivization, again became problematical. Ibrahim Beg operated out of sanctuaries in Afghanistan and in June 1930 a Soviet force penetrated 40 miles into Afghan territory before withdrawing.[33] Nadir Shah got the message. He dispatched an army and drove Ibrahim Beg and his basmachi back into the Soviet Union in April 1931. Just one day before the signing of the renegotiated 1926 neutrality treaty, Beg was caught by Soviet forces. The 1931 pact obligated each side to prevent any activities within its territories that might cause political or military injury to the other, a clause later invoked against Axis nationals in 1941.[34]

Unfortunately, the wise and effective leadership of Nadir Shah was cut short by an assassin's bullet in 1933. The assassin was apparently motivated by a personal sense of revenge since he was the adopted son of Ghulam Nabi, the former ambassador to the USSR, who had been executed by Nadir in 1932 for plotting against the throne.[35]

The period 1933–45 was a stable period in Soviet-Afghan relations. In the Soviet Union, the pre-war period was dominated by terror and collectivization. The war years were dominated by the struggle for survival. Both left little opportunity for the furthering of bilateral relations. Afghanistan during this period was dominated by nation-building activities directed mainly by the uncles of the young king, Zahir Shah. Although his government received aid from Germany up to the late 1930s, it was relatively easy for Afghanistan to ask Axis nationals to leave the country in October 1941 since this action was being supported by both the USSR and Great Britain.

In all, Soviet policy toward Afghanistan from 1918 to 45 was characterized by cordial, pragmatic, state-to-state relations, quite obviously oriented toward keeping the southern border free of turbulence and instability, while keeping Great Britain from using Afghanistan as a base for operations against the USSR. The Soviets showed that they were prepared to sacrifice these cordial relations when they found it necessary to secure their frontiers from basmachi bands which sometimes operated with tacit Afghan approval and material assistance. In 1929, the Soviets also fielded a proxy force to assist their friend Amanullah and to forestall a new leadership which might prove to be more pro-British than the last. When their efforts failed to bear fruit, they pragmatically recognized the new ruler, Nadir Shah, and continued—further basmachi problems notwithstanding—to foster good relations with Afghanistan up to 1945.

Overall, the Soviet approach was appropriate for a great, though temporarily weak, power undergoing a nation-building trauma of its own, while distracted by more pressing problems on the international scene. Up to 1945 there is little that suggests a Soviet or Imperial Russian "grand design" to one day seize Afghanistan or even to dominate its foreign policy. (The Nazi-Soviet discussions about spheres of influence in 1940 will be addressed in chapter 7.)

The most significant developments would come as a result of World War II. Two years after the war, Britain would leave India. The United States and the USSR would become the most powerful nations on earth, and Pakistan would become the custodian of Pushtunistan. A new game was beginning.

Notes

1. On the geography and climate of Afghanistan, see: U.S. Dept. of State, *Afghanistan;* U.S. Army, *Area Handbook for Afghanistan,* pp. 1–36.

2. The census was reportedly more an estimate than an actual count. For

the Afghan government's account of the census, see *Kabul Times,* October 3, 1979, p. 1.

3. Bradsher, *Afghanistan and the Soviet Union,* pp. 11–12.

4. The two quotes are respectively from: Fletcher, *Afghanistan: Highway of Conquest,* p. 262; and Fraser-Tytler, *Afghanistan,* p. 181.

5. Dupree, *Afghanistan,* p. 125–26.

6. Ibid., p. 126–27.

7. Cited in ibid., p. 415.

8. The full text of the Gorchakov Memorandum can be found in Fraser-Tytler, *Afghanistan,* pp. 333–37.

9. David Fromkin, "The Great Game in Asia," p. 940.

10. Ibid., p. 938.

11. For an explanation of the term "Great Game" which, in the widest sense, referred to Anglo-Russian rivalry in South Asia, see: ibid., pp. 936–37, and Klass, "The Great Game Revisited," pp. 1366–68.

12. Analysts have long told the tale of the lone survivor: "The solitary mounted man came reeling, tottering on. A shudder ran through the garrison. . . . Their worst forebodings seemed confirmed. There was the one man who was to tell the story of the massacre of a great army. A party of cavalry . . . brought him in wounded, exhausted, half-dead. The messenger was Dr. Brydon, and he now reported his belief that he was the sole survivor of an army of some sixteen thousand men."

Quoted from J.W. Kaye, *History of the War in Afghanistan,* and reprinted in *Parameters* 13 (March 1983), inside rear cover. For a more accurate account of the many survivors see Fletcher, *Afghanistan: Highway of Conquest,* pp. 112–13.

13. Fraser-Tytler, *Afghanistan,* p. 148.

14. Dupree, *Afghanistan,* p. 410.

15. Fletcher, *Afghanistan: Highway of Conquest,* p. 141. For a complementary analysis concentrating on Soviet weakness, see Louis Fischer, *The Soviets in World Affairs,* abridged edition (New York: Vintage Books, 1960), pp. 307–19.

16. On the origins of the Durand Line and its intended permanence or lack thereof, see: Fletcher, *Afghanistan: Highway of Conquest,* pp. 164–66; Fraser-Tytler, *Afghanistan,* pp. 181–90; and Dupree, *Afghanistan,* pp. 425–29.

17. Fraser-Tytler, *Afghanistan,* p. 179.

18. On the 1907 agreement see: Fraser-Tytler, *Afghanistan,* pp. 192–93; and Adamec, *Afghanistan's Foreign Affairs,* pp. 9–12.

19. On Afghan diplomacy in World War I, see Adamec, *Afghanistan's Foreign Affairs,* pp. 15–42. The quote is on p. 45.

20. The Manifesto, signed by Zinoviev and others, is reproduced in Spector, *The Soviet Union and the Muslim World,* pp. 182–88. Lenin repeated Zinoviev's anticlerical view at the 2d Comintern Congress in 1920. V.I. Lenin, "Theses on the National and Colonial Questions," in Tucker, *The Lenin Anthology,* pp. 619–25. For an earlier call for Muslim support in December 1917 see "Appeal of the Council of People's Commissars to the Moslems of Russia and the East,"

in Degras, *Soviet Documents on Foreign Policy,* pp. 15–17. The latter two works do not mention Afghanistan by name.

21. For a description of the Baku Congress, see Spector, *The Soviet Union and the Muslim World,* pp. 32–44. Also, Fischer, *The Soviets in World Affairs,* pp. 205–06. The latter book described the conference as "an odd gathering, a museum of Oriental costumes, a Babel of tongues, a confusion of aims and ideas." At any rate, it was unsuccessful. It was the first and last congress of its kind.

22. Lenin's stated his views against Pan-Islamic movements in his "Theses on the National and Colonial Questions" cited above. The quote is cited in Fischer, *The Soviets in World Affairs,* p. 207. For Trotsky's views on the great importance of Central Asia, see his 1919 memoranda to the Central Committee in Jan M. Meijer, ed., *Trotsky Papers, 1917–1922,* vol. 1 (London: Mouton and Co., 1964), pp. 621–27, 673–75.

23. Fischer, *The Soviets in World Affairs,* pp. 579–80. Also Arnold, *Afghanistan: The Soviet Invaison in Perspective,* pp. 10–11.

24. For a Russian language text of the agreement, see: Ministries of Foreign Affairs (USSR and Afghanistan), *Sovetsko-Afghanskie Otnosheniia, 1919–1969 gg.* pp. 28–31. The quote is from Article II of the treaty.

25. Article VIII of the treaty cited in note 24.

26. On the basmachi movement, see: Rywkin, *Russia in Central Asia,* pp. 51–62; Fischer, *The Soviets in World Affairs,* pp. 280–86; and Pipes, *The Formation of the Soviet Union,* pp. 174–84, 256–60.

27. Pipes, *Formation of the Soviet Union,* pp. 178–79.

28. Fletcher, *Afghanistan: Highway of Conquest,* p. 202.

29. Cited in Adamec, *Afghanistan's Foreign Affairs,* p. 108.

30. On the revolt see Adamec, *Afghanistan's Foreign Affairs,* pp. 148–72.

31. On the activities of Ghulam Nabi see: Arnold, *Afghanistan: The Soviet Invasion in Perspective,* pp. 18–23; Adamec, *Afghanistan's Foreign Affairs,* pp. 160–65; and Fraser-Tytler, *Afghanistan,* p. 218.

32. Cited in Joseph Castagneq, "Soviet Imperialism in Afghanistan," pp. 702–03.

33. Fletcher, *Afghanistan: Highway of Conquest,* p. 228; Fraser-Tytler, *Afghanistan,* p. 230; and Wilber, "Afghanistan, Independent and Encircled," p. 490.

34. For the text of the 1931 Treaty of Neutrality and Non-Aggression see Ministries of Foreign Affairs (USSR and Afghanistan), *Sovetsko-Afghanskie Otnosheniia, 1919–1969 gg.,* pp. 81–84.

35. For the most complete account, see Adamec, *Afghanistan's Foreign Affairs,* pp. 191–99. For a speculative account which unconvincingly argues a Soviet role in the death of Nadir Shah, see Arnold, *Afghanistan: The Soviet Invasion in Perspective,* pp. 21–23.

2
Soviet-Afghan Relations, 1945–1973

In the pre-war period, Afghanistan was "like a goat between [two] lions," but after the war one of the lions, Great Britain, retired from the field, not to be fully replaced by the United States or any other countervailing power. To cope with this situation, Afghan policy after World War II was, as Louis Dupree has noted, characterized by three goals: "nonalignment, independence, development."[1] To these goals, one must add irredentism because of the importance of the Pushtunistan issue in the postwar era. To some degree, Afghanistan's policy goals were in conflict with the goal of development, with its requirement for foreign aid, and the desire for the reunification of Pushtunistan, which required—at least for bargaining purposes—a modern military force and foreign military assistance. A modern military would also help the central government to control the country during the modernization process. At least in retrospect, the situation seemed tailor-made for an increase in Soviet influence, especially after Stalin had passed from the scene.

This chapter will argue that Soviet objectives from 1945 to 1973 were broadened to include: providing incentives for Afghanistan not to join a Northern Tier alliance, encouraging economic and trade dependence on the USSR, and using Afghanistan to support Soviet regional objectives and to serve as a model of "good neighbor" relations. The factors that permitted the broadening of these objectives were the withdrawal of Great Britain from India, U.S. refusal to fulfill Britain's balancing role in the region, the advent of modernization-oriented leaders in Afghanistan, and the general opening of Soviet attitudes toward the Third World which accompanied postwar decolonization and the death of Stalin.

1945–1963

In the period 1945–53 the Soviet Union was distracted from the problems of Afghanistan by more important issues: postwar reconstruction, the Cold War in Europe, and the Korean War. Furthermore, Soviet policy was hampered by the two-camp theory in which the Soviet leadership saw the newly independent states of Asia and the Middle East "as mere puppets of the Western colonial powers and thus incapable of formulating and implementing an independent policy—either domestic or foreign."[2] Although Afghanistan hardly fit the category of being "newly independent," it was certainly feudal, backward and, during Stalin's later years, Western-leaning.

All of this did not, however, stop the Soviets from maintaining good relations with Afghanistan. In 1950, during the first postwar flare-up of the Pushtunistan dispute, Pakistan cancelled Afghan transit rights through its territory, separating Afghanistan from port facilities and markets in India. The Soviets stepped in and in July 1950 negotiated a four-year barter agreement and provided Afghanistan duty-free transit rights for its exports.

All of this concerned the United States, but not to the point where it would move to adopt Great Britain's former role in South Asia. To examine this point and to set the stage for further analysis of Soviet-Afghan relations, it is necessary briefly to examine Afghan-U.S. relations.

While it is difficult to share fully Leon Poullada's belief that U.S. policy toward Afghanistan has been characterized by "indifference, ignorance, and appeasement," one is forced to admit that—despite its harshness—this description has, on occasion, borne some relation to the truth.[3] For example, in 1930, to silence congressional pressure to establish relations with Afghanistan, Wallace Smith Murray, chief of the State Department division of Near East affairs, told a congressman that "Afghanistan is, without doubt, the most fanatic, independent, hostile country in the world today." He added that "the British . . . have for years forbidden any white British subject to enter Afghanistan." He concluded with one final exaggeration:

> No foreign lives in the country can be protected and no foreign interests guaranteed, and in the case of destruction of either or both there would be no way for any foreign aggrieved power to bring effective pressure on Afghanistan, a landlocked Asiatic country accessible only through India or Soviet Russia.[4]

In the postwar era, the government of Afghanistan held a much higher opinion of the United States, which it viewed as the logical successor to Britain, but a successor against whom the Afghans held no grudges. In August 1946, Prime Minister Shah Mohammed Khan said that he was convinced that the United States could guarantee his country's security: "For the first time in our history we are free of the threat of great powers using our mountain passes as pathways to empire."[5] Afghanistan could, he added, now afford to concentrate its resources on bettering the people's living conditions.

Good feelings would not last. Although Afghanistan was disappointed in U.S. developmental assistance proposals, it was the issue of arms sales which destroyed Afghan hopes and left Afghanistan little alternative but to turn to the Soviet Union, which at the same time was awakening to the importance of the Third World in its global competition with the United States. In 1948 and 1951, and in 1954 after the advent of the first Daoud regime, the United States refused Afghan requests for military aid.

There are conflicting claims over just how this happened. The ultimate explanation of these events may have been buried with Mohammed Daoud. Louis Dupree maintains that

> The Daoud government officially stated the Americans refused to give Afghanistan military aid because the Afghans would not sign the required Mutual Security Agreements or join the Baghdad Pact. The unofficial American version . . . differs somewhat. According to U.S. diplomats on the scene at the time, some of the Afghan military wanted to join the pact, but demanded assurances that they would be defended by the United States if their acceptance of arms aid precipitated a Russian invasion or major subversive efforts inside Afghanistan.[6]

The reasoning behind U.S. actions was simple to understand. Up to the end of the 1970s, the United States habitually saw Afghanistan in these terms:

> For the United States, Afghanistan has at the present limited direct interest: it is not an important *trading partner;* it is not an access *route for U.S. trade* with others; it is not presently as far as is known a *source of oil or scarce strategic metals* nor does it appear likely that it will become so; there are *no treaty ties or defense commitments;* and Afghanistan *does not provide us with significant defense, intelligence, or scientific facilities.* United States policy has long recognized these facts.[7]

From the start of the postwar era, the United States was prepared to give aid to Afghanistan, but always within limits. Therefore, it was no surprise that, in the midst of a minor dispute in 1952 between the USSR and Afghanistan over the presence of a UN oil exploration team in northern Afghanistan, Ambassador Ward cabled Washington that, even if the United States were to offer arms, "we cannot guarantee Afghanistan's borders."[8]

For the United States, Afghanistan was, to use a strategic term, an economy of force area, one whose principal importance lay in its geographical position adjacent to Pakistan, Iran, and the Soviet Union, three countries which had great importance in U.S. eyes. The United States wanted an Afghanistan that was *"neutral, independent, and not over-committed to the Soviet bloc."*[9] Although U.S. officials saw aid as a potent weapon, U.S. policy was always cast in terms of a balancing act.

> We should be extremely cautious to not overplay our hand in Afghanistan. The Afghan ability to survive depends in large part on Soviet acquiescence and a policy which frightens the Soviet Union will be self-defeating. The spectrum of profitable action is small. Our goal is not to win but to hold.[10]

Accordingly, U.S. objectives in Afghanistan were habitually defined as (1) the preservation of Afghan territorial integrity and independence; (2) the creation of a viable political and economic system; (3) the prevention of Soviet influence from becoming so strong that Afghanistan would lose its freedom of action; and (4) the improvement of Afghanistan's ties with Pakistan and Iran.

The latter two objectives inhibited arms transfers and prevented the United States from playing a role similar to that which Britain had played. A 1956 National Security Council (NSC) document indicated that arms transfers might annoy the Soviet Union to the extent that countermeasures to exert full Soviet control over Afghanistan would become "a near certainty."[11] Moreover, Afghanistan was not a good candidate for a Middle East alliance and transferring arms to Afghanistan would have certainly disturbed Pakistan, which had become a member of the Southeast Asia Treaty Organization (SEATO) in September 1954 and would become a member of the Central Treaty Organization (CENTO) a year later.

Two events took place in 1953 which drastically altered Soviet-Afghan relations: the accession of Sardar (Prince) Mohammed Daoud to the prime ministership in September and the death of Josif Stalin in March 1953.

Daoud was young (forty-three), impatient, and thoroughly dissatisfied with the regimes of Zahir Shah's various uncles. Trained as a soldier, the prince wanted a planned economy, rapid development, and progress on the Pushtunistan issue. Moving closer to the Soviets was a means to these ends.

After the death of Stalin in March 1953, the Soviet Union discarded the two-camp theory. As Adam Ulam has noted, treating Third World leaders as "tools of imperialism" was tantamount to passing up "a brilliant opportunity to embarrass and outflank Western diplomacy."[12] S.N.

Rostovskii, in a 1955 issue of a Soviet journal for Asian studies, stated that

> The Asian countries have been transformed from the tools of the imperialists' policy inito states which are beginning to follow an independent international policy. . . . The extreme rear of imperialism—the colonies—has now, to a considerable degree, become its front line.[13]

E. Zhukov, writing in 1956 in *Partiinaia zhizn* went even further: "Whatever the form of national liberation of the colonies and semicolonies might be . . . this liberation is a blow to imperialism and, consequently, necessarily does not strengthen, but weakens, the world capitalist system.[14]

Countries on or near the Soviet periphery received special attention. In January 1954, in the first major Soviet move toward the Third World in the field of aid, the Soviet Union lent Afghanistan $3.5 million, repayable in eight years at a favorable 3 percent interest rate.[15] Two highly visible grain storage facilities and a bakery were purchased with these funds. Other projects began in 1954 with an additional $2.7 million loan. In May 1955, Soviet equipment began to pave Afghan roads and in September, twenty-five Soviet taxis and buses appeared in Kabul. In December Nikita Khrushchev and Nikolai Bulganin visited and announced the gift of a 100-bed hospital, an Il-14 transport plane for the king, and a loan of $100 million, with a low-interest, thirty-year repayment term. The projects which emanated from this loan included (1) two airports, one military, one civilian; (2) two hydroelectric plants; (3) a road maintenance plant; (4) a road over the Hindu Kush with a tunnel which would connect northern and southern Afghanistan for the first time; and (5) three irrigation projects. By May 1956, there were over 460 Soviet technicians in the country. In addition to the aid package described above, as a result of the Khrushchev-Bulganin visit, the 1931 nonaggression and neutrality treaty was extended for ten years instead of the usual five-year term.

None of these projects was undertaken without a view toward Soviet national security. Khrushchev later recounted in his memoirs—albeit with some self-serving exaggeration—that

> There's no doubt that if the Afghans hadn't become our friends, the Americans would have managed to ingratiate themselves with their "humanitarian aid," as they call it. The amount of money we spent in gratuitous assistance to Afghanistan is a drop in the ocean compared to the price we would have had to pay in order to counter the threat of an American military base on Afghan territory.[16]

Up to 1978, immediate Soviet objectives in Afghanistan included (1) providing incentives for Afghanistan not to join a Northern Tier alliance; (2) developing such trade and aid links as to encourage dependence on the Soviet Union; (3) conducting mutually beneficial trade relations; (4) using Afghanistan to support the programs of Soviet foreign policy; and (5) using Afghanistan as a model of relations between states with different social systems or as a model of the Soviet Union's benevolent policy toward its neighboring states.

In addition to developmental assistance, there were two other Soviet programs used to accomplish these objectives: support—though usually guarded and qualified—for the Afghan position on the Pushtunistan issue, and military assistance.

In December 1955, Khrushchev and Bulganin expressed Soviet support for Afghanistan on the Pushtunistan issue which had again flared up between March and September 1955. Bulganin said in Kabul that "we think that the demands of Afghanistan to give the population of bordering 'Pushtunistan' an opportunity of freely expressing their will are justified."[17]

Premier Khrushchev conducted a second state visit to Afghanistan in March 1960. After recounting his version of South Asian history, ("Historically, as you know, Pushtunistan has always been part of Afghanistan"), Khrushchev noted that the USSR supported every people's right to self-determination and that the Pushtun people in Pakistan should be given the opportunity to demonstrate their collective will through a referendum.[18] *Pravda,* the Communist Party newspaper, repeated Khrushchev's stand in March and again in April 1961.[19]

When the Pushtunistan issue flared up in the fall of 1961, the Soviets supported Afghanistan in what was to become a very tough, two-year-long outbreak of the problem. The crisis saw Afghan transit privileges suspended and the Soviet Union (along with the United States) gave Afghanistan airlift assistance. The USSR subsequently offered to allocate $450 million to finance the *entire* Second Five Year Plan, an offer which was politely declined.[20] When the Pakistanis, taking a page from the Afghan book, offered to hold a plebescite in Pushtunistan if the Afghans would do likewise among all of their own tribesmen, the Soviet Union issued one of its toughest statements on the Pushtunistan issue. The Soviets called the Pakistani request a "provocational plan" that had originated in the CENTO military alliance. This raised the specter of a South Asian conflict and the Soviet government newspaper *Izvestiia* added that "it would be a serious mistake on [Pakistan's] part to hope that the Soviet Union will remain indifferent to this [military conflict.]"[21] Marshal Sokolovskiy subsequently visited Afghanistan with a large group of officers. Although the substance of his activities there was never made public, the celebrated spy Colonel Oleg Penkovskiy reported that long-range contingency planning was part of his mission:

> The purpose of the trip was to study the combat readiness of the Afghan armed forces, so that we might draw up plans to improve the military skill of these forces and increase their fire power. Plans are being made, also, for extensive training of Afghan officers in Soviet military schools as well as the dispatch of large numbers of Soviet military instructors to Afghanistan. Under discussion is the possibility of sending Soviet troops into Afghanistan at the appropriate time for joint operations against Pakistan. Sokolovskiy also had orders to reconnoiter certain specific areas of Afghanistan, for selection as possible missile sites.[22]

Military assistance, mainly in the form of concessional arms transfers and advisory support, was initiated in August 1955 with an agreement between Czechoslovakia and Afghanistan for $3 million. Daoud wisely had this action and his early Pushtunistan policy approved by a *Loya Jirga,* council of tribal leaders, giving Afghanistan, which had already been refused by the United States, the freedom to get arms wherever they could be "honorably procured."[23] In August 1956, a Soviet-Afghan agreement was made public which had provided for the sale of $25 million dollars worth of military hardware at concessional terms. By October, eleven MiG–15 fighters had already been delivered. By 1965, the book value of the equipment provided, which included 100 tanks and 100 planes, was approximately $275 million although repayment terms were so concessional that only half that sum needed to be repaid. Repayment could also be effected through commodity transfer.[24] By 1962, more than 200 cadets had been sent to the Soviet Union for courses of two to four years in length. During the 1953–63 period, the Soviets also built (or were building) military airfields in Bagram, near Kabul; Mazar-i-Sharif in northern Afghanistan; and at Shindand in the central part of western Afghanistan.

Daoud's policy was meant to highlight the interdependence among Afghan objectives discussed above. Friendship with the Soviet Union without slavish obedience to its will was meant to provide support for modernization and leverage on the Pushtunistan issue. Soviet activities could also generate U.S. aid which would help Daoud to maintain national independence and also support his modernization program. One must judge that this worked fairly well for more than nine years. As Nancy and Richard Newell have pointed out, the Daoud regime was, in the main, highly successful. A base for modern economic development was built and aid—except in the military area—was received from many sources.[25] In the end, however, the problems generated by the continuing

Pushtunistan crisis, resistance within the royal family to Daoud's liberal and at times irreligious domestic policies, and his high-handed personal manner led to his undoing. On March 3, 1963 the King dismissed Daoud.

During this period, Soviet policy was also successful. Afghanistan never became a serious candidate for a Western alliance and had become, and would continue to be, dependent on the Soviet Union, both for trade and military assistance. Indeed, it must be considered a strength of the Soviet position in Afghanistan that, even when Afghanistan was under more Western-leaning leadership from 1963 to 73, its relations with the Soviet Union continued to flourish.

During the first Daoud regime, Afghanistan and the Soviet Union grew much closer in trade and in military assistance. According to a Soviet source, just in the period 1951–58, using the total value of Afghan trade as an index, Afghan interaction with the socialist world grew from 14.7 percent in 1951 to 33.9 percent in 1958.[26] Table 2–1 shows the volume of Soviet trade expressed as a percentage of Afghan exports and imports. Throughout the period, the dollar value of Soviet-Afghan trade increased from $32 million (1956) to $46.2 million (1962). During the same period, U.S.-Afghan trade declined in nominal value by more than $2 million.[27]

U.S. aid was also significant, amounting to approximately 60 percent of the total of Soviet developmental assistance. However, U.S. aid was concentrated in a few projects and was less visible in spite of the fact that some Americans considered aid as our principal weapon in the competition for influence in Afghanistan. The U.S. was also hamstrung by its alliance with Pakistan and its subsequent refusal to enter into significant military assistance agreements with Afghanistan.

In spite of nearly $400 million in Soviet developmental assistance from 1953 to 63, and more than $20 million worth of military aid, Afghanistan had not become a pro-Soviet satellite and the sobriquet "Red Prince" hardly fit Daoud.[28] In 1956, when reminded of the dangers of

Table 2–1
Volume of Afghan-Soviet Trade

USSR as Percent of Afghan	1956	1957	1958	1959	1960	1961	1962	1963
Exports	32.9	29.1	27.0	26.7	21.9	31.3	39.3	30.8
Imports[a]	34.4	25.9	25.4	29.5	27.6	35.4	35.7	25.9

Source: Adapted from Royal Government of Afghanistan, Ministry of Commerce, *Afghanistan's Foreign Trade 1335 Through 1342* (March 1956–March 1964).
[a]Does not include loans or grants from all sources which totalled more than $95 million per annum from 1956–63. Does not include military sales or equipment.

communist penetration and subsequent takeovers, Daoud, referring to a communist coup in 1948, told one U.S. historian: "Does anyone think we have not heard of Czechoslovakia?"²⁹ Even more to the point, Daoud later told two German authors,

> Our whole life, our whole existence, revolves around one single focal point—freedom. Should we ever get the feeling that our freedom is in the slightest danger, from whatever quarter, then we should prefer to live on dry bread, or even starve, sooner than accept help that would restrict our freedom.³⁰

Perhaps the most successful aspect of Soviet policy in this period was its public relations aspect. By 1960, the visible accomplishments of Soviet aid were impressive. In a typical account, the chairman of the State Committee on Foreign Economic Relations in 1960 noted that the Soviets had already completed fifteen separate industrial projects and had completed planning for a major irrigation canal, a hydroelectric station, and a vehicle repair plant.³¹ In 1961, Soviet and East European geologists discovered a large natural gas deposit in northern Afghanistan.³² Natural gas exports began in 1967.

Soviet-Afghan relations were also good press for the Soviet leaders both at home and abroad. In 1960, Khrushchev bragged on the front page of *Pravda* of his excellent reception in Afghanistan and related— "when I was riding in the same car as the king"—how impressed he was with the warm feeling of Soviet-Afghan friendship demonstrated by the people. He also noted the surprising amount of progress evident in Kabul and that—as usual—the Afghan king and his prime minister shared his "assessment of the international situation."³³

An *Izvestiia* correspondent with a talent for exaggeration even attributed the Shah of Iran's 1962 decision not to allow U.S. missile bases on Iranian soil to a visit which the Shah made to Afghanistan: "In Afghanistan [he] was able to see . . . the fruitfulness of that country's good-neighbor relations with the Soviet Union and to ascertain that the policy of peaceful coexistence . . . is bolstered everyday by concrete actions.³⁴

Although Afghanistan was not a socialist state or even a progressive one, no Soviet party congress passed without a favorable comment on the exemplary relations between Afghanistan and the Soviet Union. At the Twenty-third Party Congress, in 1966, Brezhnev was even able to compare Afghanistan and Finland, two countries where the Soviet "good-neighbor policy" was "yielding excellent results."³⁵

1963-1973

Although the Soviets lost Daoud in 1963, this did not change the direciton of Soviet-Afghan relations. Soviet economic aid continued along with Soviet developmental assistance, in spite of its aggregate decrease in value during the Vietnam War, hitting 70 percent of total Afghan aid during the period 1967–70. This was in marked contrast to the United States whose aid during this period dipped temporarily from one-third of total Afghan aid in 1967 to less than 3 percent of the total in 1969.[36] By 1973, total Soviet military and economic aid ($1.5 billion) outweighed U.S. economic aid ($425 million) by a factor of three to one.[37]

Military assistance was maintained at a very high level. A United States government handbook summed up the situation concisely and somewhat prophetically:

> Since 1956 the impact of Soviet military assistance has been great. While the quantity of Soviet aid is not known, it has been steady, and by 1967 the armed forces had become almost completely dependent upon the Soviets, not only for equipment but also for logistic support. As a consequence of their basic improvement, the military establishment has increased its effectiveness and capabilities, particularly in the role of providing domestic stability. . . .
> The acquisition of advanced types of modern air and ground equipment along with Soviet advisers to instruct in the maintenance, operation and employment of this material may eventually have a far-reaching influence on the Afghan Armed Forces. . . . The almost total dependence of the military on Soviet logistic support appears to give the Soviets a large measure of control over Afghan military operations.[38]

Between 1956 and 1970, the Soviet Union trained thousands of Afghan officers. When Marshal Grechko visited an Afghan military academy in 1969, *Krasnaia zvezda* (Red Star), the Ministry of Defense daily, could report with some degree of accuracy: "In most areas the officers teaching the classes reported to Marshal A.A. Grechko in Russian: many of them have studied in Soviet military schools."[39]

Neighborly relations were facilitated through a number of high-level visits in 1963 (L.I. Brezhnev), 1965 (Zahir Shah), 1966 (Prime Minister Maiwandwal), 1967 (N. Podgorny), 1969 (A. Kosygin, Grechko), 1971 (Zahir Shah), 1972 (Prime Minister Zahir), 1973 (N. Podgorny).[40] The results of these meetings were predictable. Both sides praised the quality of the bilateral relationship and hailed the latest economic achievement. The Soviets praised Afghan nonalignment and the Afghans gave verbal support to the latest Soviet foreign policy concern. During the period 1963–73, the Afghans voiced support or concern at one time or another for: general disarmament, the progress of decolonization, Soviet policy toward the Vietnam War, and Soviet policy toward the Arab-Israeli dispute. Both sides expressed concern over the Indo-Pakistani War and Afghanistan was described as "prepared to study" Brezhnev's collective security proposals in 1972.[41]

Afghan-Pakistani relations improved during the period of constitutional monarchy. The king muted his emphasis on the Pushtunistan issue. When India fought Pakistan in 1965 and again in 1971, and when internal disturbances hit Pakistan in 1971, the Afghan government did little to exploit the situation. With the Sino-Soviet rift in bloom,

> Moscow, though displeased with Pakistan's military alliance with the United States and its receptivity to China's overtures, counseled restraint in Kabul. It made known its opposition to any Afghan moves against the beleaguered Pakistanis, preferring quiet borders and, at a time of serious Sino-Soviet tensions, better relations with all the governments of the subcontinent. The Soviets wanted the stability of the status quo rather than the uncertainty inherent in a possible breakup of Pakistan.[42]

Afghanistan's major problem in the 1963–73 period came not in foreign policy but in domestic politics. While the 1964 constitution looked good on paper, it did not enable the government to solve problems, nor was it able to cope with the economic and social changes which Afghanistan was undergoing.

Four problems should be noted here. First, the king never permitted the long-term development of political parties. The legislature thus had no internal discipline. Second, the separation of powers was extreme. The prime minister was responsible only to the king and, in turn, had little control over parliament. Third, the king himself exercised very little leadership, hoping that the system would ultimately function effectively of its own accord. Finally, the constitution prohibited members of the royal family, many with long years of experience in government, from holding the office of prime minister. Thus, people like Daoud who could have contributed had become disaffected. Finally, all of these problems were superimposed on a country undergoing rapid urbanization and modernization. Education programs were producing hundreds of graduates, many of whom were unemployed and many of whom were easy to radicalize. A *New York Times* correspondent visited Kabul in 1973 and reported that the country had no national planning setup, no taxation system, no real banking system and no civil service. Half of the legislators were illiterate and the legislature tended to adjourn at critical times.[43]

The upshot of these problems was near-chaos. The government had five prime ministers in ten years. Serious protests took place in 1965, 1968, and again in 1971. Plotting began within the royal family and the leftist movement that would seize power began to take shape.

Evolution of the People's Democratic Party of Afghanistan

Since much of the balance of this study will concern Afghanistan under the People's Democratic Party, it is important to look at its origins and activities during the constitutional monarchy.

On January 1, 1965, the People's Democratic Party of Afghanistan (PDPA) was founded with the objective of "building a socialist society in Afghanistan based on . . . adapting Marxist-Leninist revolutionary principles to conditions in Afghanistan."[44] Nur Mohammed Taraki, a leftist intellectual, former government bureaucrat, and translator for the U.S. embassy, was named general secretary. Taraki was a Pushtun author of some reputation. Henry Bradsher had this to say of his character:

> But he was a writer and dreamer, a teahouse talker rather than a schemer or organizer, a man with lofty goals but little realistic sense of how to achieve them. Although shy and somewhat retiring, he could fire others with his mission of reform, but they had to find a way to carry out his dreams because he was incapable of following through effectively.[45]

Another prominent PDPA founder was Babrak Karmal. Karmal was a former government bureaucrat who was elected twice to the parliament. While Taraki was an introverted intellectual,

> Karmal was the fiery, dramatic leader of the leftists in the parliament elected in 1965, a man who wanted to be at the center of the political action, even if that meant splitting the Marxist movement. Chastised by time in prison, and tempered by working within the bureaucracy, he had a realistic sense of what was possible within Afghan society, if a warped sense of what ends might be acceptable to achieve it.[46]

In April 1966, the PDPA published its newspaper *Khalq* ("Masses"). To say that it was heavy with Marxist-Leninist rhetoric is an understatement. Published "for the sake of the unlimited pains of the oppressed peoples of Afghanistan," the paper proclaimed the "most outstanding subject of contemporary history" to be the international class struggle "which began with the Great Socialist Revolution of October."[47] To solve the problems of their "feudalistic system," *Khalq* recommended a planned economy, government ownership of major industries, the creation of an infrastructure based on heavy industry, protection against foreign products, the formation of handicraft and agriculture cooperatives, land reform, the creation of state farms on uncultivated land, and the development of irrigation. *Khalq*'s government was to be a "national democratic" one designed to "free [the people] from the shackles of feudalism and the influences of imperialism." The government stopped the publication of *Khalq* after only six issues.

The PDPA split into two factions—Taraki's *Khalq* (Masses) and Karmal's *Parcham* (Flag or Banner)—in 1967. The split concerned personalities and tactics but both factions remained slavishly pro-Moscow. Karmal, a member of parliament, wanted to work within the present regime, but Taraki took a harder, more revolutionary line. Parcham was definitely stronger among students and Kabul intellectuals, while Khalq would make a stronger recruiting drive among army officers.

In the early 1970s Parcham with its more flexible attitude would have the greater impact. Even before the Daoud coup, the PDPA, and mainly the Parcham faction within the PDPA, had made important gains in the urban areas. A comprehensive 1971 U.S. embassy study concluded that

> In the last four years, the leftist forces, both pro-Moscow and pro-Peking, have made important gains among students and the urban-oriented, lower-level professionnals, e.g. lycea teachers. Leftist demonstrations have become common. Essentially the increasing strength of the left is a reflection of the growing disillusionment and frustration with the existing social/economic conditions and the apparent inability or unwillingness of the leadership to tackle boldly the nation's problems.[48]

This discontent, as mirrored in the 1971 student strike, when coupled with poor agricultural performance and severe food shortages would mark the constitutional monarchy's final hour.[49]

Summary

The postwar era in South Asia was marked by the retirement of Britain from the subcontinent. Although the United States moved into this power vacuum by fostering relations with Iran and Paakistan, it viewed Afghanistan as less important strategically and too close to the Soviet Union politically and geographically to be fertile ground for a close relationship.

While U.S. objectives were limited, Soviet objectives, particularly after the death of Stalin, included keeping Afghanistan out of a Northern Tier alliance and encouraging close ties to the point of dependence. In all, the Soviet's highly visible military and economic aid outweighed U.S. efforts by a factor of three to one by 1973.

Soviet-Afghan relations were most intense during the 1953–63 prime ministership of Mohammed Daoud, but remained close and cordial during the constitutional monarchy from 1963 to 1973. This was not surprising. Indeed, it represented continuity with Soviet policy in the prewar period. Soviet success during this period can be attributed to Afghanistan's unique geopolitical position and needs, neither of which aroused U.S. interest to the extent that they did Soviet interest.

In the period from 1973 to 1978, the Daoud regime would present the Soviets with greater opportunities to make inroads into Afghanistan at the same time that relatively favorable revolutionary circumstances were developing there. Growing Soviet military strength and the salience of the Sino-Soviet rift (discussed below) would be important factors as well.

Notes

1. Dupree, *Afghanistan*, p. xx.
2. Roger E. Kanet, "Soviet Attitudes Toward Developing Nations Since Stalin," in Kanet, *The Soviet Union and the Developing Nations*, p. 27.
3. Poullada, "Afghanistan and the United States," p. 182.
4. Quoted in Adamec, *Afghanistan's Foreign Affairs*, pp. 235–36.
5. *New York Times*, August 9, 1946, p. 5. Also quoted in Bradsher, *Afghanistan and the Soviet Union*, p. 18.
6. Dupree, *Afghanistan*, pp. 510–11. Also see Khalilzad, "The Superpowers and the Northern Tier."
7. U.S. Embassy, Kabul, *Policy Review: A U.S. Strategy for the '70's*, p. 1, Annex. Emphasis in the original.
8. Quoted in U.S. Dept. of State, *Foreign Relations of the United States, 1952–54*, Volume XI: Africa and South Asia, Part 2 (Washington, D.C.: USGPO, 1983), p. 1475.
9. U.S. Dept. of State, Bureau of Near East Affairs (NEA), *Long-Term Commitment to Afghanistan's Economic Development Program*, p. 1. Emphasis in the original.
10. The quote is from ibid., p. 39. For additional material on U.S. goals, also see U.S. Dept. of State, Office of Intelligence and Research, *The Future of Afghan-Soviet Relations*.
11. U.S. National Security Council, *Expansion of Soviet Influence in Afghanistan and U.S. Countermeasures*.
12. Ulam, *Expansion and Coexistence*, pp. 543–44. On the two-camp the-

ory see the extract of Andrei Zhdanov's *The International Situation* in Alvin Z. Rubinstein, ed., *The Foreign Policy of the Soviet Union* (New York: Random House, 1960), pp. 236–40; and the "Report of the Central Committee of the All-Union Communist Party (of Bolsheviks) to the 19th Party Congress," *Current Soviet Policies: The Documentary Record of the 19th Party Congress and the Reorganization after Stalin's Death* (New York: Praeger, for the American Association for the Advancement of Slavic Studies, 1953).

13. Quoted in Kanet, "Soviet Attidues Toward Developing Nations Since Stalin," p. 28.

14. Ibid., p. 29.

15. Bradsher, *Afghanistan and the Soviet Union*, p. 24.

16. Khrushchev, *Khrushchev Remembers*, p. 508.

17. *New York Times*, February 8, 1956, p. 32.

18. *Pravda*, March 6, 1960, p. 1–3 in *Current Digest of the Soviet Press*, vol. 12, no. 10, April 6, 1960, p. 7. (Hereafter cited as CDSP–volume–number–page).

19. See *Pravda*, March 25, 1961, p. 3 and April 3, 1961, p. 4 in CDSP–13–12, 14–20 and 30, respectively.

20. U.S. Dept. of State, NEA, *Long-Term Commitment to Afghanistan's Economic Development Program*," p. 11; also, Arnold, *Afghanistan: The Soviet Invasion in Perspective*, p. 41.

21. *Izvestiia*, September 9, 1961, p. 2 in CDSP–13–36–20.

22. Penkovskiy, *The Penkovskiy Papers*, p. 77. For a brief discussion on the authenticity of these memoirs see Frank Gibney's introduction, pp. v–xx, in the same edition.

23. U.S. Dept. of State, *The Future of Soviet-Afghan Relations*, pp. 10–12.

24. For details on early Soviet military aid to Afghanistan, see: ibid.; and Hurewitz, *Middle East Politics*, pp. 301–05. For a comprehensive survey of Soviet-Afghan military relations, see Rader, "The Russian Military and Afghanistan," pp. 308–28.

25. Newell and Newell, *The Struggle for Afghanistan*, p. 42.

26. Teplinskiy, *SSSR i Afghanistan*, pp. 151–53.

27. Government of Afghanistan, *Afghanistan's Foreign Trade, 1335 Through 1342*, p. 1. Figures are in nominal dollars.

28. For a commentary on the "Red Prince" title see Fletcher, *Afghanistan: Highway of Conquest*, p. 285.

29. Ibid., p. 261.

30. Nollau and Wiche, *Russia's South Flank*, p. 136.

31. *Pravda*, February 9, 1960, pp. 3–4 in CDSP–12–6–19. Emphasis in the original.

32. *Pravda*, April 7, 1961, p. 6 in CDSP–13–14–31.

33. *Pravda*, March 6, 1960, pp. 1–3 in CDSP–12–10–6.

34. *Izvestiia*, February 2, 1963, p. 4. in CDSP–15–5–20, 21. A more realistic account of how the Shah attempted in 1962 to improve Iranian-Soviet relations can be found in Rubin, *Paved With Good Intentions*, pp. 107–10.

35. For a translation of the complete Central Committee Report by Leonid I. Brezhnev, see *Pravda,* March 30, 1966, pp. 2–9 in CDSP–18–12–12, 13 ff.

36. Newell, *The Politics of Afghanistan,* p. 148.

37. *New York Times,* June 7, 1973, p. 16.

38. U.S. Army, *Area Handbook for Afghanistan,* pp. 395–397.

39. *Krasnaia zvezda,* December 28, 1969, p. 1. in CDSP–21–52–24.

40. On the various visits see, respectively: Murphy, *Brezhnev: Soviet Politician,* pp. 181–83; *Pravda,* August 16, 1965, p. 1 in CDSP–17–33–13, 14; *Pravda,* Feb. 11, 1966, p. 1, 4 in CDSP–18–6–24; *Pravda,* June 4, 1967, pp. 1, 4 in CDSP–19–22; *Pravda,* May 30, 1969, pp. 1, 4 in CDSP–21–22 and *Krasnaia zvezda,* December 28, 1969, p. 1 in CDSP–21–52–24; *Pravda,* September 15, 1971, pp. 1, 4 in CDSP–23–38–5, 6; *Pravda,* March 22, 1972, p. 1, 4 in CDSP–24–12–10, 11; and *Pravda,* May 26, 1973, pp. 1–2 in CDSP–25–21–15.

41. *Pravda,* June 21, 1972, p. 4 in CDSP–24–25–8, 9.

42. Rubinstein, *Soviet Policy Toward Turkey, Iran, and Afghanistan,* p. 139.

43. *New York Times,* June 7, 1973, p. 16.

44. PDPA, *The Establishment of the Marxist Leninist Party in Afghanistan,* p. 2.

45. Bradsher, *Afghanistan and the Soviet Union,* p. 36.

46. Ibid.

47. *Khalq,* April 11, 1966, an unpublished mimeograph translation, page 1. The program of the Khalq can be found on pp. 7–20 of the translation.

48. U.S. Embassy, Kabul, *Policy Review: A U.S. Strategy for the '70's,* p. 5, Annex.

49. *New York Times,* June 7, 1973, p. 16.

3
Soviet-Afghan Relations, 1973–1978: From Revolution to Revolution

By the summer of 1973, the constitutional monarchy had run its course. Every sector of the government suffered from mismanagement and even the army had become disaffected from the monarchy. Mohammed Daoud, a prince, a general, and a former prime minister, executed a coup in July 1973, and quickly consolidated power.

In contrast to his first prime ministership, Daoud down-played the Pushtunistan issue and pursued a more genuine form of nonalignment. The Soviets were initially pleased that he had seized power, but they found Daoud increasingly autocratic and difficult to deal with. From 1975 to 1978, the Soviets maintained good relations with Daoud while at the same time beginning to prepare for the possibility of his downfall, skillfully burning the candle at both ends. At the same time, Afghan trade and aid dependence on the USSR increased and the Soviets continued to give a high priority to military and economic assistance to the regime. In the midst of all this, the PDPA, with Soviet assistance, grew stronger, with military recruitment becoming an important facet of its activities.

The Daoud Coup

During his ten years out of office, Mohammed Daoud had maintained a "running seminar" to discuss what had gone wrong during his regime and how to solve the problems of contemporary Afghanistan.[1] Among Daoud's students were many Soviet-trained army officers and a number of PDPA members, mostly from Karmal's Parcham faction. Discussion of a coup probably began in 1969, after election irregularities had indicated that the constitutional monarchy's days were numbered.

On July 17, 1973, Daoud struck. Supported by nearly the entire army, including the Special Unit palace guard, the coup was nearly bloodless and took less than twenty-four hours to execute. Zahir Shah, already on vacation in Italy, was exiled. His family later joined him.

Daoud quickly proclaimed the founding of the Republic of Afghanistan which was to conform "to the true spirit of Islam."² At this time, he reaffirmed his commitment to a foreign policy of *bi-tarafi* (without sides) and abjured membership in military blocs. On the Pushtunistan issue, he said, "Our relations with Pakistan, which is the only nation with whom we have a political difference . . . will be based on our continuous efforts to find a peaceful solution to the Pushtunistan problem."³

Daoud was proclaimed president and also held the defense and foreign affairs portfolios. His initial cabinet was dominated by PDPA members or sympathizers. As Anthony Arnold has noted,

> Although none of these men had been a PDPA Central Committee member or alternate in 1965, no fewer than eight out of fourteen [cabinet members] were known—then or later—as PDPA members, former members, or strong sympathizers. This category included the only two officials of ministerial rank to carry over from the previous government to Daoud's without demotion. Six of the eight leftists were to hold important positions in government under Babrak Karmal in 1980.⁴

Many of Daoud's middle-ranking military supporters were also PDPA members. Four of the supporters—Abdul Qader, Aslam Watanjar, Sayed M. Gulabzoy and S.J. Mazdooryar—were to be prime movers in the 1978 coup as well.

On July 19, 1973, the Soviet Union became the first to recognize the new republic, just as they had been the first to recognize Amanullah, Nadir Shah, and later Taraki. The complete text of the identical *Pravda* and *Izvestiia* articles on July 21st read: "Guided by its unchanging feelings of friendship for the Afghan people, the Soviet government has officially recognized the Republic of Afghanistan."⁵ Another week would pass until Brezhnev, Podgorny, and Kosygin would send their personal greetings.

One of the most complete Soviet analyses of the coup came in *Izvestiia* in January 1974. According to this article, the monarchy was simply unable to overcome the problems of a state "in which feudal and semifeudal relations prevailed." Daoud, to the *Izvestiia* correspondent, was a progressive who would give "serious attention" to land reform and "a policy of industrializing the country while increasing the state sector's share in the national economy."⁶

For the next year and a half, Daoud was preoccupied with consolidating power. By October, he had defeated two suspected coups, one which centered around General Abdul Wali, the former army commander, and another which centered around former prime minister Maiwandwal. Shortly thereafter he began to reduce the number of leftists in his cabinet. Minister of Frontier Affairs Pacha Gul, a former air force officer, was posted to Bulgaria after it became known that he had violated military law by marrying a Russian woman. Minister of Communications Abdul Hamid Mohtat was dismissed within a year for his vocal opposition to Daoud's policies. Minister of Education Nehmatullah Pazhwak and Minister of Agriculture Jilani Bakhtary were also dismissed in 1974 and 1975, respectively.[7]

The rank-and-file Parchami were dealt with in a more sophisticated fashsion. In 1974, Daoud sent over 160 Parchami to man district and subdistrict police and administrative posts. These officials

> ran headlong into the rural power elites . . . The new cadre of administrators became frustrated, and most did one of two things: accepted the fact that change would be slow and within the existing patterns, and so stayed at their posts and became effective; others, cynically, turned as corrupt as any of their predecessors.[8]

In 1975, Daoud set up his own party, the National Revolutionary Party. Afghanistan had become, in the legal sense, a one-party republic.

The Changing International Environment

Both Soviet and Afghan foreign policy during the Daoud regime were strongly conditioned by a changing international environment. Three key factors deserve mention here.

First, the United States and the Soviet Union had moderated their hostilities and were entering a period of detente. While this relationship was in its most positive phase (1972–74) the expected gains from detente exerted in some cases a moderating influence on Soviet behavior. As detente weakened, the expectation of gain disappeared and the Soviets lost an incentive toward moderate behavior. Moreover, in the Third World, the disintegration of the Portugese colonial empire, the victory of North Vietnam, and the fall of Haile Selassie provided the USSR with new opportunities to expand its influence in the Third World. This phenomenon was not one-sided. Losses in Chile, Egypt, and Somalia gave Soviet analysts reason to be flexible in their approach to new allies and only guardedly optimistic about trends in the 1973–78 period.

Second, Sino-Soviet relations had hit bottom. The year 1969 even saw fighting between Chinese and Soviet forces on Damansky Island in the Ussuri River. By 1976, all the Soviets realistically were hoping for from the Chinese was some variant of "peaceful coexistence," a term generally reserved only for nations with a capitalist system.[9] Relationships with Asian countries now took on a new meaning. Not only were the Soviets competing for influence with the United States, but they now had China to worry about as well. Both China and the Soviet Union seemed interested in ringing the other nation with its allies. The Soviets had more success on this score than the Chinese. Not only were Vietnam (and later Kampuchea), India, and Afghanistan the beneficiaries of Soviet friendship, but relations drastically improved between the Soviet Union and Pakistan (now under the leadership of Zulfikar Ali Bhutto), and Iran. The Shah even made two highly successful visits to Moscow in 1965 and 1974.

Finally, in 1973–74 the world was reminded that in the Middle East and South Asia there was a third force to be reckoned with: the oil-rich Islamic states of the Middle East. Not only had these states become—especially in the case of Iran and Saudi Arabia—a key factor in the Arab-Israeli dispute and global energy politics, but they also had become an alternate source of aid, particularly for poorer states with Islamic populations.

Soviet-Afghan Relations, 1973–1975

During the first two years of the Daoud regime, Soviet-Afghan relations in the fields of aid and military assistance appeared generally to mirror the pattern established during the first Daoud regime. On the aid front, in conjunction with the $120 million outlay in 1972, the Soviets, as a result of Daoud's visit in June 1974, agreed to a $150 million credit that supported twenty-one projects, including a natural gas pipeline over the Amu Darya to the Soviet Union.[10] This aid, when coupled with increased exports of natural gas, several Soviet moratoria on debt repayment, and remittances from Afghan workers overseas, made for favorable economic conditions during the first four years of the second Daoud regime.

In the field of military aid, the onset of the Daoud regime visibly demonstrated that Soviet-Afghan cooperation had gained in scope after July 1973.[11] While the total value of Soviet and East European arms transfers in 1971 and 1972 was $66 million, the total for 1973 and 1974 was $137 million. New tanks, personnel carriers, howitzers, and aircraft were among the equipment delivered. By 1978, the 100,000-man Afghan armed forces were, as far as equipment goes, a relatively modern fighting force, equipped even with some T–62s and MiG–21 aircraft. By 1978, at least 4,000 Afghan officers had been trained in the Soviet Union, some for as long as four years.[12]

The Pushtunistan issue, as one might have expected, flared again in the early years of the second Daoud regime. While the level of rhetoric was high from 1973–75, Daoud never pressed the issue to the point that he had in 1961. First, the Soviets, as mentioned in the previous chapter, would not support a tough policy on this issue. Second, after the advent of Bhutto in 1973 and his Moscow visit in 1974, relations between Moscow and Islamabad improved, thus creating another disincentive to support Afghanistan on the Pushtunistan issue. As stated in the joint Soviet-Pakistani communiqué of October 1974, the Soviets most fervent hope was "that the disagreements between Pakistan and Afghanistan will be settled by peaceful means, through talks based on the principle of peaceful coexistence."[13] Third, fostering a dispute with a fellow Islamic nation was not popular with Iran or the other Gulf states that Daoud was courting as potential aid donors for Afghanistan. Fourth, Daoud had had ten years to contemplate why his previous regime had foundered. It is highly likely that he came to the accurate realization that his overemphasis on Pushtunistan had wrecked his previous tenure as prime minister. Finally, some observers claim that Daoud had good reason to realize, after sending some small raiding parties into Pakistan in 1975, that Pakistan was far too strong for even a modern Afghan army.[14]

Afghanistan, in the period 1973–75, generally supported Soviet foreign policy positions and continued in its role—as a 1975 Soviet text on foreign policy stated—as "a model of fruitful cooperation between a socialist and a developing state."[15] Afghanistan was an early supporter of Brezhenev's plan for Asian collective security, but as early as June 1975, Daoud had expressed his reservations about the plan's accent on the inviolability of frontiers which served Soviet interests toward China but which did nothing for Afghanistan on the Pushtunistan issue. Daoud said that he highly appreciated Soviet thoughts on Asian collective security. "But Afghanistan believes that genuine peace can be established when the legitimate rights of the masses of people are recognized."[16] Nevertheless, the joint communiqué following Daoud's visit and subsequent communiqués in 1975 and 1977 marked Afghanistan as one of the few supporters of the Soviet call for a collective security system in Asia.

Pursuing Nonalignment: Afghan Initiatives, Soviet Reactions

Early in his second regime Daoud eliminated his domestic rivals, particularly those on the left. Beginning in 1974, Daoud also began to decrease his reliance on his Soviet benefactors for aid and military assistance. This policy was oriented toward strengthening his own power base, demonstrating his independence to his domestic audience, and also toward adjusting to what he perceived to be "new realities" in the region.[17]

In March 1974, Daoud initiated a military training arrangement with India and later Egypt. These agreements were both with nations with some reputation for independence which also were using Soviet military equipment. Additionally, in September 1975, Daoud dismissed forty Soviet-trained officers.

In the aid area, Daoud pursued and received in April 1975 a $2 billion pledge of aid from Iran, an amount equal to all of the foreign assistance which Afghanistan had received from all sources since 1953.[18] Very little of this aid (perhaps less than $10 million) was ever given, however, due to the Shah's own economic problems and a continuing bilateral dispute with Afghanistan over the headwaters of the Helmand River. China also provided a $55 million loan after Daoud's brother Naim visited Beijing late in 1974.

Diplomatic contacts widened as well. Bhutto and Zia-ul-Haq exchanged visits with Daoud in 1976 and 1977, achieving much in the way of dampening bilateral tensions over Pushtunistan. In February 1978 Daoud received U.S. Admiral Maurice Weisner, the U.S. Commander-in-Chief, Pacific, and also visited Yugoslavia, Libya, Iran, and Pakistan. In April, he visited Saudi Arabia, Kuwait, and Egypt. One analyst has indicated that Daoud was even working with Yugoslavia to block Cuban leadership of the nonaligned movement.[19]

Daoud's receipt of aid and goodwill from Pakistan, Iran, and the People's Republic of China were somewhat ironic. All three of these countries had imagined a Soviet hand in the 1973 coup and they initially saw his regime as inimical to their interests. The Shah told Secretary Kissinger in 1973 that the Soviets would try "to squeeze Iran between Afghanistan and its Iraqi client." Bhutto feared that the Soviets might "press into Pakistan and toward the Indian Ocean." Zhou Enlai related that Daoud's irredentism could weaken his neighbors and "give Moscow a corridor to the Indian ocean."[20] Thus, the willingness of these three states to deal with Daoud reflelcts more than normal interactions between neighboring states. The three states in question were all practicing their own brand of containment.

Soviet-Afghan Relations, 1975–1978

Several scholars have maintained that Daoud's pursuit of a more truly nonaligned stance severely irritated the Soviets, led them to direct the reunification of the PDPA, and—a few would add—to call for a coup against him in 1978.

Some evidence to support this thesis does exist. In 1982, a Soviet scholar bluntly noted that the Shah's 1975 offer of aid had the "purpose of weakening Soviet-Afghan relations."[21] Furthermore, in 1975 the Soviet description of Soviet-Afghan talks down-played "friendship" and introduced the term "frankness," which usually means that there is some serious disagreement between the parties. During Daoud's visit to Moscow in 1977, according to a recent book,

> Brezhnev suddenly challenged Daoud to "get rid of all those imperialist advisers in your country." Daoud replied coldly that when Afghanistan had no further need of foreign advisers they would all be asked to leave. Naim ascribed more significance to this exchange than did Daoud, who took it as nothing more than a typical Soviet gambit, designed to put him on the defensive.[22]

Finally, there is ample evidence that the PDPA reunified with some urging by the Communist Party of India (CPI). An unidentified CPI official told author Henry Bradsher that an invitation to a Khalq-Parcham meeting in India in [March] 1977 was offered "with the knowledge and consent of [the] Soviet Union; otherwise, [the] CPI would not have undertaken it."

The causes of these actions by the Soviet Union are unclear. One could speculate that the Soviets were uncomfortable with Daoud's warming to Pakistan, allied with China, and Iran, allied to the United States. Daoud's haughty personal manner and his intolerance of Afghan leftists may have been supporting factors. In any case, authoritative Soviet sources later noted that the PDPA reunited in March 1977 and held a reunification conference in July 1977.[23]

On the other hand, there is some evidence which suggests that this thesis is imprecise, if not partially incorrect. If this thesis were true, one could expect some open or veiled criticism of Daoud to have taken place in the Soviet media from 1975–78. Furthermore, trade, aid, and military assistance would probably have suffered if the Soviets had perceived that Daoud was going the way of Mao Zedong, Tito, or Anwar Sadat.

There was no criticism of Daoud or Afghanistan in the Soviet media during this period. At the Twenty-fifth Party Congress in 1976, there was a favorable reference to Afghanistan, as there had been many times before. In 1976, a highly favorable article in *International Affairs* (Moscow) proclaimed that Soviet-Afghan cooperation had "gained in scope" with the onset of the second Daoud regime and again, in that all too familiar phraseology, that "the friendly, equal relations between the USSR and Afghanistan, which have passed the test of time, are a good example of the fruitfulness of the policy of peaceful coexistence."[24] In April 1977, during the same visit when Brezhnev reportedly had his confrontation with Daoud, the term "frankness" was not used in the joint communiqué and the atmosphere was described as one of "friendship, trust, and mutual understanding." In May 1977, *International Affairs* (Moscow) published a highly complimentary article on Afghanistan with two favorable references to Daoud himself.[25]

Trade, aid, and military assistance also increased from 1975 to 1978. As table 3–1 shows, Soviet exports increased nearly 68 percent between 1975 and 1978. The value of imports from Afghanistan increased by nearly 20 percent. Furthermore, the Soviet-Afghan relationship was not maintained solely for Soviet economic gains. The Soviets funded the bilateral trade deficit with Afghanistan and development assistance also increased. In 1977, a new, twelve-year agreement on economic cooperation was signed and the Soviet Union in 1975 gave Afghanistan a credit of $425 million for Daoud's Seven Year Plan (1976–1983). This was the largest single disbursement that the Soviets had ever made to Afghanistan. Of these funds, $60 million were allocated for 1977. In all, from 1956 to 1977, Soviet economic aid (mostly loans) to Afghanistan ($1.3 billion) was exceeded in the Middle East and South Asia only by the amount given to Egypt, Syria, and India.[26]

Arms transfers also increased from 1975 to 1978. New items of equipment—the MiG–21, the BMP infantry combat vehicle, and the T–62 tank—appeared and Soviet arms transfers set a new record for single-

Table 3–1
Soviet-Afghan Trade, 1975–1977
(millions of rubles)

Trade Category	1975	1976	1977
Soviet Exports to Afghanistan			
Total	67.9	87.5	113.6
Machinery and Industrial Equipment	24.6	46.0	67.3
Oil and Petroleum Products	12.9	14.3	18.6
Rolled Steel	0.9	0.8	1.2
Wheat	1.0	—	3.2
Sugar	11.9	7.5	4.7
Soviet Imports from Afghanistan			
Total	64.3	66.8	76.5
Natural Gas	35.5	31.5	29.2
Cotton	7.9	11.9	19.1
Wool	5.3	6.0	4.6
Fresh and Dried Fruit	16.2	13.4	28.3

Sources: Adapted from *Vneshnyaya torgovlya SSR v 1976 g. (Foreign Trade of the USSR in 1976)*, pp. 212–214; *Vneshnyaya torgovlya SSR v 1978 g.*, pp. 197–198.

year deliveries to Afghanistan, with $127 million dollars worth of equipment being delivered in 1977.[27]

In January 1977, the U.S. ambassador concluded in his annual policy assessment: "The Soviets and their adherents may have lost some of their potential for influence here but, as far as we can tell, Moscow does not feel losses to any extent which would create Soviet suspicion that the United States might be threatening the USSR's vital interests. Afghan supporters of the Soviet case are virtually without influence."[28] A year later, the ambassador again concluded that "Moscow appears content with the status quo, and shows no signs that it has designs to augment significantly its political or economic position in this country."[29]

On balance, it appears that the USSR began in late 1976 to prepare for post-Daoud eventualities. No doubt they were dissatisfied with his pursuit of nonalignment, but there is no substantive evidence that they began to plot his ouster. The Soviets were preparing for an uncertain future but they were apparently prepared to continue to interact with the Daoud regime. Their long-term aid and military assistance programs seem to suggest that they believed that he would hold on for at least a few more years.

The above examination of Soviet actions also supports two other important conclusions. First, given the nature of the communiqué following the 1977 visit, it does not appear that the Daoud-Brezhnev confrontation was regarded, in itself, as serious by the Soviets. Had that been the case, in all probability it would have been reflected in the communiqué. Second, a review of Soviet sources (detailed below) suggests that the Soviets knew beyond a doubt that the PDPA wanted to launch a coup. Other signs, such as long-term aid and frequent favorable references to Daoud personally, suggest that, from the Soviet perspective, the coup would probably take place a few years in the future.

PDPA Activities

While Moscow may not have had designs, there were others who did. By their own account, the Khalq faction of the PDPA, from 1973 forward, stepped up recruiting among members of the armed forces. According to the official PDPA history of the revolution, "Comrade Taraki realized . . . that under the conditions prevailing in Afghanistan the best guarantee for the people's victory . . . depended on the cooperation of the Afghan armed forces."[30]

The task of penetrating the armed forces was entrusted to Hafizullah Amin, who had begun his rise to power after the Khalq-Parcham split of 1967, when he was appointed an alternate member of the PDPA

Central Committee. Amin was a former member of Parliament who had studied during the late 1950s and early 1960s at Teachers College of Columbia University. While Taraki was the "Great Leader," and chief theorist, Amin was an activist, and the organizer of the Khalq faction.

Amin, according to official accounts, briefed Taraki every week on his recruiting activities.[31] The impetuous Amin even recommended in 1976 that the PDPA should "seize political power from the despotic Daoud." Taraki demurred, although the official history is not clear about why he did so. The history records Taraki's reply as follows: "Comrade Taraki further guided Comrade Amin with his radiant political insight issuing concrete instructions to him on his party work among the armed forces."[32]

One reason why Taraki demurred may have been alluded to in another section of the history dealing with a different subject. Perhaps the military was not ready to move. "The armed forces' leading cadres were trained under Comrade Amin on making preparations for the revolution in such a manner that *they themselves did not feel the time for action was fast approaching* but were increasingly getting conscious of their military surroundings as well as their revolutionary tactics and strategy."[33]

Another reason why Taraki failed to move in 1976 may have been PDPA disunity. In 1976 the party was divided. In March the Parcham faction published a declaration from "The Committee of Afghan Communists Abroad" which criticized Taraki and the Khalq for "a campaign of vilification," and for claiming Khalq was the true "Communist Party of Afghanistan." The Parcham document accurately pointed out that Khalq had neither received such recognition nor had it been invited to international party conferences or "listed among the Communist Parties and working classes of the world."[34] In July 1976, Khalq distributed its secret history, *The Establishment of the Marxist-Leninist Party in Afghanistan*, which was for the most part a stinging indictment of Babrak Karmal. In this document Karmal was accused of splitting the party, supporting the monarchy, and colluding with the police and various other rightists.

What happened to heal the rift is the subject of conjecture. Given the tendency toward lifelong feuds in Afghanistan, however, this subject demands some attention.

There is ample evidence, as stated above, that the PDPA reunified with some urging by the Communist Party of India (CPI). There were also many reasons to reunify which were internal to the struggle in Afghanistan. Both parties together numbered no more than a few thousand adherents.[35] Khalq needed Parcham adherents in the bureaucracy, and even more important Parcham could not have failed to recognize Khalqi strength in the military. Even the critical Parcham document signed as "The Committee of the Afghan Communists Abroad," contains an appeal for unity. According to Parcham,

> [The Khalq] should rather work for unity among the political organizations of the working class in Afghanistan, and for strengthening democracy in that country. They should survive against Imperialism and Reactionaries and work for unity among all national and progressive forces for the achievement of peace, national independence, social progress, and socialism.[36]

Daoud was also becoming increasingly unpopular. Though economic conditions were far better than they had been in 1963 or 1973 when the last governmental changes had taken place, the country by any standard was still woefully underdeveloped. Daoud's government was highly autocratic and his move "Daoudward" had alienated many of his progressive supporters, including his brother Naim. As Louis Dupree has noted,

> By summer 1977, support for the republic had dissipated almost completely. The possibility that Taraki might succeed Daoud, legally or illegally, was widely discussed at Kabul University and throughout the Afghan intellectual community.[37]

When the factions met in July 1977, "the question of the removal of Daoud," according to Soviet sources, was placed on the conference agenda but apparently was not resolved at that time."[38] Events would soon force the PDPA's hand.

Notes

1. Dupree, "A Note on Afghanistan: 1974," p. 1–2.
2. Ibid., p. 2.
3. Ibid.
4. Arnold, *Afghanistan: the Soviet Invasion in Perspective*, pp. 56–57.
5. Page 1 in *Izvestiia*, and on page 5 in *Pravda*.
6. *Izvestiia*, Jan. 3, 1974, p. 4.
7. Dupree, "Red Flag Over the Hindu Kush, Part I," pp. 12–13.
8. Dupree, *The New Republic of Afghanistan: The First Twenty-one Months*, p. 8.
9. Leonid I. Brezhnev, *Report to CPSU Central Committee and the Party's Immediate Tasks in the Fields of Domestic and Foreign Policy*, in *Pravda*, Feb. 25, 1976, p. 2–9.
10. Dupree, "A Note on Afghanistan: 1974," p. 8.

11. Yurlov, "USSR-Afghanistan: Good Neighborly Relations," pp. 137–38.

12. On arms transfer values, see U.S. Arms Control and Disarmament Agency (ACDA), *World Military Expenditures and Arms Transfers, 1971–1980*, p. 80. On the type of equipment, see Garrity, "The Soviet Military Stake in Afghanistan: 1956–79," pp. 31–32; and Rader, "The Russian Military and Afghanistan: An Historical Perspective," pp. 316–23.

13. *Pravda*, Oct. 25, 1974, p. 4 in CDSP–26–43–16.

14. For indications of Afghan covert activities, see Eliot, "Afghanistan After the 1978 Revolution," p. 59; and Dupree, "Toward Representative Government in Afghanistan, Part 1, p. 6.

15. Ovsyany, *A Study of Soviet Foreign Policy*, p. 121.

16. *Pravda*, June 6, 1974, p. 4 in CDSP–26–23–11, 12.

17. See Selig Harrison's editorial in the *Washington Post*, February 13, 1979, pp. C1, C5.

18. Ibid. On Iranian aid, see Dupree, "Red Flag Over the Hindu Kush, Part IV," p. 1.

19. Rubinstein, *Soviet Policy Toward Turkey, Iran, and Afghanistan*, p. 150.

20. Henry A. Kissinger, *Years of Upheaval*, pp. 675–77, 687. The quoted passages are Kissinger's summaries.

21. Gurevich, "Socioeconomic Preconditions of the 1978 Revolution in Afghanistan," p. 15.

22. Arnold, *Afghanistan: the Soviet Invasion in Perspective*, p. 65. Rubinstein, *Soviet Policy Toward Turkey, Iran, and Afghanistan*, contains a similar description. Arnold's source is a relative of Daoud's who was not present at the meeting. An Afghan defector's account is in the *Sunday Telegraph* (London), June 24, 1984, p. 10.

23. Bradsher, *Afghanistan and the Soviet Union*, p. 70. For a Soviet source, see R.A. Ul'yanovskiy, "The Afghan Revolution at the Current Stage," p. 9. For a secondhand confirmation of Moscow's role, see Marie Broxup, "The Soviets in Afghanistan: Anatomy of a Takeover," *Central Asian Survey* 1 (April 1983):105, n. 10.

24. Yurlov, "USSR-Afghanistan: Good Neighborly Relations," p. 138.

25. Kunov, "Developing Good Neighborly Relations," pp. 201–5. For the text of the communiqué, *Pravda*, April 15, 1977, pp. 1, 4.

26. The text of the economic agreement appeared in *Pravda*, April 15, 1977, p. 4. On trade and aid, see CIA, *Communist Aid to the Less Developed Countries of the Third World, 1977*, pp. i–ii, 1–11, 35–36 and *Radio Liberty Research Bulletin*, RL 84/80, Feb. 25, 1980. pp. 1–4.

27. U.S. Arms Control & Disarmament Agencies, *World Military Expenditures and Arms Transfers, 1971–1980*, p. 80.

28. U.S. Embassy, Kabul, *Annual Policy Assessment 1977*, p. 2.

29. U.S. Embassy, Kabul, *Annual Policy Assessment, Additional Submission*, Airgram A–13, Feb. 27, 1978, p. 7 of inclosure 1.

30. Political Department of the Afghan Armed Forces, *On the Saur [April] Revolution*, May 22, 1978, p. 3.

31. Ibid.

32. Ibid., p. 9.

33. Ibid., p. 11. Emphasis added.
34. The document can be found in U.S. Embassy, Kabul, *History of Khalqi-Parchami Infighting Before the Afghan Revolution,* p. 7, 8, 9 of Inclosure 1.
35. PDPA membership figures can not be verified. The figure of a few thousand is taken from Dupree, "Afghanistan under the Khalq," pp. 34–50 and it generally conforms with U.S. government estimates of the same period.
36. See material cited in note 34, above.
37. Dupree, "The Democratic Republic of Afghanistan, 1979," p. 2.
38. Ul'yanovskiy, "The Afghan Revolution at the Current Stage," p. 9.

4
The Saur Revolution: April 1978–August 1979

Soviet policy in the late 1970s has been described as burning the candle at both ends: maintaining good relations with Daoud while strengthening his opponents in the PDPA. During the period covered by this chapter, this policy would bear fruit. As a result of the *Saur* (April) Revolution, pro-Moscow communists came to rule in Kabul. Although the timing of the coup was probably a surprise to the Soviets, it is apparent that they quickly decided to lend massive support to this new regime "with a socialist orientation." Increases in aid and the number of advisers shortly followed, and a friendship treaty was signed in December 1978. Despite the fact that the PDPA was on occasion slow to take Soviet advice, the Soviets continued to increase their aid and, as the insurgency grew, their military support as well.

The rationale behind this Soviet shift in policy is difficult to isolate. At this point, we can speculate that a number of factors facilitated this rapid shift. First, Taraki was known to the Soviets for at least eight years. He was probably viewed as a reliable comrade. The perception of this reliability probably increased after the Khalq-Parcham reunification. Second, the Politburo may have been encouraged and perhaps even blinded by the success of other neosocialist regimes, such as Angola and Ethiopia. Certainly, the Soviets had to do more for their Angolan and Ethiopian friends. Afghanistan appeared to have almost fallen into their laps. Finally, one must consider events in Iran. Severe outbreaks in Tabriz and Qom from January through March 1978 marked the beginning of the end for the Shah. The Soviets may have believed that a secure hold on Afghanistan was a hedge against uncertainty in Iran. (These issues and others will be addressed in more detail in chapter 8.)

Regardless of motive, April 1978 marks the start of a series of events which would take the Soviets in less than twenty months from assistance and later supervision over sectors of the Afghan government to an invasion and a costly occupation of this troubled state.

The Coup

On April 17, 1978, Mir Akbar Khyber, a former police official, a Parcham ideologue, and, in *Pravda's* words, "a well-known progressive figure" was assassinated by unknown assailants.[1] Speculation abounds on this issue. Some argued that this was the result of the intra-PDPA squabble, others claimed that Daoud and/or his secret police were more likely culprits. Even more puzzling was the relationship between this murder and the August 1977 assassination of an Ariana Airlines official who, unfortunately for him, looked like Babrak Karmal and happened to live in the same apartment complex. Were these two killings part of the same Daoudist or Khalqi plot? Given the high number of deaths in the months that followed, we will probably never know the answer to this question.

While the answer to this question is clouded, what happened next was very clear. A massive demonstration took place at Khyber's burial rites. Fifteen thousand people marched and shouted anti-U.S. slogans as they passed the U.S. embassy.[2] The ferocity of this demonstration no doubt shocked Daoud for two reasons. First, large street demonstrations were relatively uncommon in Afghanistan and their occurrence in 1965 and 1971 was associated with the downfall of two prime ministers during the constitutional monarchy. Second, the size of these demonstrations was surprising. Experts put the size of the entire PDPA at this time at about 3,000 members.[3]

The government moved quickly and on April 26 began to arrest Khalq and Parcham leaders. According to the official (and one suspects overdramatized) PDPA account,

> A few minutes after midnight on 26th April, a group of police officers of the savage Daoud Regime entered Comrade Taraki's house, searching the premises and handcuffing him. Comrade Taraki told them: "You are not police officers. On the contrary, you belong to a gang. . . . You had no right to enter my house like savages because I did not intend to flee. Should I deal you blows in self defense, the despotic Daoud Regime would use this in a special plot against the Khalqi movement".
>
> At this juncture, Mrs. Taraki pleaded with those officers to treat her husband, who had spent a lifetime in the struggle for the good of the people, like gentlemen and not as savages but to no avail. One of the officers seriously wounded Mrs. Taraki's hand with his bayonet. Sprinkling the blood onto the faces of these officers, Mrs. Taraki exclaimed "this blood would not remain unavenged!"
>
> Handcuffed and with his face covered [with] a blanket, Comrade Taraki was taken by the despotic police officers to the prison.[4]

Around the same time, officers entered the house of Hafizullah Amin and confiscated leftist printed materials. Surprisingly, Amin was not incarcerated but was only placed under house arrest. No one has been able to explain this oversight, but two theories, singly or in combination, are credible. It is quite possible that Daoud and his secret police were unaware of the depth of Amin's recruiting drive in the military and thus they thought it unimportant to bring him in with the initial wave of suspects. The fact that many key military officers with PDPA sympathies were not arrested suggests that this may be true. A second explanation from rumors in Kabul is also possible: by the time the police wagon arrived at the Amin residence, it was full. Having no room, the officers on the scene simply confiscated the evidence and left Amin under house arrest.[5] For some unexplained reason, Amin's guards were instructed not to interfere with the movement of Amin's wife or children.

The revolution owed much to this mistake. According to the official history, loyal officers had rehearsed their roles ten times and the "Great Leader" Taraki had left these instructions:

> Should imperialism, reaction, or another group topple the Daoud Regime, the Democratic People's Party of Afghanistan should wrest the political power. In case the Daoud Regime launched an offensive to incarcerate me [Comrade Taraki] in order to weaken or destroy the party members, the latter should commence the revolution to topple the Daoud Regime and wrest the political power.[6]

Amin wrote out instructions for the revolution which included twenty-two key military assignments and eight paragraphs of general instructions. Some of the coup participants even came to Amin's house to receive the orders. Amin's son, Abdur Rahman, delivered some of the other copies. At 10:30 A.M. on April 26 Amin was incarcerated but by then it was too late.

The coup began at 6:00 A.M. on April 27. This time, unlike the coup in 1973, the armed forces were divided between PDPA and Daoud loyalists and spirited fighting took place. By best estimates around 1,000 people died, including Daoud, his brother Naim, most of their families, and close to half of the 2,000-man Republican Guard.

The PDPA forces quickly hit the Arg (presidential palace), the Kabul Airport, Radio Kabul, and the central jail. By 5:00 A.M. on the 28th, PDPA forces had captured all of these objectives with only the 2,000-man Republican Guard putting up resistance at the Arg Palace.

In retrospect, the most amazing thing about the coup was that it succeeded against the odds that it faced. Table 4–1 shows the intial lineup of forces during the early stages of the coup and shows rather con-

Table 4–1
Alignment of Forces by Unit,[a] April 27

Daoud	PDPA	Undecided or Mixed
15th Armored Brigade[b]	4th Armored Brigade[b]	Misc. Air Defense Units
Commando Brigade[c]	Bagram AF Units	8th Division (Mech)[c]
32d Brigade[c]		
Shindand AF Units		
Republican Guard		
7th Infantry Division		

Source: Adapted from Louis Dupree, "Red Flag Over the Hindu Kush," Part II, pp. 5–12; Anthony Arnold, *Afghanistan*, pp. 68–74; et al.

[a] Alignments for units are approximate. Full units were generally not employed in the coup. A maximum of 5,000 troops (both sides) participated in the coup.
[b] Some refer to the 15th and 4th Armored as "divisions," but they apparently were each no more than a brigade (2–5,000 men) in strength. The PDPA used only about 50 tanks in the battle for the palace.
[c] Disarmed or neutralized early in the coup.

clusively that any pre-coup estimate of forces would, at least in the numerical dimension, favor Daoud.

In spite of limited forces, the coup succeeded because, first, the PDPA forces had a plan, and Daoud's supporters did not. Second, the PDPA was able to control the air, keeping as many as six MiG–21 or Su–7 fighters in the air at once. One Afghan pilot reportedly flew eighteen sorties, another flew thirteen sorties. Daoud's forces were unable to communicate with their air support (two MiG–21s), which flew the 400 miles from Shindand and thus had only a ten-minute loiter time over Kabul. They ultimately returned to their base with their bombloads. Third, numerous non-PDPA commanders sat out the fight, preferring to see which side would win before committing themselves.[7] Daoud, like Zahir Shah, paid the price for losing the active support of his officer corps.

The Saur Revolution was, pure and simple, an urban coup d'état against an unpopular, autocratic government. Though later propaganda would attempt to paint the coup as a popular revolt, most Kabul residents hardly recognized what was happening. Indeed the average Kabul resident was so oblivious to the events that

> Despite the danger, people queued up for buses—even in the firefight zone! Taxis honked for tanks to move over, and wove in an out as the fighting continued. At some corners, traffic policemen motioned the tanks to pull over to the curb. The tanks ignored the gestures, and rumbled on to their objectives.[8] . . .

In any case, by 7:00 P.M. on the 27th, Abdul Qader, in the name of the "Military Revolutionary Command," announced the end of "the Sultanate of the Mohammadzai [family]" and that "all power has passed to the hands of the masses."[9] The Afghan word for "masses" is khalq.

Three days mysteriously passed before PDPA loyalists and the Military Revolutionary Command passed on leadership to their civilian comrades. To date, there have been no satisfactory explanations for this delay but it does not appear likely, due to their PDPA membership, that military leaders intended to hold on to power. On the 30th, Taraki was named head of the revolutionary council and prime minister. U.S. Ambassador Theodore Eliot cabled to Washington that "the true political character of the coup leadership is now nakedly apparent to all."[10] The next day, May Day, was made an official national holiday. Also, on April 30, the Soviet Union recognized the People's Democratic Republic of Afghanistan (PDRA).

It is appropriate at this point to discuss Soviet involvement in the coup. Hannah Negaran [pseudonym], Anthony Arnold, and others maintain that the signs of Soviet complicity are there.[11] They argue that it is obvious that the Khalq-Parcham split was mended with Soviet help; that the accurate rocket fire probably came from Soviet pilots; and that the Soviet undoubtedly helped by photocopying Amin's coup instructions. Alvin Rubinstein and David Chaffetz have drawn attention to the high number of economic and aid agreements that were signed in 1978. Chaffetz said,

> The scale on which they have backed Daoud's leftist successors speaks volumes. Immediately twenty-five agreements with Comecon countries were signed by the new regime; an unusual burst of diplomacy on the part of a government scarcely secure in its own capital. While street fighting went on in Kabul, the government began contracting for Bulgarian television and East German printing equipment, together with an additional $22 million from the Soviet Union to exploit natural gas. Fidel Castro paid a brief visit shortly after the revolution, presumably to assure the new government that it is possible to run a small country entirely on Soviet aid for years.[12]

While one must admit that there was a high probability that the Soviet Union had a hand in getting Khalq and Parcham back together, there is still a wide gap between this and planning or ordering a coup. Moreover, it is not entirely clear that Moscow had written off Daoud. If it had done so, how does one explain the massive dose of developmental assistance and military aid which Moscow gave the Daoud regime in its last three years?

On the subject of air support, the equation "accurate rocket fire equals Soviet pilots" is not persuasive. Many Afghan pilots were well-trained in the Soviet Union and only a few pilots participated in the actual fighting. As previously mentioned, according to Dupree, two Afghan pilots alone accounted for thirty-one sorties.

On the issue of photocopying instructions, there is no definitive evidence that the coup order was photocopied and, if it was, there is no evidence to prove that it was done in the Soviet embassy. The PDPA predictably denied that anyone outside the party knew about the coup before it happened.[13] Again, even if this allegation were true, copying the instructions is not the same as ordering or directing the coup against Daoud.

On the subject of aid, Chaffetz's description is a bit overdramatic, perhaps deliberately so. No agreements were made and no discussions were conducted during the actual fighting. Moreover, as pointed out previously, a burst of new agreements greeted Daoud in both of his regimes. Finally, almost all of the sixty post-1978 agreements had been negotiated with the Daoud regime. Two-thirds of the funding for these projects came from pre-1978 credits.[14]

In summary, to date there is no substantive proof that the Soviets planned, directed, or participated in the coup. No doubt with 350 military advisers in the country, they knew before anyone else that the coup had begun, but it does not seem credible that they would have ordered a coup knowing that the bulk of the armed forces in the Kabul area was not PDPA commanded. The Soviets were probably guilty of burning the candle at both ends, maintaining good relations with Daoud and, at the same time, urging their PDPA supporters to come together to be in a good position for the change of regimes that many in Kabul believed was imminent. The exact timing of the coup was probably a surprise, although once it began Soviet military advisers were probably the first to know and some may have accompanied the units to which they were assigned. One can also accurately state that Soviet indoctrination and military equipment provided the infrastructure for the coup, but, overall, the coup was a "hip pocket" affair, more a monument to the disorganization and poor leadership of Daoud than to the skill, cunning, or foreign support of his undoers.

Soviet-Afghan Relations after the Coup

The Soviet Union was the first country to recognize the revolutionary government of Afghanistan. The speed of Soviet recognition surprised some U.S. observers, since it took place nearly one hour before Western embassies had received the Afghan request for such recognition.[15] To dampen speculation of Soviet domination, the Soviet note indicated, according to official Afghan sources, that "the Soviet government considers the principle of noninterference in the internal affairs of other countries as [a] mainstay of action."[16]

The first news of the coup in the Soviet Union was a Tass dispatch from Islamabad on April 29 which simply repeated the Afghan media report that power had passed to the Revolutionary Council of the Armed Forces. Brezhnev sent his personal greetings to Taraki on May 2, and the first substantive media article appeared on May 6, two days after the *Kabul Times* had resumed publishing and had announced the new government appointments. According to the Soviet media, the underlying causes of the "revolution" were land distribution problems, extreme social inequality and "exacerbation of the class struggle" which had taken place in recent years.[17] As with Zahir Shah in 1973, Daoud quickly became the villain in most Soviet analyses of the coup.

The atmosphere was a good deal warmer when Hafizullah Amin, identified as a "member of the Politburo of the Central Committee of the People's Democratic Party (PDPA), Deputy Prime Minister and Minister of Foreign Affairs," met Andrei Gromyko in Moscow a few days later. The communiqué which followed noted that power had passed "into the hands of the people under the leadership of the People's Democratic Party of Afghanistan." Noting "bonds of fraternal friendship and good neighborliness with its great neighbor," both sides expressed the hope that Soviet-Afghan cooperation "will grow stronger and broader."[18]

Though hard proof of a change in Soviet policy would follow, the Amin-Gromyko communiqué signalled a significant qualitative change in Soviet-Afghan relations. The citation of Amin as a member of the Politburo, the notation that power had passed to the people under the leadership of a vanguard party, the use of the term "fraternal," are all indicative of the fact that the Soviets now viewed Afghanistan as a progressive regime with a socialist orientation, and thus worthy of special attention.

While Soviet feelings of fraternity were in evidence, Afghan feelings were even stronger. In July 1978, Amin compared the Saur and October revolutions, and in November, he went so far as to say that the Afghan revolution was a continuation of the USSR's Great October Revolution.[19] The Constitution of the People's Democratic Party of Afghanistan, published in the summer of 1978, directed every party member, under the heading "Duties of Party Members," to "expand and strengthen the friendly relations between the Afghans and the Soviets . . . and such relations between Afghanistan and the socialist fraternity."[20] This duty was taken seriously. In the last eight months of 1978, more economic and political missions would pass between Kabul and

Moscow than in any year since the relationship began to take off in the early 1950s.[21]

In the area of economic aid, as previously mentioned, in the first twenty months after the revolution the Soviet Union signed more than sixty economic agreements with Afghanistan, including one to build a bridge over the Amu Darya. New loans or grants were also given by East Germany and Czechoslovakia, and later, in 1979, Afghanistan signed a trade agreement with Comecon. Additionally, the Soviets announced a ten-year debt moratorium. Though on the surface most of these agreements appeared to be highly favorable to Afghanistan, the Soviet Union also received many benefits, such as a ready supply of high-grade cement and nearly 3 billion cubic meters of natural gas per year at about a fourth of the world price.[22] In the military sphere, by the end of 1978, the Soviets had more than doubled their pre-Saur 350-man advisery contingent.[23]

The New Government

Taraki became prime minister and head of the Revolutionary Council. His two deputy prime ministers were Hafizullah Amin, who also held the job of foreign minister, and Babrak Karmal. The initial cabinet was divided with eleven seats for Khalq and ten for Parcham, though in actuality many cabinet officers were more flexible and independent than those two labels might suggest.[24]

The government initially (though rather inexpertly) soft-pedalled its communist sympathies, repeatedly denying that the PDPA was a communist party. Incessant Marxist rhetoric aside, the government did little in the first few months to indicate socialist policies. Indeed, most official government pronouncements were preceded by a religious invocation or quote from the Koran.

The government's major actions prior to August 1978 can best be seen by examining the "Decrees." Decrees 1 and 2 abolished the Military Revolutionary Council and set up the PDRA's government. Decree 3 abrogated the 1977 constitution and set up a system of laws or "revolutionary duties," adjudicated by military courts. Decree 4 declared racial and ethnic equality, while Decree 5 stripped the surviving members of the king's family of their citizenship. Decree 6 was more substantive. It eliminated all pre-1973 debts and severaly prorated and diminished payments on subsequent loans. This severely disrupted the rural economy. Farmers normally borrowed large amounts to plant each year. This decree cut them off from local funding and, as a result, some analysts predicted that the wheat shortfall would reach 500,000 tons in 1980.[25]

Shortly before the announcement of Decree 6 in July, Taraki and Amin purged the Parcham faction from the leadership and 800 Parcham supporters from the military. Karmal was posted as ambassador to Czechoslovakia and his brother Mahmud Barialay was sent to Pakistan. A few months later the PDPA demanded that Karmal return for trial but he refused and subsequently disappeared. In August Major General Abdul Qader and Sultan Ali Keshtmand, the minister of planning, were arrested for plotting against the government. Both were later sentenced to death. Repression continued for those outside the PDPA as well. From April 1978 to December 1979, estimates of slain political prisoners run to 20,000.[26] The Amin regime would later admit to 12,000 killed from April 1978 to September 1979 and even published a list of their names.[27]

Following the demise of the Parcham faction, the PDPA announced its three least popular decrees. Decree 6, mentioned above, abolished usury and dried up funds for sowing in the rural areas. Decree 7 introduced equal rights for women and regularized dowry practices, a seemingly innocuous policy but one which was very unpopular in the countryside. Decree 8 declared a land reform which met with widespread resistance, not only from local landowners, but from some traditional peasants as well. One report summed up the land reform problem this way:

> The centerpiece of the regime's modernization campaign was the ill-fated land reform program under which the government expropriated 3 million acres of land. . . . Due to widespread confusion concerning the legitimacy and permanence of the land redistribution scheme, much of the land went uncultivated. Some peasants refused to accept land because under Islamic law a recipient is required to provide compensation for land received; others accepted small plots only to find that they could not afford to buy seed or fertilizer due to an anti-usury campaign which outlawed the traditional credit facilities which large landowners had previously extended to small farmers to finance their planting expenses.[28]

Adding to its problems, in October 1978, the regime unveiled its new bright red flag which replaced the traditional Islamic green banner.[29]

Though it later became clear to foreign observers that the Soviets were urging Taraki and Amin to moderate the pace of their reforms, in the last quarter of 1978 numerous supportive public statements appeared. Leonid Brezhnev said in September at Baku, "a people's revolution took place [in Afghanistan]; the semi-feudal regime was toppled and the Democratic Republic of Afghanistan was proclaimed."[30]

He went on to pledge Soviet assistance and to castigate those who saw "the hand of Moscow" behind this progressive development. On

December 5, enlarging on Gromyko's characterizations in May, Brezhnev stated, in Taraki's presence, that after the Saur Revolution, Soviet-Afghan relations assumed a "qualitatively different character," changing from simple good-neighborliness into a "durable friendship, permeated by a spirit of comradeship and revolutionary solidarity."[31]

On that same day the Soviet Union and Afghanistan signed a Treaty of Friendship, Good-Neighborliness, and Cooperation which was to run for a term of twenty years. Though there were few specifics in the treaty, Article 4 contains an implicit security commitment which would be used in December 1979 to justify the Soviet invasion:

> The high contracting parties, acting in a spirit of traditions of friendship and good-neighborliness, as well as in the spirit of the UN Charter, will hold consultations and, with the agreement of both parties, take appropriate measures with a view to ensuring the security, independence, and territorial integrity of the two countries.
>
> In the interests of strengthening the defense capability of the high contracting parties, they will continue to develop cooperation in the military field on the basis of appropriate agreements concluded between them.[32]

This commitment, as vague as it was, represented the acceptance of a moderate risk by the Soviets. The Taraki regime was not secure outside of Kabul. Thousands of soldiers had deserted during the coup and subsequent purges had exacerbated this trend. The regime had alienated the large landowners, the conservative clergy, the entire Parcham faction, and many Afghan citizens whose traditional xenophobia was outraged by the large increase in Soviet civil and military advisers. As early as August 1978, *Pravda* had begun to accuse Saudi Arabia, the United States, and the People's Republic of China, by name, and Pakistan and Iran by implication, of financing and training supporters of the "Moslem Brotherhood", a right-wing Islamic fundamentalist group whose existence dated from the Daoud regime.[33] Civil unrest was also a problem. By March 1979, Nuristani rebels controlled the Kunar Valley in eastern Afghanistan and serious outbreaks had erupted in nearly half of Afghanistan's twenty-eight provinces.

The U.S. Reaction

The U.S. reaction to the Afghan coup was conditioned by a number of factors. First, it was clearly evident that U.S. state department officials in Afghanistan and Washington were hesitant to immediately classify the regime as communist. Many civilian analysts had referred to Daoud as the "Red Prince" and he had certainly proven that he did not deserve this title. Many Afghan experts felt the same way about Taraki.[34]

Second, the administration was smarting over claims that it had not adequately resisted Soviet activities in the Third World in general and in Ehtiopia in particular. Indeed, one source of this perception was Zbigniew Brzezinski, the president's national security adviser, who traced the demise of détente to the U.S. failure to react to Soviet-Cuban activities in Ethiopia and who would later strongly criticize the moderate state department approach to dealing with communist Afghanistan. He wrote later,

> I have been reflecting on when did things begin genuinely to go wrong in the U.S.-Soviet relationship. My view is that it was when at the SCC meeting I advocated that we send in a carrier task force in reaction to the Soviet deployment of the Cubans in Ethiopia. At that meeting not only was I opposed by Vance, but Harold Brown asked why, for what reasons, without taking into account that that is a question that should perplex the Soviets rather than us. The President backed the others rather than me, we did not react. Subsequently, as the Soviets became more emboldened, we overreacted, particularly in the Cuban Soviet brigade fiasco of last fall. That derailed SALT, the momentum of SALT was lost, and the final nail in the coffin was the Soviet invasion of Afghanistan. In brief, underreaction then bred overreaction.[35]

In the second memorandum to Secretary Vance written after the coup had begun, Assistant Secretary for Near East Affairs Harold Saunders accurately warned the secretary that "we will have to deal with the U.S. press and public, that the new regime is little more than a Soviet proxy."[36] Conceding that "it was too early to know whether or not the Soviets were involved," Saunders concluded: "but the public and congress may perceive this as another Soviet victory and there may be pressure to do something about it."[37] In short, coming out hard against the PDPA regime would be tantamount to declaring another Soviet victory, something the administration was loathe to do, especially since all the facts were not present. Moreover, even after the department began to refer to the PDPA as communists, they hesitated to deal harshly with the regime lest this cause them to move closer to the Soviets.[38]

Third, U.S. reaction to the coup was influenced by the level of concern expressed by neighboring countries, especially Iran. As early as 1973, the Shah had told U.S. officials that he believed that Moscow would try to squeeze Iran between Iraq and Afghanistan.[39] Summarizing a conversation between George Bush and the Shah of Iran after the coup, William Sullivan, the U.S. ambassador in Teheran, reported,

> [George Bush] said the Shah is very concerned about developments in Afghanistan and considered the coup one more example of the Soviet grand design. He had warned presidents Nixon, Ford, and Carter about Afghanistan; now he sees the coup as further proof of a communist drive to encircle Iran. He has become unsure of Pakistan now.[40]

Finally, the U.S. reaction to the Afghan invasion was conditioned by other more pressing foreign policy problems. Beginning on July 29, 1978, riots in thirteen Iranian cities drew attention to the problems of the Pahlavi dynasty. In August 1978, the Camp David meetings began and, in the first six months of the Taraki regime, the NATO long-term defense program, the final outline of the SALT II agreement, and the normalization of relations with the People's Republic of China were all negotiated or finalized. With the exception of the Dubs incident, described below, the issue of Afghanistan was eclipsed by more dangerous or apparently more important issues. Indeed, neither Brzezinski nor Vance had the time to personally debrief Ambassador Eliot when he returned from his assignment.[41]

The United States initially followed a constructive-engagement policy toward the Afghan communists. On May 6, 1978, the United States recognized the Democratic Republic of Afghanistan (DRA). In July, Under-Secretary of State David Newsom went to Kabul to discuss economic assistance. In Cyrus Vance's words,

> He returned with a pessimistic assessment of the new regime's capabilities and intentions. He believed, however, that the political situation was still fluid and that it would be a mistake for us to halt economic assistance and lose the prospect of any influence in Kabul. We decided to continue several programs and to watch the situation closely.[42]

U.S. watchfulness (and aid) continued in a calm fashion until February 1979. As was stated in 1956, at this point in time, our objective was again "not to win but to hold," hoping that time or domestic political problems would bring more favorable conditions in Afghanistan.

The Death of Ambassador Dubs

On February 14, 1979, the same day the U.S. embassy was temporarily seized in Teheran and a few days before the Sino-Vietnamese war began, Ambassador Adolph ("Spike") Dubs was kidnapped off the street and taken to a Kabul hotel. Nearly everyone from the Parcham to the KGB to the CIA was later blamed for this event, but it is more likely that the kidnappers were simply members of a dissident group whose actual purpose was to use the ambassador to gain the release of some jailed comrades.[43]

Though diplomatic contacts with both Afghan and Soviet authorities had been made to prevent a precipitous assault, the Afghan police, in the presence of several Soviet advisers, fired six AK–47 automatic rifles for about forty seconds and then stormed the hotel room where Dubs was being held.[44] The kidnappers and the ambassador were killed.

The State Department filed a formal protest with the Soviet Union and Afghanistan. Afghanistan rejected the note and described the protest as "baseless." The Afghan police leader, Sayed Taroon, who himself would later die in a shootout, said that he alone had given the order to fire.[45] The Soviet note "resolutely refute[d] as groundless all assertions that Soviet citizens in Afghanistan were in any way responsible for the tragic outcome of the incident in Kabul." Though the Soviet government condemned the murder, it did admit that there were Soviet officials in attendance, but only to protect Soviet lives. Later a Soviet correspondent claimed that Dubs had refused an Afghan government offer of protection and that the police had only rushed the room after they had heard a revolver shot.[46]

On February 22, the United States announced that it was cutting the remainder of its $20 million 1979 aid commitment. Ambassador Dubs was not replaced and henceforth U.S. interests in Kabul would be handled by a chargé d'affaires. The Peace Corps ended its twenty-year program in Afghanistan and U.S. dependents and most of the embassy staff left as well.

The Herat Massacre and Beyond

In March 1979 the insurgency against the PDPA took a significant turn. A rebel attack against the city of Herat, coupled with a local army mutiny, resulted in the capture of this important city and the wholesale massacre of the local Soviet advisery group. As many as fifty Soviet soldiers or dependents died. Patrick Garrity reported that

> Soviet advisers were hunted down by specially assigned insurgent assassination squads . . . Westerners reportedly saw Russian women and children running for their lives from the area of the Soviet-built Herat Hotel. Those Russians that were caught were killed: some were flayed alive, others were beheaded and cut into pieces . . .[47]

As might be expected, the Afghan government and the Soviets reacted strongly, On the Afghan side, domestic repression increased. In

April 1979, an Afghan army unit (with Soviet advisers in attendance) sacked the town of Kerala in eastern Afghanistan and massacred 640 of its male inhabitants.[48] On the Soviet side, an authoritative *Pravda* article of March 19, signed by the pseudonymous I. Aleksandrov, for the first time accused "some Western countries," China, Iran, and Pakistan, of instigating unrest in Afghanistan. In the same issue of *Pravda,* an Afghan dispatch blamed the Herat problem on Iranian army personnel who had infiltrated Herat and who had "organized disorder there."[49] The Afghan government also concluded that "the present reactionary religious leaders of Iran . . . are [creating] difficulties for our revolution."[50] On March 21, an authoritative article by "A. Petrov" blamed the disturbance on Pakistan, China, and Western propaganda. A subsequent *Izvestiia* article was even more blunt: "It is no secret that imperialist forces, especially the U.S. CIA., are weaving a conspiracy against the Afghan revolution."[51] Early in April rebels in Paktia province attacked four government outposts. The DRA blamed the attack on Pakistani soldiers and lodged a stiff protest to that effect. In an ironic twist, the United States, after having been accused of it for some months, began a modest, almost invisible program to aid the Afghan freedom fighters in April 1979.[52]

In a more substantive vein, in April the Soviet general Alexei Yepishev, a first deputy defense minister and chief of the main political directorate of the armed forces, was dispatched to Afghanistan along with seven other Soviet generals. After visiting loyal Afghan army units and consulting with Minister of Defense Watanjar, Hafizullah Amin, and "Great Leader" Taraki himself, General Yepishev returned home and apparently recommended an increase in military aid and advisers.[53] Among the weapons subsequently provided were 100 T-62 tanks and 12 Mi-24 helicopter gunships. Also, during the summer of 1979, a 400-man Soviet unit took over security duties at Bagram Airbase, north of Kabul. By April 1979, there were over 1,000 Soviet military advisers in Afghanistan. The Soviet diplomatic mission was also augmented in April by the arrival of career diplomat Vasiliy Safronchuk who, as deputy chief of mission, apparently had responsibility for dealing with Afghan government problems and the insurgency.

Internal problems magnified and complicated the solution to the external ones. Shortly after the Herat massacre, Hafizullah Amin engineered his own appointment as prime minister. Though the media continued to pay homage to Great Leader Taraki, increasingly real power came to rest with Amin. A Soviet analyst, the deputy chief of the International Department of the Central Committee Secretariat, writing in May 1982, noted that by mid-1978, Amin had usurped "all party and state power," and had begun to eliminate all potential rivals. Ul'yanovskiy also noted that Amin's party-splitting policies "were skillfully directed by forces of foreign and domestic counterrevolution."[54]

This development was unfortunate for the PDPA because as early as November 1978, as the U.S. embassy in Kabul had reported, Amin's high-handed manner was causing problems within the PDPA.[55] Moreover, the Bureau of Near East Affairs had begun to report growing Soviet dissatisfaction with Khalqi policy in general and Hafizullah Amin in particular. According to William R. Crawford, acting head of the bureau, in May 1979, "other reports suggest that the Soviets are already moving forward with plans to engineer replacement of the present Khalqi leadership of the DRA, perhaps with the exiled Parcham leaders including former deputy prime minister Babrak Karmal, now believed to be hiding in Europe."[56]

In Kabul, night letters, circulated in August by dissident Khalqi, accused Amin of repression, nepotism, and inefficiency. Remarkably, appeals to party head Taraki fell on deaf ears. According to the dissidents: "Although we informed the general secretary of the party of Amin's acts and behavior many times, he told us with much regret that Amin is in charge of everything and he (the general secretary) cannot do anything and every responsibility rests with Amin."[57]

As tensions within the PDPA increased and relations between the DRA and the USSR worsened, the battlefield situation deteriorated. Soviet press articles in May and June spoke of increased infiltration and warned that increased cooperation between Pakistan and China was directed against Afghanistan. The ubiquitous "A. Petrov" concluded in June 1979 that the USSR could not "remain indifferent" to this war in Afghanistan, a conflict "in direct proximity to us. . . . This is a question of actual aggression against a state with which the USSR has a common border."[58]

Notes

1. *Pravda,* May 6, 1978, p. 5 in CDSP–30–18–20.
2. Dupree, "Red Flag Over the Hindu Kush, Part II," p. 4. Former Ambassador Theodore Eliot has referred to this work as the most complete and accurate account of the coup. His remarks were made at the Harvard–State Department Conference on "The Soviet Invasion of Afghanistan: Consequences for Afghanistan and the Soviet Union," October 17, 1983, at Harvard University.

3. The U.S. Embassy used 3,000 as the approximate PDPA strength. See U.S. Dept. of State, Bureaus of Intelligence and Research and Near East Affairs, *The Coup in Afghanistan,* p. 2.

4. Political Department of the Afghan Armed Forces, *On the Saur [April] Revolution,* pp. 12–13.

5. Dupree, "Red Flag Over the Hindu Kush, Part II," p. 4–5. The Kabul rumors were related to me by Louis Dupree in an interview at West Point, February 2, 1983.

6. *On the Saur [April] Revolution,* p. 12. A KGB defector, formerly stationed in Iran, reported, apparently based on hearsay, that the PDPA consulted the Soviet Embassy before ordering the coup. See *Time,* November 22, 1983, p. 33.

7. Complete accounts of the coup can also be found in Bradsher, *Afghanistan and the Soviet Union,* pp. 74–85; and Arnold, *Afghanistan: The Soviet Invasion in Perspective,* pp. 68–74.

8. Dupree, "Red Flag Over the Hindu Kush," Pt. II, p. 8.

9. U.S. Embassy, Kabul, *Military Conflict in Kabul,* p. 2.

10. U.S. Embassy, Kabul, *Afghan Communist Leader Becomes Ruler of Afghanistan,* p. 2.

11. Negaran, "Afghan Coup of 1978: Revolution and International Security," p. 100.

12. Chaffetz, "Afghanistan in Turmoil," p. 20.

13. Amin's remarks in *Kabul Times,* July 4, 1978, p. 1.

14. Dupree, "Red Flag Over the Hindu Kush, Part IV," p. 6. See also, U.S. Embassy, Kabul, *Afghanistan's Khalqi Regime at 18 Months,* p. 3.

15. U.S. Embassy, Kabul, *USSR Recognizes New Regime in Kabul, p. 1.*

16. *Kabul Times,* May 4, 1978, p. 4.

17. *Pravda,* May 6, 1978, p. 5. in CDSP–30–18–20.

18. *Pravda* May 10, 1978, p. 4 in CDSP–30–20–17.

19. *Kabul Times,* November 8, 1978.

20. *Constitution of the People's Democratic Party of Afghanistan, the Party of the Working Class of Afghanistan,* Article 5(f), June 1978.

21. Rubinstein, *Soviet Policy Toward Turkey, Iran and Afghanistan,* p. 189.

22. Dupree, "Red Flag Over the Hindu Kush, Part IV," p. 7.

23. Rader, "The Russian Military and Afghanistan: An Historical Perspective," p. 320.

24. Dupree, "Democratic Republic of Afghanistan, 1979," pp. 1–4; *Kabul Times,* May 4, 1978, p. 1; and Arnold, *Afghanistan: The Soviet Invasion in Perspective,* pp. 72–73.

25. On the decrees, see Dupree, "Red Flag Over the Hindu Kush, Part III," pp. 3–10. On the food situation, see Chaffetz, "Afghanistan in Turmoil," p. 24.

26. On Karmal's posting to Czechoslovakia, see *Kabul Times,* July 5, 1978, p. 1. For an estimate on slain political prisoners, see the eyewitness account in *New York Times,* February 18, 1980, p. 4.

27. Dupree, "Red Flag Over the Hindu Kush, Part VI," p. 9.

28. James Phillips, "Afghanistan: The Soviet Quagmire," p. 8.

29. *Kabul Times,* October 19, 1978, p. 1.

30. *Pravda,* September 23, 1978, p. 1 in CDSP–30–38–1–4. A KGB defector, apparently without direct knowledge, has claimed that the KGB was in the forefront of the "go slow" movement and had even argued against massive aid to Afghanistan. *Time,* November 22, 1982, p. 33.

31. *Pravda,* December 6, 1978, p. 2 in CDSP–30–49–9.

32. *Tready of Friendship, Good Neighborliness and Cooperation Between the Union of Soviet Socialist Republics and the Democratic Republic of Afghanistan,* Article 4.

33. *Pravda,* August 1, 1978, p. 5.

34. For example, see Louis Dupree's letter to the editor in the *New York Times,* May 20, 1978.

35. Brzezinski, *Power and Principle:* pp. 189, 426–430.

36. U.S. Dept. of State, Bureau of Near East Affairs, *The Afghan Coup,* p. 1.

37. Ibid., p. 2.

38. U.S. Dept. of State, Bureau of Near East Affairs, *Situation in Afghanistan,* p. 2.

39. Henry Kissinger, *Years of Upheaval,* p. 675.

40. U.S. Embassy, Teheran, Subject: *Military Conflict in Kabul,* p. 1.

41. This remark was made by former Ambassador Eliot at a conference at Harvard University, cited in note 2, above.

42. Cyrus Vance, *Hard Choices: Critical Years in America's Foreign Policy,* p. 385.

43. Dupree, "Red Flag Over the Hindu Kush, Part IV," pp. 2–3.

44. Ibid. Other accounts allowed for a miscommunication between Washington and Kabul by which the Afghans may have believed that the State Department approved of the assault. See Rubinstein, *Soviet Policy Toward Turkey, Iran and Afghanistan,* p. 163, 178, n. 6. Afghanistan has never cited such a "permission" as its reason for acting.

45. *Kabul Times,* February 20, 1979, p. 20.

46. *Pravda,* February 18, 1979, p. 5 in CDSP–31–7–5. *Literaturnaya gazeta,* March 14, 1979, p. 9.

47. Patrick J. Garrity, "The Soviet Military Stake in Afghanistan," p. 33.

48. *New York Times,* February 17, 1980, p. 10.

49. *Pravda,* March 19, 1979, p. 5 in CDSP–31–11–5. The Afghan dispatch appeared in *Pravda,* March 19, 1979, p. 5 in CDSP–31–11–5, 6.

50. *Kabul Times,* March 19, 1979, p. 1.

51. *Izvestiia,* March 24, 1979, p. 4.

52. *Kabul Times,* April 9, 1979, p. 1. On U.S. aid, see the vague reference in Brzezinski, *Power and Principle,* p. 427.

53. The Yepishev visit was publicized in *Kabul Times* on April 5, 1979, p. 1; April 7, 1979, p. 1; April 8, p. 1; April 9, p. 1; April 11 and 12, p. 1.

54. Ul'yanovskiy, "The Afghan Revolution at the Current Stage," p. 11.

55. U.S. Embassy, Kabul, *Afghan Leadership Underscores Ties to USSR,* pp. 1–3.

56. U.S. Dept. of State, Bureau of Near East Affairs, *Soviet-Afghan Relations: Is Moscow's Patience Wearing Thin?* p. 2. Brzezinski briefed Carter in July 1979 that Amin might be ousted: *Power and Principle,* p. 427.

57. U.S. Embassy, Kabul, *A Second Underground Night Letter Blasts Prime Minister Amin for Creating Domestic Trouble,* p. 2.

58. *Pravda,* June 1, 1979, p. 5 in CDSP–31–21–5, 20.

5
From Revolution to Disintegration, August–December 1979

By the summer of 1979, it was clear that the Kabul regime was in serious trouble for many reasons. Like Amanullah's regime, Taraki's was hopelessly out of step with its people. Its reforms were unpopular and the government was viewed as atheistic and dominated by foreigners. The army and the state bureaucracy were similarly disaffected. In the party, the purge of the Parcham faction and the rise of Amin had narrowed the party's personnel base. Amidst all of this, the insurgency prospered and army mutinies proliferated. This brought increased Soviet military aid. The presence of growing numbers of Soviet military and civilian advisers fueled the insurgency and the mutinies, thus establishing a vicious cycle.

In the period from August to December 1979, the Soviets attempted to replace Amin and failed. Taraki's subsequent death exacerbated a situation, that in Soviet eyes was characterized by extremely primitive socio-economic conditions, an ill-conceived modernization program, lack of unity in the PDPA, a repressive leader, and an alliance between internal reaction and international imperialism. This "alliance" was a standard feature of Soviet propaganda and analysis for many years, a fact that will be explored further in chapter 7. In response to these problems, the Soviets stepped up militry aid, gathered information, and began, shortly after the death of Taraki, to prepare for a military invasion. In December 1979 the Soviets would try to solve their Afghan problem without ever understanding their own role in its creation.

Prelude to Invasion

During the summer of 1979, the security situation in Afghanistan continued to deteriorate. In the first week of August, more than 1,000 Afghan troops revolted at the Bala Hissar garrison on the edge of Kabul. Forces loyal to the regime took four hours to put down the revolt and had to use helicopter gunships and artillery against the rebels. All of this came close on the heels of Zbigniew Brzezinski's public warning to the

Soviets "to abstain from efforts to impose alien doctrines on deeply religious and nationally conscious peoples."[1] For its part, the DRA blamed the disturbance on "a number of Pakistanis and Iranians who had infiltrated into Kabul city."[2] In early September, a 2,000-man unit in Konar province defected to the rebels. By this point responsible analysts estimated that the Afghan army had lost half of its pre-coup officer strength to purges and desertions.[3]

The Soviets responded to the deteriorating situation by sending General Ivan G. Pavlovskiy, the commander-in-chief of the Soviet ground forces (and the Soviet commander in the invasion of Czechslovakia), twelve other generals, and fifty other officers to Afghanistan from mid-August to mid-October.[4] Unlike the previous visit by Yepishev, and a subsequent visit by Lieutenant General Paputin of the Ministry of Internal Affairs (MVD), the Pavlovskiy group received no local publicity. During and subsequent to this visit, the amount of military equipment and the number of military advisers increased, with the latter figure rising to over 4,000 by the end of 1979. In the fall of 1979, military advisers were posted down to the company level and Soviet pilots began flying combat missions, particularly with helicopter gunships, a highly effective weapon with which the Afghans had limited experience.[5]

It is unclear whether the decision to change horses in Afghanistan was made before Pavlovskiy arrived or as a result of his initial observations on the scene; but it is clear, in retrospect, that a definite decision was made to unseat Amin, who had become increasingly identified with repressive policies and the centralization of political power. Amin had personally taken on the defense portfolio, appointed relatives to key positions, and repeatedly purged the army and the government of those whose loyalty he questioned. In the second week of August 1979, the U.S. embassy in Kabul reported that an anti-Amin plot was developing inside the cabinet with Soviet complicity.[6]

Taraki himself visited Moscow on his way home from a nonaligned movement conference in Havana. He met with Brezhnev and Gromyko on September 10 in a "cordial, comradely atmosphere," complete with front-page photos in both Kabul and Moscow media. It was at this point that the Soviets apparently urged Taraki to oust Amin and broaden the base of his regime.[7]

On his September 11 return to Kabul, Taraki found that Amin had fired three ministers—Watanjar (interior), Gulabzoy (communications), and Mazdooryar (frontier affairs)—for plotting against the prime minister, and was attempting to arrest them. On the 14th Taraki, perhaps with some complicity from Ambassador Puzanov, managed to call Amin to the Arg Palace for a meeting. A shootout ensued but, when the smoke cleared, Taraki was in custody and Amin was in charge. The *Kabul*

Times subsequently announced that Taraki had stepped down, declaring that "due to health reasons he could not continue his work in the party and state posts." The excessive coverage in the same issue of the *Kabul Times* given to the death of "the Martyr" Sayed Taroon, former secret police chief and Taraki's *chef du cabinet,* suggests that he may have informed Amin of Taraki's intentions.[8]

A secret PDPA document, dated September 16, 1979, told the story from Amin's perspective:

> Comrade Taraki's cult of personality was the main obstacle in the way of accelerated advancement and intensified development. This cult of personality . . . overshadowed all ideological and organization principles of our party.
>
> Comrade Taraki resorted to conspiracies and anti-party groupings against the politbureau and all party organs, especially against Comrade Hafizullah Amin.
>
> A terror attempt was carried out against our scholarly principled comrade Hafizullah Amin on September 14, 1979. Our young comrade Sayed Daoud Taroon, member of the Central Committee, was martyred.[9]

For these crimes, Taraki and the three ministers were expelled from the party. In addition to his previous posts of defense and prime minister, Amin was made president of the Revolutionary Council and general secretary of the PDPA.[10]

In any other state, even the suspicion of Soviet complicity in such a plot would probably have resulted in a break between that country and the Soviet Union. Nothing of that sort happened in Afghanistan. As Amin would later state, "we are convinced that if there was no vast economic and military aid from the Soviet Union, we could not resist the aggression and conspiracies of imperialism."[11] The Soviets were similarly stuck, as a U.S. embassy cable of September 17 pointed out:

> The general impression in the diplomatic community and among knowledgeable Afghans is that the Soviets are not happy—but probably find that they have no other choices at this time but to support the ambitious and ruthless Amin. Having once reportedly been engaged in an effort to broaden the political base of the Kabul regime in order to counter better the insurgency, the Soviets now find that base even more narrowed—sharpened to a pencil point, as it were. The Soviets were also once said to recognize that the bloody-handed Amin was the primary image problem of the Khalqi regime (the avuncular Taraki had some popular support, even among some non-Khalqi circles), and were reportedly determined to eliminate him. Now Amin is all they have left. Until some other viable option becomes available, he is the only instru-

ment through which Moscow can defend a "fraternal party" and save a "progressive revolution," ideological responsibilities which local Soviets strongly profess.[12]

The Soviets immediately began to attempt a public reconcilation. Ambassador Puzanov met with Amin on September 15 for two hours. On the 17th, Brezhnev and Kosygin tersely extended their personal greetings to Amin and noted that they were "confident that fraternal relations . . . will continue to develop." Apparently as a sop to Soviet feelings, Amin commuted the death sentences of Major General Abdul Qader and Minister of Planning Sultan Ali Keshtmand, both of whom had been imprisoned since August 1978 and would later play a major role in the Karmal regime. Taraki was not so lucky. He was reportedly suffocated by Amin's henchmen on October 10, 1978.[13]

Personal relations between Amin and the Soviet staff in Kabul continued to be strained. On October 6, the deputy chief of the Soviet diplomatic mission, Vasiliy Safronchuk, was publicly embarrassed by the Foreign Minister Shah Wali in front of a meeting of friendly socialist ambassadors. According to the U.S. embassy,

> Foreign Minister Shah Wali alleged that around September 14 the Soviet embassy had harbored purged Interior Minister Watanjar. At that statement, Safronchuk displayed embarrassment and while not denying Watanjar's having been at his embassy, asked the foreign minister how he came to know about it. Shah Wali replied that they discovered it from the Kabul military commander who had been contacted by Watanjar by telephone from the embassy.[14]

In November, Amin failed to attend the Soviet reception to celebrate the Great October Revolution and various publications reported that Amin had demanded Puzanov's recall.[15] On November 19, as Ambassador Puzanov was leaving Afghanistan, the official *Kabul Times* heralded this event as follows: "H. Amin Received Puzanov, AAPSO, Cuban Teams."[16] Although minor foreign functionaries usually received their own headline when they visited Amin or any of his ministers, the Soviet ambassador had to share biling with the Afro-Asian Peace and Solidarity Organization and a minor Cuban delegation!

Publicly, on the other hand, Amin remained attentive to Moscow's wishes. He attempted to appease the Muslim clergy and faithful, supported the Soviet position on peace in Europe, and, despite verbal wishes for good U.S.-Afghan relations, continued to insist that the United States cut back its embassy staff.[17]

Militarily, from September to December 1979, the situation continued to deteriorate. On September 3, rebel forces cut the north-south road leading into Kabul and temporarily gained control of the area around the Salang Tunnel. In October, a two-day mutiny in the 7th Division in the Kabul area put the Amin regime in jeopardy. By December, more than 400,000 Afghans had taken refuge in Pakistan and perhaps half again that number had fled to Iran.

In late October, troops from all over Afghanistan were sent to Paktia province. Soviet advisers were posted to the company level and air support was reportedly provided by Soviet pilots. Predictably, the rebels fled. Within ten days, the Afghan generals ordered the troops home and rebel forces again reoccupied Paktia province. Despite "the planning and leadership provided by Soviet advisers," the Afghan army had failed to make significant progress against the resistance in Paktia Province. This may have been regarded by the Soviets as a final experiment to see if they could combat the insurgency short of invasion.[18]

The Soviet Estimate of the Situation in Afghanistan

In mid-October 1979 General Pavlovskiy returned to the Soviet Union. He undoubtedly presented a pessimistic report. While there are no public records of his briefings, there is ample evidence that after the Amin takeover the Soviet estimate of the situation in Afghanistan became even more negative. As early as mid-September a junior Soviet diplomat complained to a U.S. counterpart that "the Khalqis [had] made a mistake in trying to do too many things too fast. He thought the regime should have taken four or five years to effect what they tried to accomplish in a few months. The Soviet made it clear that he thought that the Khalqis had failed."[19]

In an analysis written shortly after the Soviet invasion, journalist Viktor Sidenko stated that four negative factors had caused an "extremely dangerous, critical situation which called for emergency measures" to develop. The most serious factor was outside interference. A second factor was that internal counterrevolution had become united with the forces of outside interference. The third factor was disunity in the party. The fourth factor was the role played by Hafizullah Amin, "a cunning individual with an inordinate lust for power." Sidenko also noted with some exaggeration that Amin "was anxious to develop secret contacts with the United States."[20]

In a more detailed analysis, R. Ul'yanovskiy, who is both a noted Soviet orientalist and a Central Committee official, noted in 1982 that "important errors took place in the practical implementation of the reforms."[21] This was exacerbated by lack of qualified leaders and the existence of "clan, tribal, local, and religious prejudices." All of this was aggravated by the Khalq-Parcham split and the rise of Hafizullah Amin. Under Amin,

> The PDPA became increasingly transformed into an instrument of Amin's personal policies, and . . . was swamped by adventurist and petty bourgeois tendencies, and by leftist demogogy and dogmatism. Amin's relatives and supporters . . . committed gross violations . . . and carried out repressions against peaceful inhabitants, including those who were loyal to the revolution . . .[22]

During all of this, according to Ul'yanovskiy, counterrevolutionary elements grew stronger. The army, led for the most part by the upper class, was unable to stop the counterrevolution because of its class background and its poor political indoctrination. Adding to this, ten purges were carried out within the armed forces. By the fall of 1979, guerrilla detachments were operating in eighteen of twenty-six provinces and the army had ceased to be of any use to the revolution.[23]

As a result of all of this, the economy worsened, providing "favorable soil . . . for the hostile activities of the counterrevolution." Food supply and routine transportation became problematical and many Soviet economic experts were recalled.[24] In all, according to Ul'yanovskiy, the imperialists were conducting an undeclared war in Afghanistan and, through that country, attempting to "approach the borders of Soviet Central Asia."[25]

What is missing from Ul'yanovskiy's fairly accurate post-factor estimate is an assessment of how Soviet judgmental errors allowed the USSR to become intricately entangled with a regime which possessed a rare talent for inflicting wounds upon itself and which had taken a relatively favorable climate of reform and turned it into one characterized, in the words of U.S. chargé Bruce Amstutz, by "an atmosphere of mortal fear . . . the alienation of the country's educated middle class . . . a widespread hatred of Amin . . . an 'anti-Russianism' often flaring into extreme violence . . . an anti-Khalqi jihad . . . [and] . . . internecine schisms, hatreds, grudges, and "scores to settle" [so deep] that violent instability will probably remain a fact of life [in Afghanistan] for years to come."[26]

In partial defense of the logic of Soviet policy, one must add that the Soviets habitually attempted to pursue their interests in Afghanistan by using the lowest level of resources possible. Information was gathered on the scene by expert observers before every escalatory effort, but each rung in this ladder of escalation brought the Soviets into deeper involvement with the Afghan problem. A relatively moderate increase in economic and military aid led to larger doses of the same. Advice and assistance led to management of the day-to-day affairs of various ministries. Military advisers were posted lower and lower in the Afghan hierarchy and by late 1979 they were routinely flying active combat missions. In a reaction which was typically Russian, as the problems grew deeper and deeper, the solution to which they turned, in an incremental fashion, was to attempt to increase Soviet control over what had started out as an Afghan operation. Increasingly larger doses of Soviet manpower and resources were applied to a problem which was sociopolitical in nature and in large measure exacerbated by the presence of those who were supposed to solve it. Like U.S. decision-makers in the Vietnam era, Soviet leaders misread the situation and incrementally moved to the point where their own troops were perceived as the last remaining instrument to achieve their objectives.

Amin's Final Days

It was past time for a new beginning in Afghanistan. Amin could not survive and there were no Marxists in Afghanistan who could take up the standard of the revolution. If anything, by late October the Soviets must have come to believe that their original desire to be rid of Amin was more than justified. New faces were needed and the Soviets had kept some on the shelf apparently for this purpose. Though no analyst has successfully pinpointed the date, place, or time,[27] in late October the Soviets apparently made a tentative decision to do three things: (1) unseat Amin, (2) install Babrak Karmal as the leader of a new Khalq-Parcham coalition, and (3) use Soviet troops to gain time for the new regime to restore order and rebuild the Afghan army.

In late October U.S. intelligence noticed an increased concentration of transport aircraft in the Turkmen and adjoining military districts. Ominously, this action took place near the home base of the elite 105th Guards Airborne Division at Ferghana.[28] In early November, reservists in the Turkmen Military District and adjoining areas were called up to fill the five Category 3 divisions (10–30 percent full-time manning, full combat equipment) in the district. Additionally, bridging equipment was brought up to the Amu Darya. In November, a headquarters for what was to become the 40th Army was established at Termez and satellite communications were established with Moscow. On December 8, an airborne regiment was posted to the Soviet-controlled Bagram Airbase. On the 20th this unit moved with its BMD carriers and assault guns to secure the area near the Salang Pass tunnel, the key choke point between Kabul and Termez. Around the same time, a small element of this unit took up security duty at the Kabul International Airport. The Soviets then controlled the road leading into Afghanistan and the two airbases closest to Kabul. The doors to Afghanistan were open and under Soviet guard.[29]

Inside Afghanistan, there were few apparent signs that the Soviets were preparing an invasion. Some of the Soviet activities in late fall 1979 could be intepreted as *maskirovka* (camouflage/deception) for the invasion. On the Afghan side, little that Amin said or did indicated that he was worried or upset about Soviet activities. Early in November, he announced plans for a gala celebration of the Great October Revolution and two weeks later, he stated that "there is no limit to the amount of Soviet help which may be extended and the level of assistance completely depends on our capacity to absorb and utilize it."[30]

Routine congratulations were extended on the early December anniversary of the signing of the friendship treaty, although there was some coolness on the Soviet part. Amin's letter was punctuated by personal messages and the "Dear Comrades" form of direct address, but the Soviet note, true to the pattern of others written earlier to Amin, was more terse and specifically sent greetings from party to party without any personal greetings. A Tass commentary stated that among the many facets of Soviet assistance were "joint measures to guarantee security, independence, and territorial integrity of the countries."[31] This went beyond the formal wording of the treaty, but, again, there was nothing happening in Afghanistan which would have caused alarm.

Diplomatic meetings took place as usual. On December 3, the new Soviet Ambassador, Fikryat Tabeyev, paid a courtesy call on Foreign Minister Shah Wali. A Soviet foreign trade team arrived on the 12th and as late as the 26th, Soviet Minister of Communications Talizin called on Amin with Ambassador Tabeyev in tow. The U.S. press later reported that in the first week of December the Soviets urged Amin to call for Soviet troops, but he demurred.[32]

The most interesting of all of these routine contacts was the visit of MVD Lieutenant General Viktor Paputin. Paputin arrived, according to official Afghan sources, on the morning of Wednesday, November 28. On the 29th he paid a courtesy call on his host, Ghulam Mustafa, the deputy minister of the interior, and on the 30th they began talks "on mutual cooperation and other issues of interest." On December 2, he saw Amin "for a courtesy call," and on the 5th he held a meeting with the minister of the interior, F.M. Faqir. He reportedly left on the 13th, although his departure was not publicized until the 16th.[33]

No one knows for sure what Paputin did with his free time in Kabul or whether he did in fact leave the country on December 13 as the newspaper stated that he did. He did speak to numerous members of the security apparat and it is clear that one of his main purposes was information gathering. It has been said that he was engaged in planning or perhaps even supervising an attempted assassination (by gunfire) of Amin and his nephew—the head of the secret police—which took place on December 17.[34] By the account of a KGB defector, the KGB had also tried and failed to poison Amin's food in December.[35] In all, the Paputin affair suggests that by the second week of December, the Soviets had irretrievably made up their mind to invade. Likewise, it is clear from the events that Amin's death or "departure" was originally supposed to have preceded the invasion. More will be said about Paputin's mysterious death in the next chapter.

Soviet diplomats in the United States were also busy around this time. Soviet Ambassador Anatoliy Dobrynin met with Secretary of State Vance to discuss the future prospects of U.S.-Soviet realtions and shortly thereafter returned to the Soviet Union, apparently to brief the Politburo on any last minute developments in his area of responsibility. In all, both in Washington and Moscow, U.S. representatives expressed concern to the Soviets over developments in Afghanistan on five occasions. Marshall Shulman, responding to a congressional query, described these meetings in the following manner:

> We did not specify what action we would take. What we said to them was that this was a matter that we regarded with great seriousness. We did say to them that it would obviously have very serious effects on United States–Soviet relations and would jeopardize the peace of the world. We did not detail to them the specific measures that we would take.[36]

Though this phase of the Afghan crisis was overshadowed by the hostage drama in Teheran, news accounts of Soviet troops in Afghanistan, when coupled with U.S. protests, forced the Soviet media and their officials to respond to the charges. On December 21, Foreign Minister Gromyko told Ambassador Watson in Moscow: "The reports are wrong. We don't know what you're talking about."[37] As late as the December 23, *Pravda* referred to claims that Soviet combat troops were in Afghanistan as "pure fabrications." Pushing journalistic license to a new limit, they even quoted Hafizullah Amin on the nature of Soviet policy: "The Soviet Union . . . has never infringed on our sovereignty, . . . is not doing so, and never will."[38]

What *Pravda* did not add, however, was that Amin, in addition to his ruthlessness, managed to be a rather unique blend of pro-Soviet leanings and fierce stubbornness, even independence. His treatment of Puzanov stands as an example. It is highly unlikely that he ever would have countenanced the introduction of even a limited contingent of Soviet troops into Afghanistan, having publicly rejected this option on numerous occasions.[39] What he told the U.S. Chargé Archer Blood in October rang true:

> If Brezhnev himself should ask him to take any action against Afghan independence, said Amin, he would not hesitate "to sacrifice even one second of his life" in opposition to such a request.[40]

He would shortly sacrifice much more.

Notes

1. *New York Times*, August 6, 1979, p. 1. On the warning, see *New York Times*, August 3, 1979, p. 1.
2. *Kabul Times*, August 6, 1979, p. 1.
3. *New York Times*, September 6, 1979, p. 2.
4. John Erickson's testimony in United Kingdom, House of Commons, *Afghanistan: The Soviet Invasion and Its Consequences for British Policy*, p. 37. See also testimony of Ambassador Marshall Shulman in U.S. Congress, House Committee on Foreign Relations, *East-West Relations in the Aftermath of the Soviet Invasion of Afghanistan*, pp. 30, 34. Hereafter cited only by title.
5. Ibid., p. 34. *New York Times*, January 1, 1980, pp. 1, 4.
6. U.S. Department of State, *Further Comments . . . About Soviet Efforts to Alter Afghan Regime*, pp. 2–4.
7. See *Kabul Times*, September 10, and September 12, 1979, p. 1 in both editions. Also, *Pravda*, September 11, 1979, p. 1 in CDSP 31–37–17.
8. An excellent account of the "meeting" between Amin and Taraki can be found in Bradsher, *Afghanistan and the Soviet Union*, p. 96–115. Also see *Kabul Times*, September 16, 1979, p. 1. A KGB defector has reported that the Soviets decided to back Amin over Taraki before the shootout. In light of the other evidence in this chapter, he was obviously incorrect. See *Time*, November 22, 1982, pp. 33–34.
9. As summarized in U.S. Embassy, Kabul, *DRA Decisions Come to Light Respecting Taraki and Others*, pp. 1–2.
10. Ibid.
11. U.S. Embassy, Kabul, *Amin Publicly Acknowledges That Soviet Support Is Essential for Khalqis' Survival*, p. 2.
12. U.S. Embassy, Kabul, *Tension Lessens in Kabul as President Amin Digests His Recent Political Gains*, p. 3.
13. *Pravda*, September 17 and 18, 1979, p. 1 both editions in CDSP–31–37–17. On Qader and Keshtmand, see *Kabul Times*, October 7, 1979, p. 1. On Taraki's death, see the Karmal government's account in *Kabul New Times*, January 23, 1980, p. 3, passim.

14. U.S. Embassy, Kabul, *Signs Continue of Strained Relations Between President Hafizullah Amin and the Soviets,* p. 2.

15. For an account of the Soviet reception, see *Kabul Times,* November 8, 1979, p. 1. On the recall, see for example, *Economist,* November 3, 1979, pp. 52–53. Neither Afghan nor Soviet sources have confirmed Amin's alleged demand.

16. *Kabul Times,* November 20, 1979, p. 1.

17. On bilateral problems at this time, see Archer Blood's comments in U.S. Embassy Kabul, *Meeting with President Amin,* p. 2–4.

18. U.S. Embassy, Kabul, *Afghanistan's Khalqi Regime at 18 Months,* p. 3. *New York Times,* January 1, 1980, p. 1, 4. Interview, Eliza Van Hollen, Bureau of Intelligence and Research, April 7, 1983 in Washington, D.C.

19. U.S. Embassy, Kabul, *Tension Lessens in Kabul,* p. 3.

20. Sidenko, "Two Years of the Afghan Revolution," pp. 20–22.

21. Ul'yanovskiy, "The Afghan Revolution at the Current Stage," p. 11.

22. Ibid., pp. 11–12.

23. Ibid., pp. 11–14.

24. Ibid., pp. 14–15.

25. Ibid., p. 15.

26. U.S. Embassy, Kabul, *Afghanistan's Khalqi Regime at 18 Months,* p. 3–4.

27. A Spanish news agency—without citing substantive proof—reported that the final decision was made on November 26, 1979. Contingency planning and preparatory measures, of course, must have begun much earlier. For a discussion of the timing, see Bradsher, *Afghanistan and the Soviet Union,* pp. 163–8; and *East-West Relations in the Aftermath,* pp. 30, 34, 37–40.

28. Ibid., p. 39. On the development and basing of Soviet airborne forces, see Bunce, "Soviet Airborne: the Quiet Revolution," pp. 4–9 and Allard, "Soviet Airborne Forces and Preemptive Power Projection," pp. 42–51.

29. *New York Times,* January 1, 1980, pp. 1, 4.

30. U.S. Embassy, Kabul, *Amin Publicly Acknowledges That Soviet Support is Essential,* p. 2.

31. In *Kabul Times,* December 8, 1979, p. 1.

32. *Kabul Times,* December 27, 1979, p. 1; *New York Times,* January 2, 1980, p. 1.

33. *Kabul Times,* December 1, 3, 6, 16, 1979, p. 1 in each edition.

34. Bradsher, *Afghanistan and the Soviet Union,* p. 178.

35. *Time,* November 22, 1982, pp. 33–34.

36. *East-West Relations in the Aftermath,* p. 30.

37. Whitney, "The View from the Kremlin," p. 91.

38. *Pravda,* December 23, 1979 p. 5 in CDSP–31–51–4.

39. Bradsher, *Afghanistan and the Soviet Union,* p. 117, 169.

40. U.S. Embassy, Kabul, *Meeting with President Amin,* p. 3.

6
Invasion, Consolidation, and Reaction

The Soviet invasion of Afghanistan was modeled after the invasion of Czechoslovakia in 1968. Both operations featured elaborate deception, subversion of an unreliable communist government, the introduction of airborne troops to seize key objectives in the capital, the movement of motorized rifle troops to link up with air-landed elements, and, finally, the replacement of a government with more reliable comrades. Generals Yepishev and Pavlovskiy, two key observers sent to Afghanistan, had performed similar duty in Czechoslovakia.

The Soviets believed that their military operation would accomplish the following objectives: unseat Amin, install a new Khalq-Parcham coalition, and frighten or deter the rebels so that Karmal would have the necessary breathing spell to rebuild an army and reestablish control over the countryside. In doing so, the Soviets would secure a hold on Afghanistan at the same time that Iran—now engaged in the hostage crisis with the United States—was in turbulence and Pakistan (and, indirectly, China) were providing a sanctuary for the Afghan freedom fighters. (As will be detailed in chapters 8 and 9, the Soviet fixation on outside interference was misplaced, since the freedom fighters were not getting and have never received the bulk of their support from abroad.)

While the Soviets have maintained a foothold, their operations in the first six months after the invasion did not follow their original plan. The Karmal government proved ineffective and the Soviet occupation has turned into a bloody lesson in counterinsurgency for the Soviet military. By June 1980, the Soviets began to adapt to the conditions in Afghanistan by modifying their force structure, replacing reservists with regular troops, and beginning the search for a peace favorable to their interests. On the international plane, the Soviets sought allies in the region and kept up a steady anti-U.S. propanganda campaign, all to no avail.

Invasion

On Christmas eve, despite prior U.S. warnings and the presence of an Afghan armored division nearby, the Soviets began landing elements of the 105th Guards Airborne Division—reinforced by elements of the 103d Guards Airborne Division and a *spetsnaz* (special-purpose commando) unit—at Kabul Airport. On December 27, following a three-day airlift which averaged 75–120 flights per day, a few hundred spetsnaz troops deployed to the Darulaman Palace outside Kabul destroyed Amin's guard and its eight tanks, and killed President Amin.[1]

Also on the night of the 27th, Soviet troops blew up the main telephone exchange, seized Radio Kabul, and captured most of the central government facilities in Kabul. Spirited fighting took place only near the radio station and at the Darulaman Palace. Soviet forces achieved complete tactical surprise. Serious fighting in the city ended by dawn of the 28th.[2]

As previously mentioned, Western analysts expected some sort of Soviet move and, by the last week of December, few people were fooled by *Pravda*'s protestations of innocence and ignorance. Early on the 27th, indeed "in the middle of the night," Soviet diplomats sent the following note to Western capitals: "We are responding to an appeal from the Afghan leadership to repel outside aggression. We are responding with limited forces and for a limited time and as soon as the need is through, we will get out."[3]

Babrak Karmal, whose career had received almost no public notice in the Soviet media up to this point, was proclaimed president of the Revolutionary Council, general secretary of the PDPA, and prime minister. In his first address to his "long-suffering countrymen," Babrak Karmal proclaimed that "today is the breaking of the machine of tortures of Amin and his henchmen, wild butchers, usurpers, and murderers of tens of thousands of our countrymen. . . ." Karmal went on to declare a holy war against the enemies of the revolution. He did not mention Soviet forces in his speech even though it was actually broadcast from a bogus "Radio Kabul" inside the Soviet Union.[4]

The details of Karmal's "election" are unclear, as is the nature and timing of the Afghan "request" for Soviet troops. Babrak Karmal himself was not seen in Afghanistan until the first week of January and some of those who allegedly elected him, like Sultan Ali Keshtmand and Abdul Qader, were in prison at the time. The Soviet propaganda apparat broke down on these points, with some accounts having Amin tendering the final of fourteen requests for aid in the form of Soviet troops. Even some of the more prestigious Soviet analysts were at a loss on how to explain these contradictions. For example, Rostislav Ul'yanovskiy noted that the decision to send Soviet troops was made before the government changed and that the arrival of Soviet troops and the change in government were merely coincidental and totally unconnected.[5]

Clearly, according to the original script, Amin was supposed to have acquiesced to the invasion before the formal invitation, or perhaps captured and then sent to the Soviet Union for "health reasons." In any case, his death under combat conditions, the degree of subsequent resistance to the Soviet occupation, and Karmal's week-long absence from Kabul created a near-impossible task for the usually more efficient Soviet propaganda machine.

On the 29th, two motorized rifle divisions—one from Kushka in the west, the other from Termez—entered Afghanistan, bringing the total of Soviet troops in Afghanistan to 50,000 by the end of the first week of January 1980. Three more divisions subsequently entered Afghanistan bringing the total number of full divisions to six and the total number of Soviet troops to around 85,000 by the end of March. Several squadrons of MiG–21 and MiG–23 aircraft accompanied the invading forces. Soviet divisions, true to the pattern established in other operations, such as the invasion of Czechoslovakia, entered the country with all organic equipment, including air defense and missile units. Interestingly, with the exception of the airborne units, these units were composed of as much as 70 percent reserve fillers on a 90-day call-up. A large number of the Soviet reservists (perhaps as many as 90 percent) were Central Asians.[6]

Soviet forces were quite methodical in the operations that followed. First, they moved to consolidate their hold over major roads and urban areas. Second, troops were deployed around the country to "show the flag" and attempt to limit infiltration from the sanctuary areas in Iran and Pakistan. Third, concurrent with the first and second steps, the Soviets attempted to disarm unreliable elements of the Afghan army or, if they resisted, as the 26th Afghan Parachute Regiment did, to destroy them. A reliable source reported that the 8th Division (Kabul area) also resisted, and that at Kandahar an entire division went over to the resistance.[7] During the first three weeks of occupation, Soviet forces were apparently ordered to keep a low profile, and it is fair to surmise that routine troop movements were tightly controlled by Soviet headquarters in Termez or at Bagram Airbase.

Deception played a great role in the initial Soviet success in Afghanistan. Four measures deserve mention. First, as previously noted, the steady arrival of Soviet ministers and technical personnel lent an air of normalcy to the situation in Kabul. Amin's meeting with the Soviet minister of communications on December 26 may have diminished any immediate fears he might have had about the Soviets. The fact that he had moved out of the Arg in central Kabul to the Darulaman Palace complex—perhaps at Soviet urging—apparently shut him off from reliable information on the situation in Kabul. Even the *Pravda* denials of imminent invasion and interference may have reassured attentive publics who did not want to believe that an invasion was imminent. Second, it is possible that some elements of the Afghan secret police helped the Soviets to disguise their movements into Kabul Airport and the Soviet-controlled Bagram Airbase, even though Amin's nephew was in charge of that organization. Third, throughout the initial phase of the operation, Soviet advisers played a key role in neutralizing Afghan army units whose loyalty was questionable. This was accomplished by Soviet control over fuel and by other measures, such as having unreliable units turn over their ammunition for inventory or having them turn in vehicle batteries for winterizing. Fourth, numerous key officials and military officers in Kabul were invited to parties on the 27th and, after having been plied with alcohol, were locked in until their reliability could be better assessed.[8] Finally, timing the invasion to coincide with the Christmas holiday again put the West off guard and insured a delayed reaction on the part of Western nations.

Any final assessment of the invasion itself must be mixed. On the positive side of the ledger, the Soviet military and security apparatus proved that (1) it is capable of rapid (though detectable) mobilization; (2) it can perform major operations without severe logistical breakdown; (3) it has suffcient ground forces to mount major conventional operations outside the Warsaw Pact or Chinese border areas; and (4) it is reliable in "political" operations, such as assassination and the disarming of unreliable "friendly" forces.

On the other hand, there were some glaring judgmental errors. The massive use of Central Asian reservists—evidently designed to facilitate movement and communication with the populace—was a mistake. Many of these reservists had probably spent their active duty in noncombat units and may have been poorly trained for fighting.[9] Moreover, most of the Soviet Central Asian troops were Tajiks or Uzbeks. This may have alienated some of the Pushtun majority in Afghanistan which tends toward ethnocentricity and ethnic prejudice. Many of these recruits were also guilty of fraternization and a few even defected.[10]

A former lawyer and present resistance leader gave this eyewitness testimony of collusion between Central Asian soldiers and their co-religionists in 1980:

> In the very beginning, when the Soviets first entered our country in 1979 . . . most of the soldiers were Soviet–Central Asians. This is because they speak a language akin to our own. And the Russians certainly thought that through the use of Soviet–Central Asian troops they could more easily control us. And these Soviet–Central Asian soldiers were told that they [were] coming to defend us in Afghanistan from American, Chinese, and Pakistan military attacks. When these people (Soviet–Central Asians) realized that the only people they were fighting

in Afghanistan were Afghans . . . then these Soviet–Central Asians began helping us. They began leaving us packages with ammunition and weapons and caches. They left it in the ground and covered it with earth and just left a little of it emerging. In the beginning we were very suspicious and cautious and poked at this with sticks, afraid that they would prove to be mines. And when we finally uncovered these things, we found out that they were parcels of weapons and ammunition that these Soviet–Central Asians were leaving for us. The Soviets (Russians) finally became aware that this was going on and [have] since withdrawn Soviet–Central Asian troops from Afghanistan and now they have just brought in their own red-faced troops.[11]

By using these Muslim reservists the Soviets may have been trying to low profile their mobilization, believing that a mobilization in a limited geographic area, especially one with an abundant workforce, might have been less noticeable than a national call-to-arms. Certainly, the Soviet high command must have viewed the Central Asian reservists as being useful for interpreting and related tasks. In any case, however, these reservists were withdrawn within ninety days, as Soviet procedure calls for.

Also on the negative side, one must again mention the Yepishev-Pavlovskiy estimate. Both of these officers were key participants in crushing the Czechoslovakian experiment, with the latter having served as the commander of invading troops in 1968. The use of airborne troops to seize key facilities, the subsequent link-up with ground forces, and the use of subversion and disinformation all suggest that the Soviets used the Czech operation as a model for their operation in Afghanistan. There is every indication that, due to the influence of these two officers, the Politburo came to believe that the Afghan operation could be a replay of their 1968 experience.[12]

Clearly, it showed a pathetic ignorance of Afghan culture and history to believe that the Afghans would not fight a foreign invasion force or that their quisling, Babrak Karmal, could ever hope to gain popular support or even acceptance in the countryside. To see Afghanistan as a replay of events in Czechoslovakia was a key error and a disastrous attempt at trying to apply historical lessons as maxims. In summary, the Soviet leadership made a fundamental miscalculation: they failed to identify the nature of the conflict and to gauge accurately the relationship between means and ends in Afghanistan. No battlefield error could have been as critical. The Soviets would have done well to remember Clausewitz, who said,

The first, the grandest, and most decisive act of judgement which the

Statesman and General exercises is rightly to understand . . . the war in which he engages, not to take it for something, or to wish to make of it something, which by the nature of its relations it is impossible for it to be. This is, therefore, the first, the most comprehensive, of all strategical questions.[13]

As a footnote to the invasion, *Pravda* announced on January 3 that a 54-year-old Lieutenant General Paputin had died under unspecified circumstances on December 28.[14] There was much speculation about the circumstances of his death. In one scenario, Paputin was killed in the assault on Amin's residence. In another, having failed in his mission with Amin, he commited suicide en route to or in Moscow. A third scenario, one popular in Moscow, had him committing suicide for personal reasons or over a power struggle with Brezhnev's son-in-law, Yuri Churbanov, also a high official in the MVD, and Paputin's eventual successor as first deputy minister of the MVD.

The first scenario is unlikely. Before becoming a high MVD official in 1974 Viktor Paputin had a long career as an *apparatchik,* not as a soldier or policeman. It is unlikely that he would be selected for a direct combat role when the GRU, Soviet military intelligence, and the KGB both had highly trained commando elements. Moreover, at least by official Afghan accounts, he had left Afghanistan two weeks before the coup.

Either of the suicide scenarios is plausible. Contrary to routine practice, Paputin's obituary appeared on the back page of *Pravda.* It was not signed by Brezhnev, and no picture accompanied the text. Normally, a first deputy minister and an alternate Central Committee member would have an obituary and accompanying photograph, usually on one of the first three pages of the paper, signed by all of the members of the Politburo.

A combat death would have borne the inscription "in the execution of his service duties." A citation of a military award would also have been appropriate. An inscription of "sudden death" would seem to correlate with natural causes or non-duty-related accidents. Although *Pravda* cited Paputin's death as "untimely," its silence on the circumstances of his death and the missing signatures suggest suicide, disgrace, or both.

In other personnel matters, some of the important officials involved in the planning for the invasion were given rewards, others were fired. On January 3, Ambassador Anatoliy Dobrynin was given the Order of Lenin for services to the state. Although this move may have been planned for other reasons well before the invasion, in light of U.S. outrage over the invasion, it certainly served the perhaps unintended function of a vote of confidence for the veteran ambassador.[15] In December 1980,

General of the Army Ivan G. Pavlovskiy was removed after thirteen years as the commander-in-chief of the Soviet ground forces. While one may speculate that this represented a censure for a faulty estimate on Afghanistan, other analysts have convincingly written of it as part of Marshal Nikolai Ogarkov's consolidation of power or as a reflection of a dispute over intervening in Poland. One analyst has also attributed twelve other general officer changes to the latter theory.[16] In any case, Pavlovskiy was removed and replaced by his former deputy, General of the Army V.I. Petrov, who had supervised the final battles of the Ethiopian-Somali War in 1977–78.[17] General Pavlovskiy was assigned to the Main Inspectorate of the Ministry of Defense and was a delegate to the Twenty-sixth Party Congress in 1981, a sign that his relief was not coupled with any personal disgrace or punishment.

The Karmal Government

As previously mentioned, the Soviet invasion was designed to unseat Amin and replace him with a new Khalq-Parcham coalition. The presence of 85,000 Soviet troops was intended to intimidate the rebels and provide the new government with a breathing spell to build an effective government and army. In effect, Soviet forces were apparently designed as an army of occupation and not a counterinsurgency force.

On the surface, Karmal was a good choice for this role. He was, prior to the Soviet invasion, genuinely popular. Amin had himself split the Khalq faction and thus one could imagine that Karmal could not possibly be any worse for intrafactional relations.

Such was not the case, however. The Karmal regime, delivered in the combat trains of the army of a foreign, atheistic power, possessed no legitimacy and was rent by internal conflicts. The Afghan government was not just a Soviet puppet, it was virtually a Soviet prisoner. Nearly every ministry except the foreign ministry was openly under Soviet control. All press releases were cleared by Soviets and eight Soviet officials were detailed to write a new constitution for Afghanistan.[18] Not even Karmal, who was president of the Revolutionary Council, general secretary of the Party, and prime minister, had any latitude in his work. According to a U.S. State Department document,

> Except for a dozen sentries at the main gate, the security of the old palace where he lives is in Soviet hands. Babrak's bodyguard, chef, driver, doctor, and six chief advisers are all Soviets. The President's isolation is described as so total that his father—said to hold the Soviets

in contempt—told Babrak never to enter the father's house with his Russian retinue.[19]

A former Afghan diplomat reported in the fall of 1980 that "even Babrak Karmal is no longer allowed to compose his own speeches."[20] Soviet domination produced one of two dysfunctional effects on Afghan bureaucrats: they either ignored their Soviet supervisors or simply let them do all of the work. In the fall, Babrak Karmal even found it necessary to remind his comrades that

> At our request the USSR has sent experts and advisers for nearly all areas of government and for the ministries and administration of Afghanistan. We ought to make very effective and maximum use of this fraternal and disinterested assistance. We will learn from the technical expertise of our Soviet comrades. Unfortunately, some of our staff close their eyes to these possibilities—I address myself to the staff and in particular to party comrades—and some of them even lay all the burden and responsibility for practical work on the shoulders of the advisors. Such acts are basically inadmissible. . . .[21]

Defection was a third course of action open to Afghan officials and dignitaries. In January, the deputy UN representative defected. In February, he was followed into exile by a diplomat sent from Kabul to a nonaligned meeting in New York. These two were followed by the national soccer team in March, numerous Ariana Airline crews, and the Olympic wrestling team.[22] In October the Afghan delegate to a UNESCO conference in Belgrade defected after informing a public session of the conference that Afghanistan "is completely dominated by our Soviet friends."[23]

Internal conflicts continued to play a leading role in Afghan domestic politics. Much like Taraki's original cabinet, Karmal's was a coalition, but this time, it was four parts Parcham to three parts Khalq, with one deputy prime minister from each wing.[24] While this might appear to have been a workable coalition, it was fraught with problems.

First, personal feuds ran deep, even inside the upper echelons of the government. A U.S. State Department report noted that

> It is understandable that the current attempts to reconcile past differences are not succeeding. Parchamis who suffered torture from their current Khalq colleagues cannot forget and forgive. One of the most hated figures is Khalqi Deputy Prime Minister Assadullah Sarwari, who was head of the secret police during the Taraki presidency and who is held personally responsible for the torture of some of the Parcham po-

litical prisoners, including the other deputy prime minister, Sultan Ali Keshtmand.²⁵

In March 1980, there were reports of shoot-outs involving Politburo members in government buildings.²⁶ In June 1980, A. Sarwari was relieved of his duties and posted to Mongolia as ambassador.

Second, a Parcham-dominated coalition was even more problematical than a Khalq-dominated one. The Khalq was particularly strong in the army and in 1980 outnumbered the Parcham by a factor of three to one.²⁷ This generated discontent over a number of specific policies. Khalq members reportedly resisted Parcham attempts to moderate their reforms and objected "to issuing [a] new, less inflammatory flag." Khalqis also objected to the presence of Soviet troops and to the signing of the spring 1980 Status of Forces Agreement, which, although it has never been published, apparently granted formal extraterritorial rights to Soviet forces in Afghanistan. In July 1980, the 14th Armored Brigade revolted when the government attempted to relieve its Khalqi commander. By the fall of 1980, many from the Khalq faction were actually fighting alongside the *mujahidin* (freedom fighters).²⁸

Third, the environment was a complicating factor, to say the least. Even an experienced, united government would have found it very difficult to solve the problems which faced the Karmal regime. Its army had disintegraged from a strength of about 100,000 to 30,000 or less. By spring 1980, more than 700,000 Afghans had fled to Pakistan or Iran. Riots in Kabul in February and April saw Soviet gunships strafing crowds of students, leaving approximately 500 and 100 dead, respectively.²⁹ The economy was totally disrupted and the Soviets were forced to deliver 140,000 tons of wheat to Afghanistan in April. In summation, the war had heated up, or as a Soviet Central Committee analyst put it in March 1980, "the armed invasion of Afghanistan [became] even more massive and open."³⁰ Major battles broke out not only around the major cities but also in Kunar and Paktia provinces on the border with Pakistan.

International Reaction

After a Soviet veto in the Security Council, the United Nations General Assembly voted 104 to 18 (with 30 absences or abstentions) to "deplore the recent armed intervention in Afghanistan." Not mentioning the Soviet Union by name, the General Assembly went on to call for "the immediate, unconditional and total withdrawal of foreign troops from Afghanistan"³¹ The most notable aspect of this vote was the sharp blow delivered to the Soviets by the nonaligned nations, more than two-thirds of whom voted against the USSR in the General Assembly. Iraq voted against the Soviets, India and Syria abstained, and Libya was absent. Conferences of Islamic foreign ministers twice condemned the invasion in January and May 1980.

Even some socialist states or fraternal parties reacted coldly to the Soviet move. Yugoslavia voted against the USSR in the UN, and Rumania failed to vote on either the January or a subsequent November 1980 motion. Rumania even implicitly criticized the Soviet Union in a joint declaration with Great Britain. Cuba did vote with the Soviets in the UN, but otherwise its support was initially lukewarm, perhaps out of anger over its loss of prestige in the nonaligned movement. For example, in January 1980, Castro made the following ambiguous remark: "The events in Iran and Afghanistan are taking on dramatic importance that worries anyone who wishes for peace based on peoples' right to sovereignty, integrity, and independence."[32] In a similar vein, while the Soviet press in January 1980 carried numerous expressions of fraternal support, Cuba's was noticeably absent. Furthermore, the invasion angered the West European communist parties to the extent that the Soviets were forced to prohibit the representative of the Italian Communist Party, Western Europe's largest, from making a speech at the Twenty-sixth Party Congress in February 1981.[33]

Iran also objected strenuously to the Soviet invasion.[34] In the case of Iran, however, the Soviet loss is best measured not by rhetoric or even by Iranian aid to the Afghan insurgents, but in terms of opportunity costs. If they had not invaded Afghanistan, the Soviets might have made great inroads with Iran during the hostage crisis. As it turned out, the Soviets were simply relegated by Iran to the position of a secondary enemy and Soviet influence with Iran was reduced by their invasion. This should not be interpreted to mean that Afghanistan was the only disputed issue between Iran and the USSR. Soviet involvement with the Kurds and the *Tudeh* party was compounded by the Soviet refusal to denounce the interventionary provisions of the 1921 Treaty of Friendship. Afghanistan simply became another serious irritant in this important bilateral relationship.

The Chinese reaction was predictable. Even before the invasion the Chinese saw Afghanistan as part of the Soviet grand design to encircle China and to cut Europe and Japan off from their energy supplies. In Chinese eyes, the Soviets, as successors of the tsars, have long "drooled" over Afghanistan for geostrategic reasons:

> To get hold of the passage leading out of the Indian Ocean and to control the strategic sea route of the West and Japan, the Soviet Union

is energetically trying to control Afghanistan to open a land route south to the Indian Ocean . . .[35]

The occupation of Afghanistan and the Wakhan corridor served to cut China off from another Third World country and increased Chinese fears of a future move against its old ally, Pakistan. Consequently, the Chinese added the removal of Soviet troops from Afghanistan to the demands that they are making of the Soviets prior to a renormalization of relations. Also, they stepped up military aid to Pakistan and completed the strategically important Karakoram Highway connecting the two countries. From October 1979 to November 1981, China and Pakistan exchanged ten high-level military and naval delegations. Although both China and Pakistan are silent on the specifics, it appears that they are cooperating on helping the Afghan freedom fighters, and reequipping the Pakistani army. One analyst noted that their close relationship may have been transformed into an alliance wherein the Chinese may have promised to come to Pakistan's aid if it were to be attacked by the Soviets.[36]

The U.S. reaction to the invasion represented one of the strongest series of actions ever taken by the United States over any specific Soviet act. Claiming that the implications of the Soviet move "could pose the most serious threat to peace since the Second World War,"[37] President Carter quickly announced a series of stiff measures: (1) blocking the export of 17 million metric tons (mmt) of grain; (2) stopping the sale of computers and high-technology equipment; (3) reducing the allowable catch of the Soviet fishing fleet in U.S. waters from 350,000 tons to 75,000 tons; (4) delaying the opening of the new Soviet consulate in New York; (5) postponing a renegotiation of the cultural agreement that was under consideration; (6) boycotting the Moscow Olympics,[38] an action later joined by fifty-five other countries, including Germany, Japan, and China.

The grain embargo was a highly controversial move, even if one disregards the contentious domestic ramifications of the issue. Many Americans—farmers, agricultural experts, economists, and election-year politicians—questioned the utility of this sanction. Though complete data are still unavailable, one must judge that the embargo was, at least from a political perspective, a partial success.[39]

The United States set out to embargo 17 mmt of grain, allowing for export a total of 8 mmt that it had promised as a minimum in accordance with an October 1975 agreement. Administration officials initially expected that Soviets would be able to pick up only about 3–5 million metric tons (mmt) of the embargoed grain from other sources.[40] Overall this would represent about a 5 percent shortfall in total Soviet grain supply but a much higher precentage of their total feed grain supply, thus delivering a sharp blow to the Soviet meat supply. The estimates of the embargo proved overly optimistic. United States Department of Agriculture (USDA) sources reported by April 1980 that the total Soviet shortfall was more in the neighborhood of 5 mmt rather than the predicted 14 mmt. Subsequent estimates would show that in 1980–81, the Soviets were able to meet their projected import targets almost in their entirety.[41] By spending much needed foreign reserves, the Soviets were able, inter alia, to make up nearly all of their shortfall from Argentina, Canada, and Australia and from "laundered" grain, transhipped to the Soviet Union from Eastern Europe. It is unknown to what extent the Soviets may also have drawn down their own stocks to offset the loss.

On the other hand, from a U.S. perspective, there were some positive effects from the grain embargo. In addition to causing a financial expense which the Defense Intelligence Agency (DIA) estimated at approximately $1 billion, the grain embargo contributed to a very poor meat supply situation in the Soviet Union.[42] It is impossible to say how much it contributed to this situation because feed grain imports are only one of many critical variables including grain stocks and the availability of fodder and other substitute feeds. It is known, however, that Soviet per capita meat consumption remained level from 1975 to 1979, while real incomes rose relatively sharply during the same period.[43] In a period where consumers might have purchased more meat, there was no more to purchase.

The Soviet government was forced to double meat imports from 1979 to 1981, but, overall, the USDA estimates that

> Meat production declined 3 percent in 1980 and milk production fell by the same percentage. Despite record meat imports during 1980, per capita meat consumption in the Soviet Union dropped by at least 2 kilograms from the 1979 level of 59 kilograms, to about the same consumption as in 1975—half the U.S. level, and 28 percent lower even than Poland's.[44]

Had the Soviets not faced the U.S. embargo, they might have chosen to increase their grain purchases to offset these problems. Under the embargo their 1980 import target bacame a ceiling beyond which they could not go. Since the first purpose of U.S. sanctions was to impose a heavy price for Soviet aggression, one can judge the embargo as being partially successful. The psychological effect of the boycott on the Soviet population is another matter and beyond the scope of this inquiry.

In a related area, the reaction of U.S. allies was less consistent and impaired alliance cohesion. Industrial exports from Western Europe to the Soviet Union actually increased in nominal value in 1980 and both the Federal Republic of Germany and France took over—albeit in a slightly changed fashion—major industrial projects in the USSR which were to have been completed by U.S. companies. Verbal support to the contrary, U.S. allies in Europe and Japan did not signal their objection to the Soviet invasion to the same extent that the United States did. Not only were there varying estimates of the importance of the Afghanistan invasion, but the Europeans also faced significant economic problems and were thus unable to participate to the extent that the United States did. At the root of all this, of course, was a fundamental problem for the Western alliance: agreeing on the importance of Third World conflicts for alliance interests and the course of East-West relations in general.[45]

In a move which the Soviets could have predicted, President Carter also withdrew the SALT II treaty from active consideration for ratification by the Senate and announced the Carter Doctrine: "An attempt by any outside force to gain control of the Persian Gulf region will be regarded as an assault on the vital interests of the United States of America. And such an assault will be repelled by any means necessary, including military force."[46] In related moves, the United States reaffirmed its 1959 agreement "to help Pakistan preserve its independence and its integrity,"[47] but U.S.-Pakistani dealings in 1980 were troubled. Due to budgetary problems and Pakistan's "dubious record on human rights and on nonproliferation," the United States wanted to hold aid to a low level.[48] Pakistan wanted a much larger package and also desired the 1959 pledge to be extended to cover an Indian attack. Although the Carter administration's offer of $400 million was rebuffed by President Zia and called "peanuts," the Reagan administration in 1981 announced a $3.2 billion, five-year aid package for Pakistan. Finally, the Soviet invasion accelerated the development of the U.S. Rapid Deployment Force which had been under consideration since 1977.[49] Worst of all, from a Soviet perspective, the invasion contributed to greater Chinese-U.S. cooperation. In the years that followed, the United States granted China most favored nation status and agreed to sell the People's Republic "nonlethal" military equipment which included eleven advanced computers with military applications. Discussions on actual military purchases continued.

Consolidation and Damage Limitation, January–July 1980

The Soviets no doubt were surprised by the severity of the international reaction. Their military and diplomatic moves after the invasion suggest a damage-limiting strategy and a search for different means to their more constant ends.

On the military front, the Soviets quickly realized that they were not an army of occupation, but rather that to survive they would have to pursue a more active policy. Not possessing enough troops to control the ground, the Soviets adopted what amounted to a modified enclave strategy. More specifically, Soviet strategy was directed at holding the major centers of communications, limiting infiltration, and destroying local resistance strongholds at minimum cost to their own forces. In essence, the Soviet strategy was one wherein high technology, superior tactical mobility, and firepower were used to make up for an inadequate number of troops and as a means to hold friendly casualties to a minimum. By intent or in effect, Soviet policy was a combination of scorched earth and, in anthropologist Louis Dupree's words, "migratory genocide." From January to April 1980, close to an additional half million Afghans became refugees.[50]

In response to the battlefield situation, the Soviets also sought to modify their force structure in Afghanistan. In June 1980, in a move timed to coincide with a Western summit and to follow closely an Afghan peace initiative, the Soviets removed 5,000 troops, more than 100 tanks, and much of their air defense and extraneous missile units from Afghanistan.[51] The troops were replaced by additional infantry and Soviet materiel was augmented by an influx of Mi–24 gunships, which reached a total of 240 by the end of 1980. In addition to these changes, according to U.S. intelligence sources, during their first six months in Afghanistan, Soviet troops improved on their infrastructure by (1) constructing permanent logistics facilities and barracks; (2) beginning the construction of a bridge over the Amu Darya; (3) improving airfields, in particular to accommodate the Mi–24 gunship; and (4) constructing permanent communications and fuel storage facilities.[52]

To date, it is impossible to estimate accurately Soviet casualties in Afghanistan. Most estimates are in the range 5–7,000 casualties in the first year, with at least a third of these being killed. In addition to Paputin, it is possible that as many as six Soviet general officers may have died in (or in connection with) operations in Afghanistan during the first six months of military operations.[53]

On the diplomatic and propaganda fronts, the Soviet Union attempted to counter the adverse effects of the invasion with claims of outside interference and by justifying its invasion through the Soviet-Afghan friendship treaty and the UN Charter. A consistent attempt was made to shift the blame for the invasion to the United States and to convince the attentive public that outside interference was the cause of the problem. On January 6, *Pravda* noted the U.S. reaction to the Afghanistan crisis was a result of its plans for turning that country into an "anti-Soviet military staging ground."54 In a related theme, many Soviet analyses pointed to the fact that the United States had taken up the "big stick" approach and that they were using the hostage crisis as a pretext to make their military presence in the Indian Ocean a permanent fact of life.55 In February, Central Committee official Leonid Zamyatin said that "it would be enough for the United States President to issue a command for ending thrusts into Afghanistan's territory," and the infiltration—and the reason for the Soviet presence—would then cease.56 Brezhnev himself noted, "It is the Americans, together with the Chinese, who are directing this intervention, which has created a serious threat to the Afghan revolution and the security of our southern border."57

The USSR also made a deliberate attempt to separate the United States from its allies on the issues of sanctions in particular and detente in general. One approach was to remind the West Europeans and Japanese of the financial benefits of detente and to suggest that sanctions would not work and would only benefit the United States. Vitaliy Kobysh, a Central Committee official, noted that U.S. sanctions were really designed to deprive the Germans and the Japanese of their trade advantages and to restore the U.S. economic dominance in the alliance.58

Brezhnev himself was more sophisticated. Echoing the European perception that the United States had become an "unreliable partner," he pointed out in January 1980 that the United States was "not content . . . to poison Soviet-American relations," but that it also wanted to spoil Soviet–West European relations as well. He went on to say that the European people, because of their experience with war, knew that their fundamental interests were "bound up with detente."59 Brezhnev went on to remind the Europeans of the importance of the Conference on Security and Cooperation in Europe (CSCE) meeting in Madrid (September 1980) and Soviet efforts to end the dangerous and expensive arms race in Europe, the latter subject being much more important to Soviet–West European relations than the war in Afghanistan. The message was simple: distance yourself from U.S. actions, and Soviet-European detente can continue. As proof of good faith, the Soviets backed off on their threat not to discuss the issue of Eurostrategic missiles without NATO's cancellation of the deployment of the Pershing II and cruise missiles, and they also redeployed two tank divisions and 700 tanks from East Europe to the USSR early in 1980.

The Soviet Union also sought regional allies on the issue of the invasion. Soviet diplomats met with Iranian officials to attempt to calm their fears, but this action met with little success. Although the Soviets had supported Iran, before the Afghan invasion, against U.S. "flagrant military and political pressure," in A. Petrov's words, Iran reacted sharply to the Soviet invasion.[60] The Iranian foreign minister said shortly after the invasion that

> The Islamic government of Iran cannot agree with military intervention . . . by a superpower in a small country. . . . Because Afghanistan is a Moslem country and a neighbor of Iran, the military intervention of the government of the Soviet Union . . . is considered a hostile measure not only against the people of the country but against all Moslems of the world.[61]

Soviet-Iranian relations deteriorated even more when, in the Gulf War, the Iranians perceived a pro-Iraqi tilt on the part of the Soviets. By the spring of 1983, relations were at an all time low.

India, once again under Indira Gandhi, was a more likely target for Soviet influence, especially since U.S. plans to renew arms sales to Pakistan affected its security. In spite of some earlier pro-Soviet remarks, and in spite of a generous aid package and a visit by Gromyko in February and Brezhnev in December 1980, the only verbal concession from India was a joint declaration which condemned U.S. activities at Diego Garcia and contained this remarkably ambiguous sentence: "The Soviet Union and India reiterate their opposition to all forms of outside interference in the internal affairs . . . of that region."[62] Although "outside interference" was a common Soviet formulation, the remark can certainly be taken two ways.

The Soviet treatment of Pakistan was much less tactful. Although the U.S. and China came in for even harsher treatment, the Soviet media left no doubt that Pakistan was one of the chief "instruments of interference," "dragged in" by the United States. Pakistani explanations, in large part accurate, that they were unable to halt incursions into Afghanistan were, in Gromyko's words, "unconvincing" and "not to be taken seriously."[63] With Saudi and U.S. funding, and training assistance from Egypt and China, Pakistan was portrayed by the Soviet media as maintaining "dozens of camps" which facilitated the infiltration of 1,500 "armed bandits" per month by the fall 1980.[64]

Soviet pressure on Pakistan was not limited to gentle persuasion. Threats, overflights, and limited hot pursuit of guerrillas into Pakistan took place. Babrak Karmal himself said in November 1980, "I warn [the Pakistanis] that conditions have changed and no forces . . . can divert us from our course. If they persist, they will get a reply that they will never forget."[65]

The Soviet Union did refrain from taking stiffer actions against the Pakistanis. It did not directly threaten Pakistan with invasion and it did not decisively move to arm or incite Baluch separatists. The USSR needed Pakistani help to extricate itself from Afghanistan. For its part, Pakistan, mindful of India to its rear and the burden of millions of refugees, has had to at least consider Soviet peace proposals.

The Soviet peace position began to emerge in Brezhnev's RSFSR (Russian Soviet Federated Socialist Republic) Supreme Soviet election speech of February 23, 1980. According to Brezhnev, U.S. and Chinese intervention brought Soviet forces into Afghanistan. Soviet forces could begin to withdraw when the outside intervention ceased. If the United States, Iran, and Pakistan would guarantee the cessation of interference, "then the need for Soviet military assistance [would] no longer exist."[66] Rejecting a German scheme for the neutralization of Afghanistan, Vitaliy Kobysh of the Central Committee reaffirmed Brezhnev's position in March, but noted that a guaranteed cessation of infiltration would have to take place before the Soviets would be able to begin their withdrawal.[67] Three days later, Gromyko assured the Afghan foreign minister, S.M. Dost, that the Soviet Union would do nothing behind Afghanistan's back and that they would approve no plans which ignored the status of the PDPA's "legitimate government."[68]

Brezhnev's original ideas were broadened by Karmal's "May fourteenth Proposals." Karmal proposed (1) separate bilateral talks between Afghanistan, Iran, and Pakistan on normalization of relations; (2) the immediate cessation of armed interference during these talks; (3) the return of refugees with amnesty; (4) U.S. and Soviet guarantees to any bilateral agreements; (5) the withdrawal of Soviet troops, depending "on the resolution of the question of effective guarantees for [the] bilateral accords."[69]

An unsigned and presumably authoritative editorial in the July 2, 1980 issue of *Pravda* elaborated on the May 14th proposals right after the USSR's token June troop withdrawal and noted that the two preconditions for a political settlement were a cessation of infiltration and the institution of "effective measures" to guarantee that "subversive actions from abroad will not be resumed in any form." On the critical issue of the pace of Soviet troop withdrawals, the editorial vaguely added only that the size and pace of withdrawal "is determined by the need to support . . . Afghanistan in the struggle."[70]

Talks under these provisions never took place. They would have constituted de facto recognition of the Karmal regime and they would have legitimized the Soviet presence. Iran remained hostile and Pakistan would not move to jeopardize its pending U.S. aid commitment or to break faith with the other Islamic nations who rejected both the Karmal government and its proposals. No real progress was made on a peace proposal in the first six months after the invasion.

During the same period the Soviet Union learned that its forces would not simply be an army of occupation and that their stay in Afghanistan would be neither short nor without costs. The Karmal government was ineffective, the Afghan army useless, and the situation in Afghanistan nearly hopeless.

Slowly, the Soviet Union began to react to its new and unexpectedly hostile military environment. Diplomatically a search was made for allies and measures were taken both to shift the blame for the conflict to the United States and China and also to reassure nations in the area that the Soviet Union had no designs on their territory, resources, or interests. In all, Soviet diplomacy and propaganda had very little effect during the first six months after the invasion. Soviet efforts to develop a favorable peace agreement began in February 1980 but were also unfruitful.

This inquiry now turns to the examination of the factors which were critical to the Soviet decision to invade Afghanistan.

Notes

1. The low flight estimate is cited in Valenta, "From Prague to Kabul," pp. 124–27. The high estimate comes from Charters, "Coup and Consolidation." On the death of Amin, see *Time*, November 22, 1982, pp. 33–34. Again, the defector was not an eyewitness, but his account of this particular incident generally coincides with other reports. For the account of an Afghan diplomat, see *Sunday Telegraph* (London), June 24, 1984, p. 10.

2. For a detailed description of Soviet actions in December 1979, see Bradsher, *Afghanistan and the Soviet Union*, pp. 175–88; and U.S. Dept. of Defense, Joint Special Operations Command, *Special Operations: Military Lessons from Six Selected Case Studies*, pp. 205–12.

3. *East-West Relations in the Aftermath*, p. 35. U.S. contingency planning for a Soviet invasion began in September 1979. Brzezinski, *Power and Principle*, p. 427.

4. For official Afghan announcements, see *Kabul New Times*, January 1 and 12, 1980, p. 1 in both editions. On the fake "Radio Kabul," see U.S. Dept. of State, *Soviet Invasion of Afghanistan*, p. 1.

5. Ul'yanovskiy, "The Afghan Revolution at the Current Stage," p. 16.

6. On Soviet equipment, see John Erickson's memorandum in House of Commons, *Afghanistan*, Appendix 2. On ethnic composition, see Shulman in *East-West Relations in the Aftermath*, p. 39. Also, Kruzhin, "The Ethnic Composition of Soviet Forces in Afghanistan," p. 1–2. Kruzhin is skeptical about the 90 percent figure. Two Rand analysts have cast doubt on these figures as well, but their objection is based on the following weak rationale: (1) Central Asians or other Muslims do not dominate combat units, and (2) many observers may have mistaken Tartars, Armenians, and Georgians for Central Asians. While their arguments have some merit, in light of numerous reports and the Afghan

testimony noted below, the vast majority of the reservists appear to have been Central Asians. Wimbush and Alexiev, *Soviet Central Asian Soldiers in Afghanistan*, pp. 1–10.

7. *New York Times*, January 14, 1980, p. 5; Also, John Erickson's memorandum in House of Commons, *Afghanistan*, Appendix 2.

8. Valenta, "From Prague to Kabul," p. 134; Luttwak, "After Afghanistan, What?" pp. 46–47; and Arnold, *Afghanistan: The Soviet Invasion in Perspective*, pp. 94–96.

9. Wimbush and Alexiev, *Soviet Central Asian Soldiers in Afghanistan*, pp. 10–15.

10. Bennigsen, "Soviet Muslims and the World of Islam," pp. 46–49.

11. *Soviet Human Rights Violations in Afghanistan*, pp. 21–22.

12. Freistetter, "The Battle in Afghanistan," p. 37. On the common methodology in the 1968 and 1979 events, see Valenta, "From Prague to Kabul," pp. 114–40.

13. Clausewitz, *On War*, p. 121.

14. Paputin's obituary appeared without photograph on the last page of *Pravda*, January 3, 1980. For an analysis of obituaries and rumors concerning Paputin, see U.S. Embassy, Moscow, *USSR First Deputy Interior Minister (MVD) Paputin Dies—In Afghanistan?* and U.S. Embassy, Moscow, *Churbanov and Paputin—Recent Gossip*. For an analysis of high-ranking casualties, including Paputin, see Haselkorn, *Analysis of Soviet Casualties in Afghanistan*, esp. pp. 13–17.

15. *New York Times*, January 4, 1980, p. 6.

16. Anderson, "Soviet Decision-Making and Poland," pp. 22–27.

17. Hosmer and Wolfe, *Soviet Policy and Practice Toward Third World Conflicts*, p. 92. For a description of a Pavlovskiy appearance made after the 26th Party Congress, see Foreign Broadcast Information Service (FBIS)–Soviet Union–III–64–4/3/81–vi.

18. U.S. Dept. of State, *Soviet Dilemmas in Afghanistan*, p. 3.

19. Ibid.

20. *Frankfurter Allgemeine Zeitung*, October 31, 1980, in FBIS, Daily Report—South Asia, 8, no. 217, November 6, 1980, p. C7. FBIS hereafter cited as: FBIS–Publication–Volume–Number–Date–page.

21. Speech translated in FBIS–South Asia–8–223–11/17/80–C3.

22. On the subject of defections, see U.S. Dept. of State, *Afghanistan: A Year of Occupation*, pp. 4–5.

23. *New York Times*, October 27, 1980, p. 6.

24. U.S. Dept. of State, Bureau of Intelligence and Research, *Political Feuding in Afghanistan*, p. 2.

25. Ibid., p. 4.

26. *Time*, March 10, 1980, p. 30.

27. U.S. Dept. of State, *Political Feuding in Afghanistan*, p. 3

28. Ibid., p. 5. Also *New York Times*, November 7, 1980, p. 3. For further information on factional feuding see Khalilzad, "Soviet-Occupied Afghanistan," pp. 26–9.

29. *New York Times*, May 11, 1980, p. 3; and *Time*, March 10, 1980, p. 30. Also, U.S. Dept. of State, *Soviet Dilemmas in Afghanistan*, p. 4.

30. *Literaturnaya gazeta*, March 12, 1980, p. 9 in CDSP–32–10–7.

31. The text of the resolution is in *New York Times*, January 15, 1980, p. 8.

32. Quoted in Rand, "Cuba Continues To Take an Ambiguous Stand on Soviet Actions in Afghanistan," p. 1. On Rumania and Great Britain, see *New York Times*, March 15, 1980, p. 20.

33. *New York Times*, March 1, 1981, p. 3.

34. For excellent surveys of the relationship, see Zalmay Khalilzad, "Islamic Iran: Soviet Dilemma," *Problems of Communism* 33 (January-February 1984), pp. 1–20; and Dawisha, "The USSR in the Middle East," pp. 438–52.

35. *Renmin Ribao*, June 11, 1979, in FBIS–China–I–118–6/18/79–F2.

36. F. Yaacov Vertzberger, *The Enduring Entente: Sino-Pakistani Relations, 1960–80* (New York: Praeger with Georgetown Center for Strategic and International Studies, 1983), pp. 63–75.

37. In his State of the Union Address, January 23, 1980 reprinted in U.S. Dept. of State, Current Policy, 132, p. 2.

38. Ibid.

39. On the effectiveness of the embargo, see the following: Hajda, "The Soviet Grain Embargo," pp. 253–8; Paarlberg, "Lessons of the Grain Embargo," pp. 144–62; and John C. Rovey, "Grain Embargo as a Diplomatic Lever: A Case Study of the U.S.-Soviet Embargo of 1980–81," in U.S. Congress, Joint Economic Committee, *Selected Papers Submitted to the Joint Economic Committee on the Soviet Economy in the 1980's, pp. 124–40*.

40. U.S. Congress, House Committee on Foreign Affairs, *An Assessment of the Afghanistan Sanctions: Implications for Trade and Diplomacy in the 1980's*, pp. 39–45.

41. Ibid. See also Paarlberg, "Lessons of the Grain Embargo," pp. 154–55.

42. U.S. Congress, Senate Committee on Banking, Housing, and Urban Affairs, *Hearings on the Suspension of United States Exports of High Technology and Grain to the Soviet Union*, p. 2. The DIA did not and has not released information on its computational methodology.

43. See Gregory Grossman's statement in ibid., pp. 98–9.

44. For an analysis of meat imports, see Marshall I. Goldman, *USSR in Crisis: The Failure of an Economic System* (New York: W.W. Norton, 1983), p. 64–74. The quote is from Roney, "Grain Embargo as a Diplomatic Lever," p. 135.

45. *New York Times*, October 5, 1980, p. F7–8. Also U.S. Congress, *An Assessment of the Afghanistan Sanctions*, pp. 98–109; and *New York Times*, September 18, 1980, p. D5. For an informed discussion of the West's problems with Third World conflict issues in Southwest Asia, see George E. Hudson, "Nonregional Impacts of Southwest Asian Policy: The U.S.–Soviet–O.E.C.D. Triangle," in S. Tahir-Kheli, ed., *U.S. Strategic Interests in Southwest Asia* (New York: Praeger, 1982), pp. 142–55.

46. *State of the Union Address*.

47. See Carter's address, reprinted in *New York Times*, February 4, 1980, p. 6.
48. Z.K. Brzezinski, *Power and Principle*, p. 448–49.
49. *New York Times*, January 25, 1980, p. 6.
50. On "migratory genocide," see Wade, "Afghanistan: the Politics of Tragicomedy," pp. 521–23. On refugees, U.S. Dept. of State, *Soviet Invasion of Afghanistan*, p. 2.
51. *New York Times*, July 4, 1980, p. 4.
52. U.S. Dept. of State, *Soviet Dilemmas in Afghanistan*, p. 3.; and U.S. Dept. of State, *Afghanistan: A Year of Occupation*, p. 3.
53. Haselkorn, *Analysis of Soviet Casualties in Afghanistan*, pp. 13–17.
54. *Pravda*, January 6, 1980, p. 5 in CDSP–32–1–5.
55. *Izvestiia*, January 16, 1980, p. 5 in CDSP–32–2–6.
56. Quoted in *New York Times*, February 27, 1980, p. 10.
57. In *Pravda*, February 23, 1980, p. 1 in CDSP–32–8–1.
58. *Literaturnaya gazeta*, December 3, 1980, p. 9 in FBIS–Soviet Union–III–245–12/18/80–3.
59. *Pravda*, January 13, 1980, p. 1 in CDSP–32–2–4.
60. *Pravda*, December 5, 1979, p. 5 in CDSP–31–49–4, 26.
61. Quoted in Rubinstein, *Soviet Policy Toward Turkey, Iran, and Afghanistan*, p. 107.
62. *Pravda*, December 12, 1980, pp. 1–2 in CDSP–32–50–7.
63. *Pravda*, April 26, 1980, p. 1 in CDSP–32–17–1–4, 17.
64. Tass in FBIS–Soviet Union–III–247–12/22/80–D1.
65. *New York Times*, November 7, 1980, p. 3.
66. *Pravda*, February 23, 1980, pp. 1–2 in CDSP–32–8–1–4. For Soviet "evidence" of Western and other types of support, see: *The Truth About Afghanistan*, pp. 33–80; and Grachev, *The Undeclared War: Imperialism Against Afghanistan*, pp. 38–70.
67. *Literaturnaya gazeta*, March 12, 1980, p. 9.
68. *Pravda*, March 15, 1980, p. 4.
69. Reprinted in *Pravda*, May 15, 1980, p. 5 in CDSP–32–20–6.
70. *Pravda*, July 2, 1980, p. 4 in CDSP–32–26–12.

7
Soviet Motives for the Invasion of Afghanistan: The Background Factors

To this point, it has been demonstrated that the Soviet invasion was influenced by a number of implicit assumptions. First, the Soviets probably believed that the PDPA would provide Afghanistan with a government with a socialist orientation and that it had—with generous Soviet inputs—a good chance of success. Secondly, the Soviets apparently believed that outside interference was an important factor in explaining the insurgency. Third, the Soviets believed that—given regional developments, internal leadership problems, and outside interference—a decisive invasion (as in Czechoslovakia in 1968) would deter the guerrillas and provide a new Afghan leadership with an opportunity to rebuild an army and to regain control of the country.

In the chapter which follows, the source of these assumptions will be addressed, as will the factors which served as the background causes of the invasion. It will be argued that many Soviet explanations of the invasion were untrue and that many Western hypotheses were unsupported by the available evidence. Furthermore, Soviet civil and military thinking about the Third World, strongly influenced by successes in Angola and Ethiopia, served as a background factor in the decision to embrace the PDPA, causing the Soviets to see great promise in an Afghanistan with a "socialist orientation," a title that "required" the Soviets to increase their assistance to that country. Military thinking was quite obviously influenced by the successes of the 1970s and the generally improved military balance. Soviet analysts saw military aid from socialist governments as a key to the survival of states with a socialist orientation.

Spurious and Unsupported Explanations

Whatever the critical factors may have been in the Soviet decision to invade, they were hardly clarified by the Soviet and PDPA announcements immediately after the invasion. The Soviets claimed to have been invited fourteen times to send troops into Afghanistan, but Amin declared in September 1979 that such a move was not under discussion, and that it had never been considered. His foreign minister, Shah Wali, repeated this as late as December 1979.[1] Karmal's claim that other PDPA officials convinced Amin to profer the invitation distorts the nature of the governmental structure in late 1979: Amin was in total, dictatorial control of the regime. (Taraki might have added that this was true as early as late summer of 1979.)[2] Moreover, Babrak Karmal, if he did repeat a request for Soviet troops on December 28, did so from within the Soviet Union, and in any case it was after the fact. Most Soviet accounts then have two "invitations" being made: one by a man who died in a vicious fight with his "guests," the other by an expatriate who did not arrive in Kabul until nearly a week after the invasion began.

Afghan and Soviet claims that Amin was either a CIA agent or an "agent of imperialism" were transparently false. As Marshall Shulman has pointed out, "why a CIA agent would have sought to impose a Marxist regime upon his country" and "why a CIA agent would call for a massive Soviet military intervention" has never been satisfactorily explained.[3]

In a similar vein, Soviet and Afghan claims that Amin was about to sell out the revolution to the U.S. and/or Pakistan were false. *Pravda's* citation of Amin's talks with U.S. Chargé Archer Blood in October 1979 are weak evidence. At that time, the Afghans were insisting that the U.S. cut their diplomatic staff in Afghanistan. Blood reported the substance of that forty-minute discussion as follows:

> I do not think that in the near future Amin realistically expects any substantial forward movement in U.S.-Afghan relations, such as the resumption of aid. My guess is that he will be content for the time being with the less rancorous discourse we are having with his government, agreeing to avoid confrontational actions provided we do the same. In this connection he seconded with some alacrity my observations that sometimes two countries can work toward a better relationship simply by refraining from doing each other mischief. Perhaps, this is all we should strive for . . .[4]

No doubt the Soviets were privy to the substance of these talks. Furthermore, although Amin was talking with the Pakistanis up to his death, it was over the upcoming visit of the Pakistani foreign minister and not an attempt at a coup. To think that any Afghan leader could have hatched a plot involving some use of the Pakistani armed forces is far-fetched, to say the least.

Western analysts also made speculative assertions about the invasion that are difficult to substantiate. The origin of these speculations has much to do with disputes concerning the nature of decision-making in the USSR. For years, the decision-making level of analysis in Sovietology was dominated by the totalitarian model, which saw the necessary emergence of a single strong leader who would completely dominate the party and society and brutally turn them to the accomplishment of state objectives. The death of Stalin saw numerous changes that accentuated collective leadership in the USSR. Western theorists ultimately attempted to adapt to this development by applying the bureaucratic-politics or group approach which emphasized the "pulling and hauling" and the strain toward compromise that is so essential to the understanding of the Western political process. Jiri Valenta even applied this model to the case of the invasion of Czechoslovakia in 1968. This emphasis on "groups," and later on, "factions" led some analysts to make statements concerning the invasion which will not stand up to rigorous examination. In other words, some analysts tried to apply a generally acceptable model to a case in which it did not apply.[5]

One such theory, put forth by George Kennan and others, speculated that the "moderate" Brezhnev was overruled on Afghanistan and that the invasion heralded the succession of or at least a strong initiative from a new, more militant Soviet leadership faction. George Kennan wrote that the invasion was not "in character" for Brezhnev or Kosygin. Gromyko—according to Kennan—was "unlikely to have approved." All of this reflected a new dominance by "hard-line elements" unconcerned with "world opinion" and "much less experienced" than the older figures.[6] Later, rumors would emerge that even Andropov and other KGB officials were against the invasion.[7]

There is very little evidence to support these assertions. The first Politburo member to vigorously support the invasion was Brezhnev himself on January 13. In the second and third week of February, Gromyko and Andropov, citing Brezhnev's explanation, strongly voiced their support for the invasion and sharply condemned the U.S. reaction to it. Kosygin, in a speech devoted to economic issues, voiced support of the invasion on February 21, and the day before, Mikhail Suslov had made a spirited defense of Soviet policy, attributing U.S. reaction to the machinations of the military-industrial complex.[8] Gromyko, Andropov, and Suslov spoke in greater detail than Kosygin, but otherwise there was little in the initial public reactions of the key memebers of the Politburo to suggest that any were virulently opposed to the invasion. Furthermore, the thesis advanced by Alfred Monks that Suslov and other, unnamed, "hard-line elements" were "in ascendancy" before the invasion, does not appear to be accurate.[9] Granted—as will be discussed in detail later in this chapter—there was noticeable stiffening of Politburo positions on détente and international relations in the latter half of 1979, but there was hardly any noticeable differentiation between Politburo members on this point. If there were differences of opinion over major policy issues, they did not result in any personnel changes or even any noticeable proxy debates over related issues.

On the issue of Brezhnev's power and whether or not the invasion was in character or not, it should be remembered that the Brezhnev regime is the same one that invaded Czechoslovakia in 1968, did nothing to stop the outbreak of the Yom Kippur War in 1973, conducted a successful military operation in Angola in 1975, and armed both the attackers and the defenders in the Ethiopian-Somali War in 1977–78. This record gives one little reason to believe that Brezhnev would be "constitutionally unable" to approve an invasion of Afghanistan. Furthermore, there is little evidence to suggest that his political power was fading in 1979. In a demonstration of his political strength, Brezhnev, just one month prior to the invasion, was able to install his close associate, Nikolai Tikhonov, as a full member of a Politburo already packed with Brezhnev's other lifelong associates. Even given limited working hours, it is unlikely that he was overruled on such a critical issue. Politburo members may have differed on how to solve the Afghan problem, but they all supported the final decision.

In a similar vein, the analysis of events in Afghanistan does not seem to favor a bureaucratic-politics interpretation of the Soviet decision-making process in this case. Jiri Valenta contrasted the Czech and Afghan cases as follows:

> A preliminary analysis of the Afghan case seems to indicate the emergence of a somewhat different mode of decision-making, one definitely more centralized, more coordinated, and less affected by bureaucratic politics and factional infighting. Unlike during the Czechoslovak crisis, there was neither an intense media debate nor reports about a serious division in the leadership. While in 1968 one could detect the pressures being exercised on the Politburo in favor of the invasion by such elements as the leadership of the Soviet non-Russian republics in the West, particularly the head of the Ukrainian Party, P. Shelest, various intergroups in the Party apparatus, the armed forces, and the KGB, these pressures did not exist or were well concealed in 1979.[10]

Valenta attributes this to Brezhnev's personal power and his ability to outmaneuver and replace his most serious rivals.

In the case of Afghanistan, we would be hard pressed to discover any group or individual who would have spoken with authority against the invasion. We might hypothesize, for example, that the USSR Academy of Sciences Institute for the Study of the USA and Canada might have, given its knowledge of the public mood in the United States, objected to the invasion. However, with one of its chief spokesmen, Georgiy Arbatov, sidelined with a heart attack, the institute apparently did not have a major input into the decision-making process. Referring to the moderate "foreign policy elite," Robert Legvold of the Council on Foreign Relations wrote "as one of them speculated after the invasion, when the crunch came late in the fall, 'the old bosses' had no need of their musings—'the old bosses' felt in their bones what they must do."[11] An institute analyst reinforced this statement in 1983 when he said in an interview "Only a very few know the details" of how the final decision was made.[12] Even if this were not the case, it is still doubtful that the so-called moderates could have overcome the position which was apparently supported by firsthand observers such as Generals Yepishev and Pavlovskiy and former ambassador Puzanov. In summary, the remarkable consensus orientation of the Brezhnev regime apparently did not falter over the issue of Afghanistan.

Many analysts were also mistaken in their attempts to fit the invasion into a Soviet grand design to capture or control Persian Gulf oil, or perhaps to invade Iran for this or other purposes. If these were immediate Soviet reasons for invading (or even part of a long-range plan), holding Afghanistan would have to offer significant military or economic advantages that could facilitate these objectives.

Numerous analysts drew the conclusion that the Soviet invasion of Afghanistan was aimed at capturing or at least controlling Persian Gulf oil. President Carter—perhaps with an eye toward garnering support for future policy moves—said in January 1980,

> The Soviet effort to dominate Afghanistan has brought Soviet military forces to within 300 miles of the Indian Ocean and close to the Straits of Hormuz—a waterway through which most of the world's oil must flow. . . . The Soviet Union is now attempting to consolidate a strategic position, therefore, that poses a grave threat to the free movement of Middle East oil.[13]

No one can totally rule out future moves in this direction, nor can one conclusively prove that Soviet operations in Afghanistan are not being directed at this long-range objective. However, there is much evidence to suggest that this was not a principal factor in the Soviet decision to invade Afghanistan. On the petroleum issue, the projected Soviet oil shortage also seems not to have provided an important impetus for the Soviet invasion. For one thing, the CIA's original position that the USSR would soon become a net importer of oil has not been validated. While production may have temporarily peaked, the current situation has not yet reached crisis proportions. Indeed, by the 1990s, the Soviets may even be able to exploit a favorable energy situation in their foreign policy dealings with the West.[14] While Brezhnev's declaration that "it is the colonialists that are attracted by the smell of oil," not the USSR, should be taken as a rhetorical flourish, it does remind one that Middle East oil is much more a U.S. obsession than a Soviet one. The Soviets would no doubt enjoy any sort of leverage they could get over the OPEC nations, but using armed force toward Afghanistan does not appear to be a preferred method.

Contrary to many claims, the possession of existing facilities in Afghanistan has only marginally improved Soviet military capabilities in the oil-rich Persian Gulf region. For example, from their nearest bases at Shindand or the smaller one at Farah, the Soviets are *not* within 300 miles of the critical Straits of Hormuz; rather, they have closed only to within 540 statute miles (sm), the distance to major Iranian cities being even greater. This distinction is not simply academic. Were the distance 300 miles, it would be theoretically possible for nearly all modern Soviet fighter aircraft to reach the Straits of Hormuz. At 540 sm, given the aircraft and ranges in table 7–1, only the S–24 Fencer (none of which are in Afghanistan) could reach this area. Even this aircraft would have

Table 7–1
Ranges of Selected Soviet Aircraft

Tactical Aircraft	First Year in Service	Combat Radius (Miles)[a]
Su–7 Fitter	1959	200–300
MiG–21 Fishbed D	1962	200–300
Yak–28 Brewer	1964	200–300
MiG–21 Fishbed J	1970	300–400
MiG–23 Flogger B[b]	1971	300–400
MiG–27 Flogger D	1973	400–500
Su–17 Fitter C/D	1971/76	300–400
Su–24 Fencer[c]	1975	500–600

Sources: Adapted from Keith Dunn, *Soviet Constraints in Southwest Asia: A Military Analysis*, SIRM 81066 (Carlisle, Pennsylvania: Strategic Studies Institute, U.S. Army War College, 1981), p. 9.

[a]Combat radii are for flight profile of hi-lo-hi and no external fuel tanks. If aircraft were forced to fly lo-lo-lo, combat radii would be reduced by as much as 50 percent. Aircraft shown cannot be refueled in the air.

[b]Using other sources, such as *Jane's All the World's Aircraft 1981–82*, the MiG–23 also has under ideal conditions the range to reach the Strait of Hormuz.

[c]The *Fencer's* combat radius is where one sees the most disagreement. The estimates range between 200–1000 plus miles. Varying assumptions on mission profile and weapons load, as well as limited information, account for the difference in estimates.

only a short time over its targets and would also lack the ground guidance and controllers with which Soviet forces habitually operate. Furthermore, to accomplish this mission Soviet fighters might have to deal with hostile Iranian air defenses and would be subject to monitoring by Saudi AWACS aircraft. Finally, one must consider the current situation in Afghanistan. Could the Soviets launch daring operations from bases which are insecure due to insurgent activity? Longer range aircraft—the Backfire bomber, for one—can already reach critical targets in Iran from deep inside the USSR.[15]

Control of Iran itself is another issue which has been raised in connection with the motives behind the Soviet invasion of Afghanistan. In 1921 and after World War II, the Soviet Union tried to establish a puppet state in that country. In November 1940, in response to a German initiative to clarify the Nazi-Soviet Non-Aggression Pact and to divert the Soviets from East European objectives, the Soviet foreign minister asked the Germans, using language that the Germans had suggested, to recognize "that the area south of Batum and Baku in the general direction of the Persian Gulf [be] recognized as the center of the aspirations of the Soviet Union.[16] Putting the specific context of this statement aside, many analysts saw the invasion of Afghanistan as a step toward the fulfillment of the long-term goal expressed in this document.

This was apparently not the case. First, if one draws on a map the area in the Nazi-Soviet communication, it directly includes only western Iran and eastern Iraq, not Afghanistan, which the Soviets never saw fit to occupy in either World War. Secondly, the use of Afghanistan as a staging area for an invasion of Iran is an exaggerated threat. For an effort to secure either Tehran or the Iranian oil fields, Soviet forces based in Afghanistan would have to choose between negotiating the narrow roads that run through the Elburz Mountains or crossing the nearly trackless Kavir or Lut deserts for a distance of nearly 600 miles. This is not an impossible task, but it is a logistical nightmare, one which any rational planner would shy away from. Third, if this option were ever to be chosen, the Soviets would, for the foreseeable future, be relying on long and insecure lines of communication. Even before the Soviet invasion of Afghanistan, the risk of directly colliding with U.S. forces in an attack on Iran would have been great. Finally, a Soviet attack from Afghanistan would be of little help to a larger thrust from the Transcaucasus. Although Iran might err and split its forces to meet both attacks head on, the two prongs of the Soviet forces would be virtually unable to support one another. Indeed, a single concentrated thrust through the Transcaucasus would probably be safer and certainly easier from the standpoint of command and control and logistics. Unless Soviet leaders were willing to risk World War III, a classic invasion of Iran would be a low probability option, one that, in any case, would be better accomplished from Soviet bases in Azerbaijan than ones in Afghanistan. Genrikh Trofimenko, a Soviet expert on U.S. foreign policy, said,

> If one speaks about Soviet action in Afghanistan, was it a prelude . . . towards action against Western oil interests in the Gulf, then I say that it is patent nonsense, because every strategist knows that there are quicker approaches than the approaches via Afghanistan—the gateway to the Persian Gulf from Soviet Transcaucasus is much more easy and much more obtainable.[17]

Explanations based on Soviet desire to secure a warm-water port—an idea which dates to Peter the Great—suffer from many of the same limitations as the notions concerning oil or Iran. Few would argue that this long-range goal has been continuously pursued by the Soviets and their Imperial forbears. Moreover, while the Soviets have shown concern for the security of their Black Sea–Suez–Indian Ocean–Pacific Ocean route to the Far East, the last direct Soviet move toward securing a warm-water port ended with Stalin's attempts to get control of Libya and the Dardanelles-Bosporous at the end of World War II. Since then, changes in air transport, the naval balance, and maritime technology suggest that a new warm-water port is less than critical for the Soviets. As an Indian scholar said, "the plain truth is that the Soviets now possess a sizable, modern, and self-reliant navy whose efficacy does not depend on physical control of warm-water ports. . . . It has been operating in the Indian Ocean since the late 1960s without any visible handicap."[18] Furthermore, it is not clear why the Soviet Union would pursue the dangerous search for warm-water ports in Pakistan or Iran when it already has access to anchorages or bases at Aden, Socotra, and on Dahlak Island in the Red Sea. Again, the issue is not whether such facilities would be nice to have, the issue is whether the Soviets invaded Afghanistan to get them. This is much less clear.

Would Afghan bases be of use in an attack on Pakistan? The answer is decidedly affirmative. Although there is a significant mountain barrier in the north, the central and southern parts of the Afghan-Pakistani border could be easily penetrated. Moreover, many key targets, such as the capital, are less than 150 miles from the border and within easy range of bases in Afghanistan. On the other hand, to attack Pakistan, the Soviets must prepare for stiff and probably direct U.S. and Chinese response. Is there anything in Pakistan for which the Soviets would contemplate a multi-front World War III? In any case, Afghanistan could prove useful as a base from which to subvert the fragile Pakistani government, a topic which will be addressed in chapter 9.

None of this suggests that the Soviets could not use Afghanistan as a base from which to invade Iran and/or Pakistan or that they would let pass a more graceful opportunity to move into Iran or subvert Pakistan, but it does seem to indicate that their immediate motives for invading Afghanistan lay elsewhere. Furthermore, many of the above noted scenarios confuse effect with motive. There are many minor political and military benefits—improved aerial reconnaissance over the Indian Ocean, for one—which the Soviets would gain from a prolonged occupation of a pacified Afghanistan, but none of them seem important enough to have had a motivational role. Finally, hypotheses such as "invade Afghanistan to flank Iran," tend to deemphasize the reactive nature of Soviet foreign policy and exaggerate the Soviet ability to control the future. Henry Kissinger said in 1969,

> It is always tempting to arrange diverse Soviet moves into a grand design. The more esoteric brands of Kremlinology often purport to see each and every move as part of the carefully orchestrated score in which events inexorably move to the grand finale. Experience has shown that this has rarely if ever been the case. From the Cuban missile crisis . . . to the invasion of Czechoslovakia, there has been a large element of improvisation in Soviet policy.[19]

One final explanation of the Soviet move into Afghanistan concerns annexation. According to Lieutenant General G. S. Miraki, a high-level defector from *Khad,* the Afghan secret police, Karmal was directed by Moscow in December 1981 to hold a PDPA congress to legitimize his leadership. With this done, Karmal could use his increased legitimacy to call for reinforcements and, subsequently, he could request annexation by the Union of Soviet Socialist Republics (USSR). According to Lieutenant General Miraki, the congress failed and Leonid Brezhnev then threatened to dismember Afghanistan, absorbing the nine northern provinces into the USSR, leaving the rest "to its fate." According to the general, a "high-ranking member of the government and a highly placed Soviet source from Tajikistan" told him this tale.[20]

Although Afghanistan is potentially rich in minerals, one has to be skeptical of the desire for annexation as a serious factor in the Soviet decision to invade Afghanistan. A direct annexation of all or part of Afghanistan would probably generate more cost than benefit. Most importantly, an annexed Afghanistan would be able to lay claim to a standard of living equal to that of the other Central Asian republics of the Soviet Union. Given Afghanistan's dismal pre-war GNP, the cost of raising this to a level compatible with the Central Asian republics of the USSR would be staggering. Decades hence the Soviets might be able to recoup this investment by exploiting Afghanistan's mineral wealth, but ultimately the Soviets would have to address the needs of the population, as they have done in Soviet Central Asia. When quizzed on this point, a Soviet analyst dismissed the annexation option and told an American scholar, "look . . . all we need is another 15 million mouths to feed."[21]

Background Factors

Of the many background factors that have been mentioned in connection with the Soviet invasion of Afghanistan, two deserve detailed examination: Soviet thinking about the Third World, and Soviet military capabilities and thought.

Soviet Thinking about the Third World

It is not easy to demonstrate a cause and effect relationship between Soviet doctrinal thought and Soviet policy. First, doctrine is only one input among many in the policy process. Environmental constraints, domestic political considerations, and the global balance of power exist alongside doctrine, giving a complex, multicausal explanation for even the simplest events. Second, Soviet doctrine is intricately entwined with propaganda. The Soviets do not always say what they mean. Moreover, doctrinal pronouncements on international issues are sometimes directed at domestic audiences, either inside or outside the leadership, and thus are doubly difficult to decipher. Third, thought not only precedes action, it also occurs after it. What may appear as a doctrinal prescription may in fact be a doctrinal justification for an action taken for other reasons. Later on, a justification such as the Brezhnev Doctrine may be (accurately or inaccurately) interpreted as an indicator of the direction which future policy may take. Fourth, the analysts's problems are complicated by a simple question which often has a very complex answer: what is Soviet doctrine on a particular subject? Even on issues with relevance to contemporary policy, debates between analysts take place in the Soviet media. Even on important issues, the Soviet media sometimes present less than a united front and, again, it is never clear to what extent an analytical debate may reflect differences of opinion at the highest level. Fifth, it is literally impossible to establish the final link between doctrine and policy. Policy-makers exist in a hectic world where, especially at the highest levels, they must routinely make important decisions on matters that they might have great difficulty in fitting into one or another doctrinal niche. "Staff theologians" no doubt can recite the accepted line on matters in their area of interest, but it is not similarly clear that Brezhnev or even the more lettered Andropov could do likewise. Finally, since doctrine serves an important legitimizing function, many analysts have noted that decision-makers have a strong incentive to insure that doctrine can accommodate many realities.[22]

A complete review of Soviet theoretical writing concerning the Third World is beyond the scope of this inquiry. Rather, the following material will address some aspects of Soviet doctrine that have relevance to the case at hand.[23]

After a rather optimistic phase in the Khrushchev era, Soviet thought concerning the Third World entered an era of realism, flexibility, and more modest expectations. Having suffered setbacks in Africa, Indonesia, and a number of other places, the Soviets began to take a more complicated and realistic view of their prospects in the Third World. Rather than classifying every progresive movement as incipient socialism, the Soviets began to see an intermediate stage: development along the "noncapitalist" path, a stage which could take "several generations." The purpose of this period was "to create the prerequisites for the eventual transition to socialism.[24] At this stage of development, countries on the noncapitalist path could follow in varying degrees the path of Mongolia or the Central Asian republics since, like these two areas, the states on the noncapitalist path had the assistance and protection of a relatively strong socialist entity.[25]

States which have chosen the noncapitalist path—referred to now as states with a socialist orientation—characteristically "carry out deepgoing social transformations" which feature some state ownership of industry, industrialization, land reform, and the diversification of agriculture, all done within an atmosphere characterized by a united front of progressive forces and a high degree of national unity.[26] In the foreign policy realm, the activities of these states, referred to as "positive neutrality," "demand convergence with the socialist countries.[27] According to this theory, setbacks are possible and these states have to guard against bourgeois and religious reaction as well as "attempts made by international reaction to deprive people of their right to wage a struggle for their national liberation and social emancipation.[28]

Over time, the alliance between socialism, the forces of national liberation, and the progressive states went through three stages, very similar in the Soviet analyses to the major shifts in the world correlation of forces. The first phase, from 1917–1945, produced a secure socialist state. The second phase, which lasted until the mid-1950s, saw socialist revolutions in Eastern Europe and China and a "steadily growing" Soviet influence in the world.

The third stage, which continues today, began in the mid-1950s, when world socialism began to have a decisive influence on the whole system of international relations, and the swift collapse of the colonial system began.[29]

By the late 1970s more than ninety new states had emerged. Following the principle of proletarian internationalism—"the basis of the socialist countries' policy vis-à-vis the young . . . states"[30]—the Soviet Union offered economic, political, and moral support to these states in their fight against neocolonial economic arrangements and the forces of reaction. Although all of the developing countries benefited from Soviet policy, Soviet authors noted that outside the Warsaw Pact there were less than twenty nations on the noncapitalist path.[31]

Soviet assistance was a key factor in the success of progressive movements in the late 1970s. The following analysis by alternate member of the Politburo B. N. Ponomarev echoed Brezhnev's remarks at the Twenty-fifth Party Congress that Soviet strength and the policy of detente provided fertile ground for progressive movements in the Third World. Among the major changes in world politics in the 1970s were

> New shifts in the ratio of forces in the international arena in favor of socialism and national liberation; [and] major successes achieved by the policy of detente as result of which the so-called "maneuvering freedom" of most aggressive imperialist forces was substantially restricted,

In this environment, the "anti-imperialist struggle" flourished and colonialism was crushed. With Soviet support, Vietnam, Laos, and Kampuchea were freed. "The people's revolutions" in Afghanistan, Nicaragua, and Ethiopia, according to Ponomarev, represented "powerful blows" to imperialism.[32]

In the midst of these victories for the forces of peace and socialism, the forces of imperialism launched inevitable counteroffensives to keep nations of the Third World in their neocolonial status. Even before the events in Afghanistan, the forces of imperialism tried to throttle progressive regimes, sometimes succeeding, as in the case of Chile. In analyzing the lessons of the Chilean experience, Seweryn Bialer noted that among the lessons learned by the Soviets were that "present-day revolutions never occur in an international vacuum and the importation of counterrevolution is an ever-present fact of life of overwhelming importance. For revolutions to succeed, such an importation must be counterbalanced by extensive and timely help from abroad."[33]

The Soviet orientalist, G. Kim, noted on more contemporary cases that the imperialists were "trying to strangle" the newly independent states. Angola and Ethiopia were early examples, and

> In late 1979 revolutionary Afghanistan was threatened when the U.S. together with the PRC, organized open intervention using Afghan reactionaries and employing Pakistan as a staging ground.[34]

The progressive regimes also had to help themselves. The Soviets recommended the following measures: (1) the formation of a revolutionary party; (2) the strengthening of central governmental authority and armed forces; (3) the formation of loyal cadres; (4) the improvement of living conditions; (5) the strengthening of links to the masses; and (6) the development of relations with the socialist countries.[35]

This analysis does not provide one with a roadmap to the Soviet decision to invade Afghanistan. It does suggest however, that the Soviets were (and will be) flexible in their dealing with Third World countries and that they would offer great amounts of assistance to those that profess a "socialist orientation." Moreover, it is clear from this brief examination of contemporary thinking that the Soviets view their dealings with Third World countries in light of the global competition with the United States, perhaps even overestimating the Soviet contribution to the development of a favorable environment for the development of Third World forces. Finally, it is clear that in the late 1970s, Soviet thinkers did gain some degree of satisfaction from the emergence of semi-allies in the Third World and from the victories of Soviet arms and indigenous progressive forces in Vietnam, Angola, and Ethiopia. In light of all of this, it is less surprising than it otherwise might have been that the Soviets quickly and tightly embraced the PDPA in Afghanistan. Indeed, at least in the beginning, it may have seemed likely that the PDPA would follow the optimum program for the development of states with a socialist orientation that has been described above. Moreover, Soviet political analysts spoke of assisting states with a socialist orientation as a duty and thus may have been prone to support great increases in economic and military aid for them.

Soviet Military Power and Thought

No objective analyst could fail to note the growth of Soviet military power under the Brezhnev regime. While one can debate the rationale for this, the build-up and the consequent change in the military balance are unassailable facts. In every conceivable category of forces, as shown in table 7–2, there was progress from a Soviet perspective. In addition

Table 7–2
Soviet Build-up in Nuclear and Conventional Forces, 1964–1980
(billions of FY 1980 dollars)

Forces	1964	1980
Strategic		
ICBMs	190	1,398
SLBMs	29	950
Bombers	170	156
Total weapons (warheads)	400	6,000
Land		
Tanks	30,000	45,000
Divisions	145	170
Artillery tubes/rocket launchers	11,000	20,000
Tactical air		
Fighter/attack aircraft	3,500	4,500
Naval		
Major surface combatants and amphibious ships	260	360
Other naval vessels	1,440	1,200
Total naval tonnage	2,000,000	2,800,000
Total military manpower	3,400,000	4,400,000
Total defense spending	$105	$175
Military investment (procurement, milcon, R&D)	$49	$80

Source: U.S., *Department of Defense Annual Report, Fiscal Year 1981* (Washington, D.C.: U.S. Government Printing Office, 1980), p. 37.

to the strategic nuclear realm, Soviet land and projection forces grew as well.

Total manpower increased by one million troops, the ground forces increased by twenty-five divisions, the navy added 100 surface combatants and put close to an additional one million tons on the seas during the 1964–1980 period. Between 1965 and 1977, airlift capacity increased 132 percent.[36] Qualitative improvements more than kept pace with quantitative improvements.

The political utility of their new-found military power was not lost on the Soviets. Indeed, the Soviets may have overestimated the importance of their military power. While their doctrine of the correlation of forces formally ridicules an overreliance on the military factor isolated from its social and political context, it is easy to find Soviet civilian and military analysts who went so far as to state that "the growing might of the Soviet Union," and a changing "alignment of forces . . . in favor of socialism" had driven the imperialists to accept peaceful coexistence.³⁷ Colonel V. M. Kulish even stated in 1972 that

> The establishment between the USSR and the USA of a dynamic balance in strategic forces will substantially limit the military activities of imperialism in the international arena and force it to take into account the peaceful policies of the socialist community . . .³⁸

None of this is meant to argue that there is a direct relation between the Soviet military build-up and the invasion of Afghanistan. The invasion itself did not severely tax Soviet capabilities and the amount of force used was not great when compared to the total that was available. As early as 1968, the Soviets launched an invasion of Czechoslovakia which was nearly five times greater in total scope than the Afghan invasion. Certainly, the Brezhnev-era build-up, by itself, did not cause the invasion because the Soviets have had, since 1945, more than enough troops to perform such a mission. Rather, this data is meant to provide a background for a murkier subject: Soviet thought about the use of force in the Third World.

It is doubly true for military writings that the relationship between doctrine and policy is not always clear. While all military writing has the Party's imprimatur, it is not clear in many cases to what extent it represents current leadership thinking, especially since much of it appears in military journals written for a military audience. For example, V. D. Sokolovskiy's classic *Military Strategy* is regarded as a basic Soviet text. It went through three editions and has never been revoked, replaced, or even revised since 1968. A retired Soviet general has suggested publicly that it is outdated but again no actions have been taken to change its status.³⁹ Moreover, much analytical writing on contemporary subjects in military journals is camouflaged as lessons from the Great Patriotic War or even as the distilled viewpoint of Western military thinkers. Although at times this is a rather transparent method, it does successfully conceal any official support which may be present for such thoughts.

With this in mind, the thesis here is simple: with qualification and some degree of ambiguity, Soviet military thinkers began to write more concerning the use of force in support of Third World states, especially the relative handful that were classified as having a socialist orientation. While the Third World has not replaced strategic nuclear or NATO–Warsaw Pact issues as the major subjects of Soviet military thought, in the 1970s it became a secondary topic, which suggested increased interest in the Third World by some in the military leadership and increased confidence in the military as a tool of Soviet foreign policy.

The first major work to evidence a new interest in using force in the

Third World was the 1968 edition of Marshal V. D. Sokolovskiy's *Military Strategy*. Although the second edition only spoke of ideological, political, and material support for wars of liberation, the third edition, published at the height of the Vietnam War, stated in a one-sentence paragraph that: "The USSR will render, when it is necessary, military support as well to people subject to imperialist aggression."[40]

The 1968 version of the authoritative *Marxism-Leninism on War and Army* also included a statement which legitimized military assistance for states with a socialist orientation:

> In their struggle for the noncapitalist road of development . . . these peoples rely on the comprehensive assistance of the Soviet Union and other socialist countries, including also their help in setting up and developing their national armed forces and in organizing the armed defense of their countries against imperialist aggressors. The Soviet Government has repeatedly declared that it has always given and continues to give various assistance to peoples fighting against imperialist intervention in their affairs, and will assist victims of imperialist aggression by all, including military, means.
>
> In modern conditions, when the relation of forces in the world continues to change in favor of peace, democracy and socialism, while imperialism intensifies its aggressive ventures, the defensive might of the USSR and other socialist countries, [and] the combat efficiency and readiness of their armed forces are a most important factor in securing historical progress.[41]

One thought continually stressed in nearly all accounts was the deterrent nature of Soviet military power, which, in effect, induced moderation on the part of the imperialists and provided incentives for them not to initiate local wars which, even in the post-Khrushchev era, according to Marshal Ogarkov, carried a dangerous possibility for escalation to global war.[42] Moreover, the class basis of each society, in the Soviet view, lent a different purpose to an activity when it was carried out by a socialist power than when it was carried out by the forces of imperialism. The former, of course, was progressive and moral by definition, while the latter was inherently reactionary and evil.

One Soviet work which directly examined these questions was retired Colonel V. M. Kulish's *Military Force and International Relations*. Published in 1972, Kulish's work was, however, never printed beyond its 10,000 original copies and was rarely cited by any of his successors in the field. Moreover, the principal topic of the book, as noted by its subtitle, was "Military Aspects of U.S. Foreign Policy Concepts." In any case, Kulish and his collaborators stated,

> At the present time the principal means for retraining imperialist aggressors in all regions of the world is the ability of the USSR to deliver nuclear missile weapons to any point on the earth's surface. . . . However this form will not always be effective in those situations that could develop into limited wars. . . .
>
> In connection with the task of preventing local wars and also in those cases wherein military support must be furnished to those nations fighting for their freedom and independence against the forces of internal reaction and imperialist intervention, the Soviet Union may require mobile and well-trained and well-equipped armed forces. In some situations the very knowledge of a Soviet military presence in an area in which a conflict situation is developing may serve to restrain the imperialists and local reaction. . . .[43]

Kulish went on to applaud the "power and mobility of the Soviet navy," which "radically changed the military-strategic situation on the world's oceans." Lest the USSR be lumped together with the United States, Kulish noted that the Soviet Union "was forced" into employing this technique by the aggressive, resource-hungry imperialists.[44]

Around the same time that Kulish's book was published, more authoritative spokesmen began to speak of a broadened mission for the Soviet armed forces. In 1971, Marshal Grechko spoke of the mission of the Soviet armed forces as "defending the entire socialist community and the worldwide historical values of socialism." The only Third World countries with whom "military collaboration" was even discussed were Mongolia, North Korea, North Vietnam, and Cuba.[45] In May 1974, Marshal Grechko, by then a full member of the Politburo, went further and declared that the functions of the Soviet armed forces were not limited to the defense of the socialist world:

> In its foreign policy activity the Soviet state purposefully opposes the export of counterrevolution and the policy of oppression, supports the national liberation struggle, and resolutely resists imperialists' aggression in whatever distant region of our planet it may appear.[46]

Grechko's 1974 statement was followed two years later by Gorshkov's tome *Seapower of the State* in which he saluted the peacetime "presence" role of naval forces and argued for a balanced fleet. Significant studies on the nature of modern local wars were also conducted. One key study, conducted by the head of the General Staff Academy, concluded that an analysis of local wars showed that the outcomes of these wars favored the forces of socialism.[47]

Analysts also made numerous studies on the lessons of Vietnam. As time progressed more and more of these works concentrated on the technical and tactical lessons of the U.S. experience. Two experienced U.S. analysts concluded—on the basis of a content analysis of over 850 articles—that, while the lessons that the United States drew from Vietnam would have counselled restraint by the USSR in Afghanistan,

> The lessons the Soviets drew, however, did not warn them of the dangers of such an intervention by Soviet forces. On the contrary, the frequent assertion that aid from the Soviet Union and other socialist countries had been important in Vietnam may have increased their propensity to intervene in Afghanistan.[48]

Leonid Brezhnev, following Soviet victories in Southeast Asia and Angola—two victories which required massive logistical assistance and, in the latter case, proxy troop support—obliquely reinforced the comments of Kulish, Grechko, and Gorshkov when he said at the Twenty-fifth Party Congress in 1976 that detente only referred to relations between states:

> Detente does not in the slightest abolish, and it cannot abolish or alter, the laws of class struggle. No one should expect that in conditions of detente the communists will become reconciled to capitalist exploitation or that monopolists will become supporters of revolution. . . .[49]

After the Twenty-fifth Party Congress in March 1976, Soviet military authors continued to discuss military aid to the Third World in increasing detail, usually waiting for a successful act before describing the theory behind it.[50] As detente with the United States faded and Soviet military activities in the Third World increased, the Soviets began to write more openly about Soviet support for nations with a socialist orientation. In 1977, "supporting the struggle of people for national liberation and social progress, [and] preventing wars of aggression" were listed in the new constitution as aims of Soviet foreign policy.[51] Increasingly, Soviet authors came to stress the salience of Soviet support for indigenous movements. One work, written in a military-political journal on the eve of the invasion of Afghanistan, cited "reliance by forces of national liberation on comprehensive support of world socialism" as one of the two keys for success for countries with a socialist orientation.[52]

In November 1978, in *Voyenno-istoricheskiy zhurnal (Military-Historical Journal)*, an article by a well-known military theorist stated that due to the success of Soviet foreign policy, the imperialists and China had stepped up their efforts to turn back "social and national liberation." He went on to suggest that this activity had produced a new type of local war, a variety of class liberation wars hitherto only implied by Soviet military writing:

> In an era when the world revolutionary process of transition from capitalism to socialism is being completed, the forces of imperialist reaction attack countries which have taken or are taking a socialist path of development. In response, the latter wage wars to defend their socialist homelands. . . .[53]

According to Soviet sources, the former colonial powers, led by the United States, had transformed their colonial policy into a neocolonial policy. The battle for national liberation would not be the last for many developing countries. Although the article contained no specific aid promises, it repeatedly used Angola as an example of excellent cooperation between the Soviet Union and a developing country in a class liberation war.

In a comprehensive review signed to the press on December 4, 1979, and recommended for pedagogical use by political cadres in the military, Colonel Malinovskiy was more specific. The contemporary struggle for liberation "is linked directly with a further growth in the might of world socialism as the deciding factor of the social progress of mankind."[54]

In remarks which were probably directed at the situation in Afghanistan, Malinovskiy cited imperialism's modus operandi as favoring the use of neocolonial measures, promoting conflict among the less-developed countries, an "ever-increasing transfer of functions of suppressing the national liberation struggle to reactionary regimes," and using the services of the PRC, which, he added, is "in the same harness" as the neocolonialists. Malinovskiy also noted that support from socialist states was of "inestimable importance" to the states battling the forces of reaction.[55] Again, Vietnam, Angola, and Ethiopia stood as prime examples.

After the invasion, an unsigned editorial in the Soviet weekly *New Times* summarized much of what Soviet military and political thinkers had been leading up to, albeit not always in such direct language:

> What is the internationalist solidarity of revolutionaries? Does it consist only of moral and diplomatic support, of verbal wishes of success, or also of material assistance, including military help, given in definite, extraordinary circumstances, and especially in a situation of manifest massive outside interference?
>
> The history of the revolutionary movement confirms the moral and political legitimacy of this form of assistance and support. Such was the case, for instance, in Spain in the 1930s, and in China in the 1920s and 1930s. Today, when there exists a system of socialist states, it would be simply ridiculous to question the right to such assistance. . . . To refuse to use the possibilities at the disposal of the socialist countries would signify virtually evading performance of the internationalist duty

and returning the world to the times when imperialism could throttle at will any revolutionary movement.[56]

The above analysis of political and military thinking yields no empirically verifiable conclusion concerning the Soviet decision to invade Afghanistan. Rather, it does suggest the possibility that at least some of the Soviet politico-military leadership had come to place increased emphasis on the small number of beleaguered states with a socialist orientation and that they had come to see an important, even critical role to be played by Soviet assistance, including military aid. Indeed as detente waned, the successes of Soviet foreign policy in the late 1970s were brought with the use of armed force, not by economic aid or moral support. Favorable circumstances, a flexible doctrine, armed force, and proletarian internationalism had favored Soviet policy in the late 1970s; but they also may have somewhat lulled the Soviet leadership into complacency, leading them to think that the general principles derived from other cases might be applied, and even amplified, in the case of Afghanistan. Perhaps even more to the point here are the subjects and issues which were *not* being talked about in Soviet politico-military writings in the late 1970s. One does not find articles on the limits of Soviet military power, the overriding importance of local conditions in Third World conflicts, or the problems generated by excessive proletarian internationalism on the management of peaceful coexistence. In this respect the Soviet invasion of Afghanistan was not only a military miscalculation in its initial phase, but it was a failure too of the entire Soviet conceptual apparatus.

All of this is not meant to suggest that doctrine provided a principal factor behind the Soviet decision to invade. The situation in Afghanistan and the general state of Soviet foreign policy in the latter half of 1979 produced more immediate, critical, and proximate factors.

Notes

1. Bradsher, *Afghanistan and the Soviet Union*, p. 117, 173.

2. U.S. Embassy, Kabul, *A Second Night Letter Blasts Prime Minister Amin*, pp. 1–4.

3. U.S. Department of State, *Tales of Afghanistan, Moscow Style*. The "CIA agent" claim appeared often in Afghan sources and was quoted by the Soviets who also referred to Amin as "an agent of the U.S. Special Services." See editorial in *Pravda*, January 29, 1980, p. 4.

4. For the Soviet claim, see *Pravda*, January 17, 1980, p. 5 in CDSP–32–3–4. Archer Blood's analysis is in U.S. Embassy, Kabul, *Meeting with President Amin*.

5. For an analysis using the totalitarian model, see Merle Fainsod, *How Russia Is Ruled,* revised edition, (Cambridge, Massachusetts: Harvard University Press, 1967). The group approach is thoroughly examined in H. Gordon Skilling and Franklyn Griffiths, *Interest Groups in Soviet Politics* (Princeton, New Jersey: Princeton University Press, 1971). For an important critique of the applicability of the group approach, see William E. Odom, "A Dissenting View on the Group Approach to Soviet Politics," *World Politics* 28 (July 1976): 542–67. For an application of the group approach to a case in Soviet foreign policy, see Jiri Valenta, *Soviet Intervention in Czechoslovakia, 1968: Anatomy of a Decision* (Baltimore: Johns Hopkins University Press, 1979). For an essay on the Brezhnev era that argues that the key process in the USSR is coalition maintenance at the top through the minimal satisfaction of key institutional actors on every issue, see Dennis Ross, "Coalition Maintenance in the Soviet Union," *World Politics* 32 (January 1980): 258–80.

6. *New York Times,* February 1, 1980, p. 28.

7. See the account of the KGB defector in *Time,* November 22, 1982, pp. 33–34.

8. For Andropov's view, see *Pravda,* February 12, 1980, p. 2; for Suslov's view, *Pravda,* February 21, 1980, p. 2; on Gromyko, *Pravda,* February 19, 1980, p. 2; and on Kosygin, *Pravda,* February 22, 1980, pp. 1–2.

9. Monks, *The Soviet Intervention in Afghanistan,* pp. 18–30.

10. See Jiri Valenta's comments on the model in *Studies in Comparative Communism* (Winter 1980), p. 338.

11. Legvold, "Containment Without Confrontation," p. 82.

12. Interview with a Soviet analyst, Moscow, January 5, 1983.

13. *State of the Union Address,* January 23, 1980.

14. Tyrus W. Cobb, "Energy and East-West Relations", an unpublished paper presented at the 1981 NATO Colloquium. On the significance—and the lack thereof—of Afghan natural gas to the Soviet Union, see Marshall Goldman's letter to the editor, *New York Times,* April 7, 1980.

15. On this point, the author wishes to acknowledge the advice of Keith A. Dunn of the Strategic Studies Institute of the U.S. Army War College. See Dunn, *Soviet Constraints in Southwest Asia,* p. 1–12.

16. The Soviet document can be found in George Kennan, *Soviet Foreign Policy, 1917–1941* (Princeton, New Jersey: D. Van Nostrand Co., 1960), pp. 184–85.

17. On the British Broadcasting Corporation domestic service, February 27, 1982 at 2110 hours (GMT).

18. M. S. Agwani, "The Saur Revolution and After," in Misra, *Afghanistan in Crisis,* p. 14. Mr. Agwani is a Professor at Nehru University in New Delhi.

19. Kissinger, *White House Years,* p. 161.

20. *Guardian* (London), December 16, 1982, p. 13.

21. Tyrus W. Cobb, "From Russia with Doves," p. 14. Quoted with the permission of the author. On Afghanistan's considerable mineral wealth, see John F. Shroder, Jr., *The USSR and Afghanistan Mineral Resources,* Occasional Paper no. 3 of the University of Nebraska (Omaha), pp. 125–43.

22. Seweryn Bialer, "Ideology and Soviet Foreign Policy," in Schwab, *Ideology and Foreign Policy*, pp. 86–7.

23. Two modern Soviet books which are instructive on the general subject are Ul'yanovskiy, *National Liberation*, and *Present-Day Problems in Asia and Africa: Theory, Politics, Personalities*. Both books were published in Russian two years before their translation into English. For a Western source, see Kanet, *The Soviet Union and the Developing Nations*.

24. P. I. Manchkha, *Current Problems of Contemporary Africa*, as quoted in a review by Anatoliy Gromyko and G. Starushenko, *Kommunist*, no. 2 (January 1980), translated in JPRS 75384. Ul'yanovskiy, "The 'Third World'—Problems of Socialist Orientation," p. 27.

25. Ibid., p. 29.

26. Nikolayev, " 'Third World': Choice of Path," p. 35–36.

27. Ul'yanovskiy, "The 'Third World'—Problems of Socialist Orientation," p. 29.

28. Krasin, "The Immutable Principles of Soviet Foreign Policy," p. 83.

29. G. Kim, "The Soviet Union and the National Liberation Movement," pp. 19–33 in CDSP–34–41–10.

30. Zagladin, "Revolutionary Forces and Their Ideological and Political Unity," p. 67.

31. Ul'yanovskiy, *Present-Day Problems in Asia and Africa*, p. 83; and Malinovskiy, "National-Liberation Movement at the Present Stage," in JPRS 75264, March 1980, p. 30.

32. Ponomarev, "Joint Struggle of the Workers and National-Liberation Movements," pp. 30–44 in JPRS 77341, February 1981, p. 33.

33. Bailer, *Stalin's Successors*, p. 273.

34. Kim, "The Soviet Union and the National Liberation Movement," p. 28.

35. Ponomarev, "Joint Struggle of the Workers and National-Liberation Movements," pp. 43–5.

36. Berman, *Soviet Air Power in Transition*, p. 36.

37. Arbatov, "On Soviet-American Relations," pp. 101–113 in CDSP–25–15–1, 3.

38. Kulish et al., *Military Force and International Relations*, p. 171.

39. See the interview with retired Lieutenant General Mil'shtyn in *New York Times*, August 25, 1980.

40. Sokolovskiy, *Soviet Military Strategy*, 3d edition, p. 184. The Soviet title translates literally as *Military Strategy*. The 3d edition first appeared in 1968.

41. Byely, *Marxism-Leninism on War and Army* (in English) (Moscow: Progress Publishers, 1972), p. 166.

42. Nikolai Ogarkov, "Voennaia Strategiia," (Military Strategy), in *Soviet Military Encyclopedia*, vol. 7, 1979.

43. Kulish, *Military Force and International Relations*, p. 103. In comparison, a recent monograph by Chief of Staff Ogarkov was initially run in 100,000 copies.

44. Ibid., p. 105.

45. Grechko, *On Guard For Peace and the Building of Communism,* in JPRS 54602, December 1971, p. 74–5.

46. Grechko, "The Leading Role of the CPSU in Building the Army of a Developed Socialist Society," *Problems of History of CPSU* (May 1974), as quoted in Harriet Fast Scott and William F. Scott, *The Armed Forces of the USSR,* 2d edition (Boulder, Colorado: Westview Press, 1981), p. 57.

47. Shavrov, "Local Wars and Their Place in the Global Strategy of Imperialism."

48. Zimmerman and Axelrod, "The 'Lessons' of Vietnam and Soviet Foreign Policy," pp. 19–20.

49. Brezhnev, *Report to the CPSU Central Committee,* in CDSP–28–8–11.

50. Katz, *The Third World in Soviet Military Thought,* pp. 138–54.

51. *Constitution (Fundamental Law) of the Union of Soviet Socialist Republics,* Article 28, p. 30.

52. Malinovskiy, "National-Liberation Movement at the Current Stage," p. 31.

53. Rybkin, "The 25th CPSU Congress and Wars of Liberation of the Contemporary Era," pp. 10–17 in JPRS 7253, January 1979, p. 39. Peter Vigor predicted the development of "wars of fraternal aid" in Soviet military theory. See *The Soviet View of War, Peace and Neutrality,* pp. 56–58.

54. Malinovskiy, "National Liberation Movement at the Current Stage," p. 29.

55. Ibid., p. 38.

56. "World Communist Solidarity With the Afghan Revolution," p. 10.

8
Soviet Motives for the Invasion of Afghanistan: The Immediate Factors

The most immediate and important factors—the proximate causes—behind the Soviet invasion of Afghanistan can be subsumed under three headings: the pressure of events in Afghanistan; Soviet security concerns, commitments, and prestige; and the absence of constraints.

The Pressure of Events

As previously stated, it would have been very easy to have concluded that the Amin regime could not hold on much longer. With the Parcham leaders dead or exiled, the likelihood of another Marxist government emerging "spontaneously" was slight. Armed intervention may have been seen as the only alternative to uncertain developments which probably would have militated against Soviet national interests, especially in light of recent developments in the area which will be discussed below.

Although the timing of the invasion was no doubt influenced by the Pavlovskiy estimate and the failed October-November offensive, it was, in all probability, also designed to catch the West off guard during the holiday season and to take advantage of the confusion generated by the hostage crisis in Teheran. Surprise was also enhanced by another factor: weather. The harsh winter was an apparently unfavorable time for an invasion, which would have logistically been much easier in the warmer months. On the other hand, a decisive move in the early winter made it difficult for the resistance to mount a counteroffensive.

Understanding the events of September to December 1979 and the timing of the Soviet invasion does not totally elucidate why the Soviets believed it necessary to use force in Afghanistan. The Soviet sense of its own security and its commitment to Afghanistan answer this question.

Soviet Security Concerns and Commitments

Soviet officials and analysts went to great lengths to indicate that Soviet security was at risk in Afghanistan. For Leonid Brezhnev, "a hotbed of serious danger to the security of the Soviet state was created on our southern border." For Yuri Andropov, it "was necessary to protect the interests of our homeland." Mikhail Suslov said that U.S. actions prior to the invasion were directed toward "using Afghanistan's territory for provocations against the Soviet Union." Andrei Gromyko spoke of those "who wanted to turn Afghanistan into an American military bridgehead." "A. Petrov," four days after the invasion, spoke of a U.S. attempt to mend holes in the strategic arc on the USSR's southern border by subjugating the Afghan people.[1]

It is not entirely clear how the Soviets imagined that an Afghanistan without the PDPA would affect their security. However, two things are clear. First, the Soviets have traditionally demonstrated an exaggerated fear of encirclement and a great sensitivity to their borders, even those shared with small Third World countries. This was evidenced in 1952 by their objections to Afghanistan about the presence of Western UN specialists in northern Afghanistan, their behavior toward the U.S. reaction to the hostage crisis in Iran, and on many other occasions. Soviet sensitivity to disorders on their frontiers was highlighted when an institute analyst with alleged KGB connections personally (with some apparent exaggeration) told this author that the alternative to sending troops into Afghanistan would have been permanently to increase the size of the Soviet ground forces by as much as "thirty divisions!"[2] Georgiy Arbatov said,

> No U.S. leader would exchange his strategic situation for our strategic situation—say, having on the U.S. northern border the Warsaw Pact nations; on the Mexican border something like China with a billion people, nuclear armaments, and claims to territory beyond the Rio Grande, and somewhere offshore, Japan.[3]

Second, the Soviets maintained radically different perspectives than Westerners on the indigenous nature of the Afghan resistance. From the beginning the Soviets believed that it was more of a fundamentalist Islamic movement than it truly is, usually stressing the dominance of the Islamic resistance and placing an unwarranted emphasis on groups which they claimed to be "Maoist." They also overestimated the scope and importance of outside support. This neatly dovetailed with the writing (discussed above) of civilian and military theorists during the 1970s, which stressed the universal connection between "internal reaction" and "the forces of imperialism," a fact to which revisionist Soviet historians now attribute even the origins of the original basmachi movements.[4] There is no doubt a strong dose of propaganda mixed in with these Soviet analyses, but the strength and frequency of these thoughts in Soviet writing suggest that Soviet officials would probably attribute local resistance to interference rather than to culture or local circumstances.

One way in which many analysts speculated that Soviet security was connected to the situation in Afghanistan was through the linkage between the Islamic resurgence and the status of the 40 million citizens of Muslim heritage in the USSR.[5] By itself, however, the evidence to support an "invade Afghanistan to insulate Soviet Muslims" hypothesis is mixed. Supporting the null hypothesis is the fact that many Central Asian reservists were used to man the initial attacking divisions. Furthermore, recent newspaper accounts indicate that the Soviet leadership has not experienced any problems over the invasion from their Muslim population. In addition to journalists, some scholars have also been skeptical over a threat to the USSR from its Muslim subjects. As Martha Brill Olcott has pointed out, Islam in the Soviet Union "is a social force, but it is not a political force."[6] Indeed, Islam is intensively "managed" by the Soviets, who have organized religious boards to manage the two Islamic seminaries and the 200 official showplace mosques which exist in the country. Central Asian diplomats are routinely posted to Asian countries and Soviet mullahs have held international religious gatherings in the Soviet Union.

The relative passivity of Soviet Muslims can be attributed to a number of factors. First, the living standards in Soviet Central Asia are very high for the Islamic world. Iranian or Afghan Muslims can hardly provide a model for Soviet Muslims in this regard. Second, Soviet Muslims are subject to atheistic indoctrination and to close scrutiny by communist authorities. There is only a very low level of unauthorized samizdat literature in the Muslim areas of the USSR and on being interviewed by Western journalists, many Central Asians even quoted Soviet propaganda on the events there. Third, many in the West exaggerate the homogeneity of Soviet Muslims, while at the same time deemphasizing the very real ethnic differences between various Muslim nationalities.

An unidentified Soviet diplomat in Washington—alleged to have KGB connections—summed up one school of thought on the possibilities for an Islamic resurgence in the USSR by saying:

> The threat by Islamic fundamentalism has been very much exaggerated. The Muslims, these are humble people. We have 40 million of them in our country, and we do not have any trouble with them. . . . Nor

will we be getting any trouble with them in Afghanistan. What do the Muslims want except a little freedom for their cult?[7]

On the international scene, the Soviet attitude toward Islam has been flexible. Although Lenin cast aspersions on the reactionary nature of Islamic clergy, Brezhnev and his colleagues have taken a more differentiated stance.[8] Iran's Islamic revolution was heralded as an anti-imperialist movement and a favorable development. Brezhnev said at the Twenty-sixth Party Congress in 1981,

> Of late, Islamic slogans are being actively promoted in some countries of the East. We Communists have every respect for the religious convictions of people professing Islam or any other religion. The main thing is what aims are pursued by the forces proclaiming various slogans. The banner of Islam may lead into struggle for liberation. This is borne out by history. But it also shows that reaction, too, manipulates with Islamic slogans to incite counterrevolutionary mutinies. Consequently, the whole thing hinges on the actual content of any movement.[9]

Although Brezhnev may have been contrasting Iran and Afghanistan, a subsequent article by a local scholar in a Kazakh periodical left no doubt:

> In Iran, for example, Islam unified the people in the struggle against the regime of the shah. However, counterrevolutionary elements opposing the legal government of Afghanistan have collected under the broad banner of Islam.[10]

Although there is little evidence that would prove that the Soviets were vitally concerned about "their" Muslims in December 1979, after the invasion there were a number of expressions of concern by Soviet officials or analysts in Central Asia, although it is less than clear whether the Soviets feared their Muslim populations at the time or were simply working against the vigorous U.S. propaganda directed at them after the invasion. Most of these comments emanated from border republics and many were made by agitprop personnel or security officers. For example, in an article heralding the work of local KGB personnel, Major General Yusif-Zade, chairman of the Azerbaijan SSR KGB, singling out "young people" as especially vulnerable, stated in a *Bakinsky Rabochy* article that

> In view of the situation in Iran and Afghanistan the U.S. special services are trying to exploit the Islamic religion—especially in areas where the

Muslim population lives—as one factor influencing the political situation in our country.[11]

Less than a week later, G.A. Aliyev, Azerbaijani party chief and candidate member of the Politburo, echoed the general's concerns in the same newspaper.[12] An official of the Tajik SSR Central Committee Secretariat put the blame more on U.S. propaganda designed to "spread . . . the 'Islamic revival' into the southern regions of the USSR."[13]

In any case, one must believe that Brezhnev and his colleagues were aware of and interested in the connection between Soviet Muslims and their co-religionists (some of whom are descendants of the original basmachi) in Afghanistan. Time may be the factor which allows resolution here. It is quite possible that the future, long-term effects of an Islamic republic in Afghanistan were feared by a Soviet leadership which, at the same time, perceived no immediate threat from exposing Central Asian reservists to their fellow Muslims.

Soviet security, in their perspective, was also affected by regional and global developments, especially those unfavorable to the Soviet Union, which took place in the latter half of 1979. These developments put the deteriorating situation in Afghanistan in a bad light. Events outside Afghanistan made losing that troubled country appear to be much more devastating than it might have otherwise.

For many reasons, South and Southwest Asia have always been a key geopolitical concern for the Soviet Union, not only because they touch its southern border, but also because they were a critical area of competition between the USSR and Great Britain, the leading imperialist power of the time. There is perhaps no more telling proof of this than the fact that some of the most important activities of early Bolshevik diplomacy resulted in treaties with Turkey, Persia, and Afghanistan in 1921. More recently, problems with China and the renewed Soviet concern over the Soviet–Black Sea–Pacific lines of communication have highlighted their interest in his area.[14]

After World War II and the Soviet withdrawal from Iran in 1946, an uneasy status quo emerged. Iran became a CENTO member but maintained "correct" relations with the Soviets, which improved tremendously after the Shah's declaration in September 1962 "not to permit the establishment of foreign rocket bases of any sort on its territory" and to "never permit Iran to become a tool of aggression against the Soviet Union."[15] Subsequent to this the Shah made two visits to Moscow and even began to import sizeable quantities of Soviet arms. Afghanistan accommodated the Soviets and, although Pakistan was hostile to the USSR (and was both a SEATO and a CENTO member), it was checked by a friendly India and at times by Afghanistan. In the late 1960s,

Pakistani-Soviet relations began to improve and Soviet aid to Pakistan began. In retrospect, even superpower naval activity in the Indian Ocean, prior to the fall of the Shah, seems to have been relatively insignificant. Preliminary talks had been initiated by the superpowers to demilitarize the entire area, but were terminated after the fall of the Shah.

The onset of 1979 saw a rather favorable situation for the Soviets in the region. Turkey was alienated from the United States, due to the latter's arms embargo over Turkish behavior in the Cyprus crisis. Pakistan, although it had moved closer to China, was also under a U.S. arms embargo for human rights violations and its attempts to develop a nuclear weapons capability. The Shah was toppled by a progressive, virulently anti-American revolution and Afghanistan was clearly on a socialist path, the revolt not yet having reached crisis proportions.

This favorable situation did not last long. The situation in Iran began to complicate U.S.-Soviet relations. U.S. fleet deployments increased and as early as January 1979, *Izvestiia* accused the United States of conducting a "show of force directed against the Iranian people."[16] The United States and Soviet Union traded charges of interference in Iran's internal affairs and a *Pravda* article warned that "the USSR would regard any intervention . . . in the affairs of Iran—a state that borders on the Soviet Union—as affecting its security interests."[17]

Soviet-Iranian relations also began to sour. In March 1979, the Soviet press echoed the Afghan charge that Iranian soldiers had infiltrated Herat and thus indirectly charged Iran with complicity in the murder of Soviet advisers there. By September, open criticism of the Ayatollah's regime began to appear in the Soviet media, especially after Iranian authorities began to pressure the Tudeh party by closing its newspaper. One of the earliest pieces along these lines was written in September 1979 by Alexander Bovin who criticized the regime's human-rights, economic, and foreign policies and noted that, with regard to the Iranian revolution, "hopes have given way to anxiety and trepidation, to uncertainty and disappointment."[18]

The situation in Afghanistan began to slide quickly downhill in March 1979. The USSR began to stress Chinese-Pakistani and U.S. complicity in interfering in the affairs of Afghanistan and charged that the United States had begun to abandon its evenhanded policy by tilting toward the PRC in the triangular relationship. More will be said below about the deterioration of U.S.-Soviet and Sino-Soviet relations.

The Soviets had previously been able to live with a pro-Western Iran, but losing Afghanistan would now create a bigger problem. If not kept solidly in the Soviet camp, Afghanistan could become the linchpin in an encirclement of the Soviet Union, with NATO in Turkey abutting a hostile Iran and Afghanistan. The latter would undoubtedly come under the influence of the United States and the adjacent PRC as well. In Soviet eyes, the U.S. fixation on its problem with Iran was in part a cover for grander purposes. As one Soviet analyst said,

> U.S. ruling circles also hope to divert world attention from its dangerous action with respect to Iran, to justify the vast concentration of U.S. naval forces in the Persian Gulf area, and the Pentagon's efforts to set up new pro-Western military . . . alliances in Asia, spearheaded against the Soviet Union. . . .[19]

Even more to the point was an article by the pseudonymous A. Petrov, which used a term popularized by Zbigniew Brzezinski. After the fall of the Shah, "holes were found in the . . . 'strategic arc'," that series of alliances that the United States had been building around the southern border of the USSR. Subjugating the Afghans, according to the article, was just one of the ways that the United States was trying to replace the Shah in the region.[20]

In retrospect, the Soviet miscalculation of immediate U.S. aims in Iran was probably an important element in the Soviet decision to invade. Toward the end of 1979, the Soviets—again using A. Petrov—began to warn that "there are more than enough facts to indicate that preparations are underway for the use of force" to solve the hostage crisis in Iran.[21] A 1981 U.S. International Communications Agency report, based on 160 proxy interviews of middle-level Soviet officials and analysts, reported that many Soviet analysts believed that the U.S. build-up in the Indian Ocean presaged a full-scale invasion of Iran. When reminded that the United States did not invade Iran, "the Soviet response generally was to the effect that 'Yes, but you should have!' or 'Yes, but we had every reason to believe that you would. . . . We had to gain a foothold to match the one the United States was going to obtain'."[22] It may also have occurred to the Soviets that U.S. action in Iran could—as with the Hungarian invasion and the Suez Crisis—divert some of the more troublesome aspects of the international reaction to their move.

Soviet concern over a deteriorating strategic position was reinforced by a security commitment to Afghanistan. Article 4 of their friendship treaty stated that, when necessary, both parties will "take appropriate measures with a view to ensuring the security, independence, and territorial integrity of the two countries."[23] While this represents far less than an ironclad guarantee of Afghan security, one can imagine the great loss of prestige that the Soviets would face if a regime with a socialist orientation on the Soviet border were to fall to "reactionary forces." What sort of lesson would such a defeat teach to Angola and Ethiopia—both beset by internal revolts—and Vietnam, threatened by China? This commitment to Afghanistan and the subsequent involvement of Soviet prestige was accentuated by the lessons learned from the loss of Chile, which—true to the pattern discussed above—was attributed in 1973 to "the subversive activities of Chilean reactionary circles . . . with the support of foreign imperialist forces."[24]

Brezhnev himself justified the invasion in a widely reprinted interview in *Pravda* which indicated the force of the Chilean example in Soviet thinking. To have refrained from the invasion would have "allow[ed] aggressive forces to repeat here what they were able to do, for example, in Chile, where the freedom of the people was drowned in blood."[25]

It seems probable that the deterioration of Sino-Soviet and U.S.-Soviet relations which accelerated in the second half of 1979 played a contributory role in the Soviet decision to invade Afghanistan. This role included (1) enhancing the general Soviet perception of encirclement and insecurity concerning regional developments; (2) contributing to the perception that the Soviet Union had "nothing to hope for and nothing to fear" from the United States and to a lesser degree China; and (3) contributing to a decision-making climate apparently characterized by "intense emotionalism . . . anger . . . [and] frustration."[26]

Soviet relations with the PRC in 1979 never recovered from China's abortive attempt to teach the Vietnamese a lesson for invading Kampuchea in late December 1978. This was done in face of the friendship treaty between the Vietnam and the USSR, signed in November 1978. Just as bothersome to the Soviets was the apparent collusion in this incident of the United States, which had resumed full diplomatic ties with China. The visit of Deng to the United States, which ended only sixteen days prior to the invasion of Vietnam, intensified Soviet concerns. A. Petrov reminded his readers that "during his trip to the West and Tokyo, Teng Hsiao-ping talked bluntly about plans 'to teach Vietnam a bloody lesson'." Petrov noted that Teng may even have disclosed his plans to his "American friends."[27]

A Soviet commentator writing in April 1980 was even more direct: "Washington was fully aware of the scope and scale of the intervention Peking was preparing and of the meaning of China's threat addressed to Vietnam."[28] To further complicate matters, in late 1978, the PRC and Japan normalized relations in the midst of renewed Japanese interest in recovering the Kurile islands.

Even more than the United States, China, which shares a short border with Afghanistan, was singled out as the main impetus behind support for the Afghan resistance. Chinese efforts to complete the Karakoram

Highway and numerous visits by high level officials to Pakistan were seen as Chinese moves against Soviet foreign policy in the region. When the commander of the PRC air force visited Pakistan, *Izvestiia* noted that China was moving in to fill the void created by the cutoff of U.S. aid and that "by promising the Pakistani administration new supplies . . . Peking is pitting Pakistan against Afghanistan and India."[29]

To complicate matters, the PRC announced in April 1979 that it would not renew the 1950 Sino-Soviet Treaty of Friendship, Alliance, and Mutual Assistance, which was scheduled to lapse in April 1980.[30] The Chinese offered at the same time to conduct negotiations on bilateral issues of interest, which could have resulted in a new agreement based on the principles of peaceful coexistence. The Chinese motives for doing this are unclear but the negotiations which began in mid-September never generated much enthusiasm in Moscow. First, the treaty itself was long since a dead letter. Second, the Sino-Vietnamese war had poisoned the well. What further proof of Chinese bad faith was necessary than their attack on a Soviet ally? Third, in mid-July 1979, both sides admitted to yet another border clash in Central Asia. Even before talks began, the pseudonymous "I. Aleksandrov," in an obvious reference to Vietnam, described the upcoming talks as a Chinese attempt to "pressure states of the socialist commonwealth."[31]

The talks appeared doomed from the start and, amidst Chinese insistence on Soviet troop withdrawals from the border, they foundered. At the same time, the Soviet perception of an embryonic U.S.-Chinese alliance grew. Numerous Soviet reports in the summer and fall of 1979 charged the U.S. and the PRC with interfering in Afghanistan. In September, heralding "The Speech that Was Applauded in Peking," *Pravda* highlighted Vice-President Walter Mondale's visit to Peking, quoting his statements that the United States was "determined to join you in advancing our many parallel strategic and bilateral interests" and that the key task was "to establish concrete political ties in the context of mutual security."[32] In October, the United States announced that Harold Brown, the secretary of defense, would visit China in January 1980. This trip would ultimately reveal U.S. willingness to sell China "dual use" military-civilian technology. In Soviet eyes, the facade of evenhandedness had passed through a "tilt" on its way to making China a "factual ally." A senior Western diplomat in Moscow noted that Foreign Minister Gromyko "seemed almost obsessed by a threat to Soviet security from the United States and China."[33]

Although Sino-Soviet relations were problematical, U.S.-Soviet relations further deteriorated in the second half of 1979, completing a steep descent which had begun in 1975 over Soviet activities in Angola. While many U.S. analysts saw the Soviet invasion of Afghanistan as the first decisive battle of a new Cold War, Soviet analysts found the origins in the domestic political scene in the United States and in U.S. behavior prior to the crisis.

Detente, by Soviet analysis, came about because the might of the Soviet Union forced American "realists" to see the Cold War as an irrelevant relic of the past. But it saw the battle between the realists and the reactionaries in the United States as never permanently settled. Two months after the Soviet invasion, Georgiy Arbatov, head of the USSR Academy of Sciences Institute for the Study of the USA and Canada, wrote that the "most aggressive circles" in the United States—especially in the military-industrial complex—were angered over the loss of U.S. military superiority and the people's "negative attitude" toward overseas adventures.[34] Illusions linked to the PRC contributed, according to Arbatov, to the U.S. error of believing that China could change the balance of power and obviate the need for detente. All of this was "favorable soil" for the concept that the United States should use its economic and military might in a more direct fashion.[35] Brezhnev and Arbatov noted that the change of course was also facilitated by U.S. electoral politics.

The policies dictated by this shift signified to the Soviets that the United States was returning to Cold War tactics: a drive for military superiority, stronger rhetoric, the development of "positions of strength" around the Soviet periphery, and confrontation. Realistic moderation was replaced by a U.S. intention "to create a network of military bases in the Indian Ocean and in the Middle East and Africa."

The litany of events which "proved" these theses became familiar after the January 1980 Brezhnev interview in *Pravda*. The "course hostile to the cause of detente" began in 1978 with the NATO countries' decision for 3 percent real growth in their defense budgets, and continued through the formation of the Rapid Deployment Force.[36] Even SALT II was used by the U.S. No sooner than the treaty was signed, "aggressive circles" began to derail its ratification. According to a highly placed Soviet diplomat, it became clear to the Soviets that efforts to create a crisis over Soviet troops in Cuba was interpreted by the Soviet leadership as an attempt to derail the treaty.[37]

A particularly frightening manifestation of the new U.S. attitude from a Soviet perspective was the NATO plan to station Pershing II and cruise missiles in Europe to offset what NATO saw as a growing Soviet advantage in Eurostrategic missiles. While the plan was not yet officially approved, *Pravda* (around the same time that the final preparations to invade Afghanistan were being made) reported that German, British, Italian, and Belgian acquiescence had been received. Gromyko, on a visit to Bonn, loudly and threateningly complained of the same thing in a news conference on November 25.[38]

The leading Soviet Americanist, Georgiy Arbatov, summarized the Soviet view by saying that "it was before the events in Afghanistan" that the U.S. derailed the SALT II treaty, "sharply heightened the pitch of anti-Soviet hysteria and accelerated rapprochement with Peking on an anti-Soviet basis."[39]

In short, U.S. "interference" in the affairs of Afghanistan was seen as part of a more dangerous and comprehensive policy shift. Soviet analysts were quick to point out that it would be to no avail. Alexander Bovin confidently noted after the invasion that the United States would be forced to return to the policy of detente and to acknowledge Soviet strength and the Soviet Union's "principled positions and policies." His remarks also reflected Soviet anger over U.S. reaction to the invasion and Soviet pride in their military might: "In general, it is time that the United States learned to behave more modestly."[40]

To summarize, by the fall of 1979, it was the Soviet view that their relations with both their principal and secondary adversaries had deteriorated significantly. Chinese hostility had brought about a direct attack against one Soviet ally and, in Soviet eyes, the potent subversion of another. In the United States, reactionary circles were ascendant and support for the policy of detente had evaporated. The United States had abandoned even the appearance of evenhandedness and had apparently supported Beijing in the Sino-Vietnamese war. Even SALT II, the fruit of seven years of negotiations, was being disowned by its U.S. parents. In Southwest Asia, it appeared, at least to some Soviet officials, that the United States was about to use force to reestablish a position of strength in Iran at the same time the Soviets were on the verge of losing theirs in Afghanistan.

When superimposed on the deteriorating situation in Afghanistan, Soviet relations with its principal adversaries in 1979 appeared to magnify Soviet fears and uncertainties. With apparently nothing to lose in their relations with major adversaries, the Soviets apparently calculated that they had no reason not to resort to a quick intervention to shore up their position in Afghanistan.

Absence of Constraints

The Soviet invasion of Afghanistan was apparently viewed as a low-risk operation. From an empirical perspective, there were few constraints either from external or internal sources. This subject has, of course, not been the topic of any published Soviet analyses, so we are limited here to an inferential reconstruction of Soviet thinking on military, economic, and domestic and international political constraints.

Military constraints were few. With the hostages in Iran, the United States was distracted. Furthermore, the type of force it had in the Persian Gulf was ill suited to deter or combat the invasion of a landlocked country by Soviet ground forces. Pakistan possessed neither the will nor the forces to combat directly a Soviet army which ultimately could cause Zia to moderate his "interference." U.S. moves to aid Pakistan could be (and were to some extent) offset by Soviet moves toward India. China could do nothing directly. Its army was not deployed to move into Afghanistan and, barring use of Pakistani territory, its approach would have been limited to the Wakhan corridor which at any rate was impassable by December. Moreover, the finite limits of the Chinese army had been severely tested in Vietnam, leaving the world to wonder who was the student and who the teacher in that bloody lesson.

Politically, the Soviets apparently calculated the costs as moderate or at least containable. U.S. reactions to the Hungarian and Czechoslovakian invasions proved to be more smoke than fire, and short-term smoke at that. Reactions to Angola, Ethiopia, and to previous moves in Afghanistan may have caused some to believe that the U.S. reaction would be less than substantive. To the contrary, one could argue that strong U.S. measures in support of the Yemeni Arab Republic in its border war with the People's Democratic Republic of Yemen (PDRY) in February 1979, the overreaction to the Soviet brigade in Cuba, the increased U.S. naval presence in the Persian Gulf, and multiple warnings about Afghanistan in the fall of 1979 should have signaled the Soviets that the United States was emerging from the "post-Vietnam syndrome" and that its patience had been worn thin. Even if these signals were taken into account in Moscow, however, it was not clear that the United States had the means to make the Soviets feel its anger.

As discussed, direct military measures were hard to imagine. Politically, it was even hard for many Americans to believe that the president would order a grain embargo during an election year. Trade with the East builds its own constituency and President Carter had been a trade expander in his term in the White House. Facing an uphill battle for reelection, would he use a weapon that might be politically damaging to his own campaign?

Tough U.S. moves in the foreign policy realm were also hard to imagine. Moving closer to a Pakistan that in November had been unable to prevent a crowd from burning the U.S. embassy in a burst of misdirected Islamic frenzy seemed unlikely. Further use of the "China card" was probable but the damage in this area was already nearly complete from the Soviet perspective.

The response of the Third World and the value attached to it by the Soviets would have been hard to gauge. Soviet decision-makers may have accurately calculated that the twenty or so states with a socialist orientation would, for the most part, support the move. The importance and weight that the Soviets attached to the reaction of the "capitalist roaders" in the Third World is impossible to gauge. It is also possible that the Soviets may have believed that the tough reaction of Islamic states would have been diverted or offset by an impending U.S. military action toward Iran, much as the world's attention to the Suez Crisis diverted attention from the Soviet invasion of Hungary in 1956.

Internal constraints—either in the USSR or in Afghanistan—were few. As previously mentioned there does not appear to have been a united group in the Politburo which was against the invasion and which might have extracted some political cost for intervening in Afghanistan. Moreover, the invasion promised to be a low-cost operation, using less than 4 percent of the total ground forces, and, using Czechoslovakia as a guide, the Soviets may have calculated that the complete occupation of key areas in Afghanistan would not take more than a few months.

In Afghanistan, the army was politically divided and ill-disposed to counter a strong thrust. Moreover, Soviet advisers controlled its logistical strings. Before the disunited resistance could respond, they would be faced with a fait accompli, and during the winter, it would be hard to respond effectively. By spring, Soviet forces could easily have been (and were) entrenched to the point where their physical survival was unassailable.

If the Soviet leadership took account of these considerations in the Politburo and/or the Defense Council, it is clear from the events which followed that they miscalculated, both in their estimate of the situation in Afghanistan and in their calculation of the effects of the invasion. One must add at this point that although this miscalculation was serious, it does not stand alone in the annals of Soviet foreign policy. From Stalin's decisions on the Korean War, to Khrushchev's actions in the Cuban Missile Crisis, to Brezhnev's policy toward Somalia and Egypt, miscalculation has been at least as much a part of Soviet policy as it has been of U.S. policy. Indeed, as Edward Crankshaw has pointed out, we often give the Soviets credit for an omniscence which neither they nor any other people have ever possessed:

> One of the most serious mistakes of the West . . . has been to overrate, often to an absurd degree, the knowledge and understanding of the world enjoyed by the Soviet leadership . . . The mistake is serious because it has led us again and again to attribute great subtlety and

exactitude of calculation to manifestations of Soviet government behavior which often arise from ignorance and muddle.[41]

Notes

1. See *Pravda*, January 13, 1980; February 12, 21, 19, and 22 (respectively), 1980, p. 2 in each issue; and December 31, 1979, p. 4.
2. Interview with a Soviet analyst, Moscow, January 5, 1983.
3. *New York Times*, October 5, 1980, p. E3.
4. See P.G. Kim's review of A.I. Zevelev et. al., *Basmachestvo: Origin, Essence and Collapse*, in *Obshchestvennyye nauki v uzbekistana (Social Sciences in Uzbekistan)*, no. 6 (June 1982), pp. 47–8, in JPRS 81918, October 1982, pp. 96–8. Kim concludes that "the history of the basmachi movement . . . has much in common with the . . . basmachi in Afghanistan. Kim claims that both were supported by international imperialism. For an opposing Western view, supported by earlier Soviet historians, see Pipes, *The Formation of the Soviet Union*, pp. 178–81.
5. A precis of the Soviet nationality problem can be found in Paul Cook, *The Soviet Conglomerate*, reprinted in U.S. Department of State, Special Report 67, March 1980. The relationship between the nationality problem and the stability of the Soviet government is addressed in Bialer, *Stalin's Successors*, pp. 183–227. On the issue of linkages, see Corcoran, *Soviet Muslim Policy; Domestic and Foreign Policy Linkages*, pp. 1–22.
6. Olcott, "Soviet Islam and World Revolution," p. 500. For a contrary view see Alexandre Bennigsen, "Mullahs, Mujahidin, and Soviet Muslims," *Problems of Communism* 33 (November-December 1984), pp. 28–44.
7. *Die Welt* in FBIS–Soviet Union–III–010–1/15/80–A4.
8. Lenin, "Theses on the National and Colonial Question," pp. 622–25.
9. *Documents and Resolutions: The 26th Congress of the Communist Party of the Soviet Union*, pp. 18–19.
10. K. Tazhikova, "Islam and the Contemporary Ideological Struggle," *Kazakstan Ayelderi* (Alma Ata), no. 3 (March 1982), pp. 25–6 in JPRS 82081, October 1982, p. 1.
11. *Bakinsky Rabochy* (Baku Worker), December 19, 1980, p. 3. in FBIS–Soviet Union–III–4 1/7/81–R1.
12. *Bakinsky Rabochy*, December 25, 1980, p. 1.
13. *Kommunist Tadzhikistana* (Dushanbe) (Communist of Tajikistan), July 31, 1982, p. 2 in JPRS, *USSR Republic Political and Social Affairs*, no. 1307, September 21, 1982, p. 20.
14. For a Soviet appraisal of the importance of the Indian Ocean to the Soviet Union see Volsky, "A Strategy Without a Future," p. 405; and also Alexeyev and Fialkovsky "Peace and Security for the Indian Ocean," pp. 51–55. See also A. Lodozhsky, "The USSR's Efforts to Turn the Indian Ocean into a Zone of Peace," pp. 40–6. Also, see the interview with a Soviet diplomat in the Seychelle Islands in New York Times, April 20, 1981, pp. 1, 12.

15. *Pravda*, September 17, 1962, p. 3.
16. *Izvestiia*, January 5, 1979, p. 4 in CDSP–31–1–15.
17. *Pravda*, January 7, 1979, p. 4 in CDSP–31–1–15.
18. *Nedelya*, ["Week," a supplement to *Izvestiia*] September 3–9, 1979, p. 6.
19. Mikhailov, "Provocatory Campaign Over Afghanistan," p. 99.
20. *Pravda*, December 31, 1979, p. 4 in CDSP–31–52–5, 6.
21. *Pravda*, December 5, 1979, p. 5 in CDSP–31–49–4, 26.
22. U.S. International Communications Agency, *Soviet World View and Perceptions of the United States*, pp. 34–35.
23. *Treaty of Friendship*, Article 4.
24. *Pravda*, September 14, 1973, p. 1 in CDSP–25–37–18.
25. *Pravda*, January 13, 1980, p. 1 in CDSP–32–2–2. Brezhnev had given a similar analysis of the Chilean situation at the 25th Party Congress in 1976. See *Pravda*, February 25, 1976, pp. 2–9.
26. *East-West Relations in the Aftermath*, p. 37. The hope-fear analogy is from Lowenthal, "Dealing with Soviet Global Power," p. 90.
27. *Pravda*, February 20, 1979, p. 5 in CDSP–31–7–1, 2.
28. Kuznin, "China in the West's Aggressive Policy," p. 34.
29. *Izvestiia*, April 15, 1979, p. 4 in CDSP–31–15–19.
30. *Pravda*, April 5, 1979, p. 5 in CDSP–31–14–1. Also, see "I. Aleksandrov" in *Pravda*, April 7, 1979, p. 4 in CDSP–31–14–2.
31. "I. Aleksandrov" in *Pravda*, July 11, 1979, pp. 4–5.
32. *Pravda*, September 2, 1979, p. 4 in CDSP–31–35–15.
33. For use of the term "factual ally," see Petukhov, "PRC–USA: A Threat to Peace and Security," p. 60. On Gromyko, see *New York Times*, February 16, 1980, p. 6.
34. *Pravda*, March 3, 1980, p. 6 in CDSP–32–9–2.
35. Ibid.
36. *Pravda*, January 13, 1980, p. 1 in CDSP–32–2–1.
37. Interview with Marshall D. Shulman at West Point, December 11, 1981. See also, *Pravda*, October 9, 1979, p. 4 in CDSP–31–41–5.
38. *Pravda*, November 16, 1979, p. 5 and November 25, 1979, p. 1.
39. *Pravda*, March 3, 1980, p. 6.
40. *Izvestiia*, January 16, 1980, p. 5 in CDSP–32–2–6, 7.
41. Edward Crankshaw in his foreword to Khrushchev, *Khrushchev Remembers: The Last Testament*, pp. vii–viii.

9
The Use of Force in Afghanistan, June 1980–December 1984

In previous chapters, it has been shown that the Soviets believed that their occupation of Afghanistan would provide a reinvigorated PDPA with the opportunity it would need to quickly restore order in Afghanistan. This was obviously wishful thinking. By June 1980, the withdrawal of some armor and missile units and the construction of bases indicated that the Soviets were attempting to adapt to the counterinsurgency environment and to adopt a long-term perspective toward the problems in Afghanistan.

From June 1980 to December 1984, Soviet strategy appeared to be to hold the major centers of communication, limit infiltration, and destroy local strongholds at minimum risk to its own forces. The use of helicopters, chemical weapons, and the use of what may accurately be called terror tactics are all key instruments in the Soviet strategy, as is the training of thousands of new cadres and bureaucrats in the USSR. Although the Soviets have inflicted hundreds of thousands of casualties on the Afghan populace and have driven one third of the population into exile, their hold on Afghanistan has not improved. The resistance has from 1981 to 84 stepped up its activities. Perhaps even more surprising, many Soviet units have performed badly and Soviet soldiers appear to be undisciplined and poorly motivated.

The USSR was generally unsuccessful on the diplomatic front in its search for regional allies and its efforts to gain a favorable peace were fruitless. In all, however, the Soviets, to the end of 1984, were not prepared to give up on Afghanistan and seemed prepared to accept a peace only on their terms or to continue their war of attrition for the foreseeable future.

The Domestic Political Situation in Afghanistan

Unfortunately, from a Soviet perspective, the domestic political situation in Afghanistan provided the Soviets with little reason for confidence during the period following the invasion.

As has been shown, the Soviet invasion had all the hallmarks of a quick thrust, designed to support a short-term occupation. This move would have provided Karmal with a stable environment in which to build an effective government and a loyal army. The Karmal government made little progress toward this goal in the period from June 1980 to December 1984.

Khalq-Parcham fighting—and this word is used literally—continued unabated. In July 1980, the 14th Armored Brigade revolted when the government attempted to relieve its Khalqi commander. By fall 1980, many lower-ranking Khalqi were actually fighting alongside the mujahidin. The Parcham faction attempted to increase its strength in recruiting, by PDPA accounts, more than 40,000 new members (for a total of over 100,000) but Khalq numerical advantage seems to have been retained since many of the new candidates were in the military. Although the actual size of the PDPA is subject to question, experts still put Khalq numerical superiority at more than two to one. Rivalries—factional and personal—continued as well.[1] Early in 1981, the Soviets apparently decided to divest party head Karmal of the prime ministership in favor of a Khalqi. When the "competition" ended, however, the post went to Sultan Ali Keshtmand, the deputy premier and minister of planning, who was from the Parcham faction. Keshtmand, an ethnic Hazara, was a rival of Karmal's and a potential successor. In a similar move, in early 1982, Abdul Qader—an officer with a reputation, perhaps undeserved, for being above the Khalq-Parcham rivalry—replaced M. Rafie as minister of defense. None of these measures slowed factionalism in the PDPA.[2] Plots, real and imagined, dominated intraparty relationships. In February 1981, unnamed sources reported the arrest of 2,000 officers and bureaucrats, followed by another purge of equal magnitude in March 1982. In September 1982, the Khalqi general commanding the Central Army Corps was found shot to death in his office under circumstances apparently not connected with combat with the rebels. In May 1983, the Khalqi deputy defense minister physically assaulted the defense minister after having been passed over for promotion. Military mutinies and defections are still commonplace, and, in December 1984, the Defense Minister was replaced after a year of criticism of the military by the leadership.[3]

The atmosphere in the PDPA and the problem of factionalism have been addressed by Karmal many times. In his speech to the Fourth PDPA Plenum in November 1980, he said,

> Some of the staff to whom the party has entrusted high and responsible posts abuse their position and rank. The Central Committee has received information that some of the staff have embarked on acts of factionalism, bribery, repression, suffocation, law breaking, threats and

oppression, promises and other unsuitable activities outside their authority. What can be said in this regard? . . . The Saur Revolution was carried out to realize the hopes and the well-being of the people, not to enhance personal glory and create a new rich bureaucratic strata, not for self-praise and administration, not for factionalism. . . .

The beleaguered president made a similar plea in January 1984.[4]

Karmal was no more successful in generating national unity than he was in generating PDPA unity. The Karmal regime attempted to restore national unity by forming Defense of the Revolution Battalions and a National Fatherland Front. The former were regarded as unreliable despite high pay and the latter, a throwback to the old national tribal assemblies, took six months to organize its initial meeting. The initial congress lasted only one day and numerous delegates were later assassinated by the resistance. As a further sop to local, non-PDPA elites, in August 1981 the regime loosened its land reform policy to enable clerics and army officers to keep their larger holdings.[5] In a similar vein, the government renewed its verbal support for Islam and early in 1981 formed a Supreme Council of *Ulema* and Religious Leaders, a move which again brought little support.

The regime—even more than in 1978—suffered from the popular (and accurate) perception that it was a Soviet puppet. Karmal and his colleagues were less than efficient in cultivating an image of independence. At the Fourth PDPA Plenum, Karmal said, "The pursuance of eternal friendship and solidarity with the Leninist Communist Party of the USSR and friendship between the countries and our peoples, are the basic measures and yardsticks for the appraisal of the work of every member of the party . . . and government. . . ."[6]

Out of necessity, Soviet interference in the Afghan economy has also increased. More than 140 industrial facilities are being built (or rebuilt) with Soviet assistance, and the value of Soviet aid since 1978 has allegedly doubled, reaching 80 percent of the Afghan total. Furthermore, total trade with the Soviet Union has seen a 100 percent increase since 1977. The Soviets claim to have trained some 60,000 Afghan workers of all types, and, at present, there are more than 9,000 Afghan students enrolled in institutions of higher education in the USSR. Because of the Soviet "fraternal assistance," food is now critically scarce in some areas. A British organization has estimated recently that 500,000 Afghans are in imminent danger of starvation.[7]

Afghanistan is an extremely poor country. However, in P. Gentelle's words, Afghanistan is not "underdeveloped," but "nondeveloped."[8] The Soviets are presently doing their best to change this situation. Indeed it has become obvious that furthering development of Afghanistan's extractive industries is clearly part of a larger Soviet strategy designed to defray the costs of their "fraternal assistance" to Afghanistan.

An estimated 1 percent of Soviet natural gas production is being met through deliveries of Afghan gas, paid for by the Soviets at half the world price. No one is sure how much the Soviets have imported since the invasion because all of the gas meters are across the Amu Darya in the USSR. The deflated value of the Afghan gas is being subtracted from the total of $3 billion owed by Afghanistan to the Soviet Union. At least 200 Soviet geologists are in Afghanistan, surveying its mineral wealth. Deposits of chrome, lead, zinc, and copper are all being examined.[9]

Perhaps the greatest indicator that the Karmal regime has little support among the population is its inability to field an improved army. Disillusionment with the government has produced defections of whole units to the rebel side. In fact, even the paltry force that is left is more burden than boon to the Soviets. In August 1980, fearing further defections, the Soviets were forced to remove all anti-air and anti-tank weapons from the Afghan forces to preclude their falling into rebel hands. In April 1981, fearing further unrest within the Afghan army, Soviet forces expelled some of the Afghan garrisons from the Kabul area and took over many of their local security duties.

To bolster their forces, to take the pressure off Soviet units, and perhaps to regain some autonomy, the Karmal government has repeatedly resorted to desperate measures. Press gangs have reportedly been rounding up teenagers as young as fourteen years of age for military service. In some cases, young men have been taken off of buses in Kabul or even from villages known to be insurgent strongholds. Despite this and other measures, defections have kept pace with enlistments and the size of the army has remained around 30,000 effectives.[10] In July 1981, the government, by design or incompetence, committed some 300 cadets of the Afghan Military Academy to combat only sixteen miles from Kabul. The results were devastating: as many as 70 were killed and 200 defected.[11] The government lamentably televised the funerals of some 30 cadets. In a similarly tragic vein, more than 100 young party activists were killed in ambushes when they were sent in June 1982 to the explosive Panjsher Valley to support a military operation there. The militia, despite high pay, is similarly unreliable. Nearly 3,000 militia defected to the resistance in the fall of 1984 and guerrilla leaders regard the militia as one of their prime sources of weapons.[12]

The effects of the war have also complicated matters for the regime. The population of Kabul has doubled and more than 30 percent of the pre-war population now resides in Pakistan or Iran. As table 9–1 shows,

Table 9–1
Number of Registered Afghan Refugees in Pakistan

Date	Number of Refugees
April–December 1978	18,329
January–December 1979	389,072
January 1980	427,580
February 1980	538,099
March 1980	599,050
April 1980	650,076
May 1980	720,495
June 1980	779,059
July 1980	839,260
August 1980	926,216
September 1980	996,872
October 1980	1,054,148
November 1980	1,148,470
December 1980	1,232,253
January 1981	1,310,928
February 1981	1,490,301
March 1981	1,560,912
April 1981	1,688,289
May 1981	1,812,001
June 1981	1,835,894
July 1981	1,859,639
August 1981	1,887,639
September 1981	1,906,826
October 1981	1,913,412
November 1982	2,800,000

Source: Official Pakistani Data, cited in the testimony of Dr. Zalmay Khalilzad before the Senate Committee on Foreign Relations, March 8, 1982, p. 84; and *New York Times*, November 22, 1982, p. A5.

the refugee population in Pakistan continued to increase up to the end of 1982. Despite much international aid, the living conditions in some of the 300 camps in Pakistan are very difficult.

One U.S. scholar reported in 1982 that

> Life in many of the refugee camps is extremely difficult. For example, at the Panya Camp in Haripoor, which I visited, some 80,000 Afghan refugees reside. As of 6 weeks ago the people in this camp had only 250 tents and 1,000 blankets. So there were thousands without either tents or blankets. Two Pakistani officials who run the camp told shocking stories of human tragedy that they witnessed every day. A number of refugees have come to Pakistan believing that life in the camps would be very different than it actually is. The exodus of large numbers of the

Afghans helps the Soviets, as it results in the emptying of the areas of resistance.[13]

The refugee situation also represents a brain drain for the government and serves as a very clear mirror of its illegitimate status in the eyes of the Afghan people. On the other hand, the internal and external refugees represent an erosion of the guerrillas' support base, and thus the regime's only claim to progress.

Current Military Operations

The current situation in Afghanistan pits roughly 120,000 Soviet and 30,000 Afghan troops against 85–100,000 freedom fighters. Soviet forces (the 40th Army), according to unclassified sources, are composed of six divisions, at least one Air Assault Brigade (about 2,000 men), and four or five separate regiments or brigades, backed up by an undisclosed number of spetsnaz, (commando) units, around 240 gunships, 400 other helicopters, several squadrons of MiG–21s and 23s, and at least one squadron of Su–25 attack aircraft. The deployment of this latter aircraft is significant in that the Soviets have chosen Afghanistan as the location for its first operational deployment.[14] Recent reports indicated MiG–25s configured for reconnaissance may also be in the country. Persistent reports also have an unknown number of Cuban, Vietnamese, and East European advisers and troops in Afghanistan.[15]

Soviet forces in Afghanistan include up to 80,000 ground troops, 30–40,000 general support troops, and 10,000 Air Force personnel. These forces are supported by 50,000 ground force and air force personnel in the southern part of the USSR. Divisional deployments are geographically balanced with about one-third of the ground force total in the Kabul area with other major deployments at Mazar-i-Sharif and Quonduz in the north, Herat and Farah in the east, Kandahar in the south, and Jalalabad in the east. Major air bases are located in Herat, Shindand, Farah, Kandahar, Kabul, Bagram, and Jalalabad.

The insurgents are generally affiliated with seven loosely organized, shifting, and disunited resistance groups which included in 1983 two factions of the Hezbi Islami, the Harakat-Enkelab, the Jamiat Islami, the Jabbha-e Najat-e Melli Afghanistan (Professor Mojaddedi), the Gailani and M. Nabi parties, and the Shiite Shura group. All of these groups fight in anything from platoon to regimental strength and most have both village militia and full-time fighting units. Armaments vary, with some units having one Kalashnikov (AK) automatic rifle per platoon, while others have nearly all of their fighters equipped with AKs.[16] Fire support is limited, in the main, to rocket-propelled grenades, machine guns, and mortars. Although some analysts put foreign aid to the insurgents at around $350 million (1980–84) from the U.S. alone, relatively little materiel has found its way to fighting units.[17] Some observers have noted that the open market price of an AK in Pakistan—about $2,800—did not decline appreciably from 1979 to 1982. The best source of arms is still the Soviet and Afghan forces and most observers agree that foreign assistance accounts for no more than 20 percent of the weapons supplied to even the more active and well-connected resistance groups. The insurgents obtain their arms from deserters, battlefield casualties, and even from enlisting in government militias until they are issued them.[18]

Overall, since mid-1980, the Soviet position in Afghanistan has deteriorated, though not yet to the point where it might jeopardize the entire operation. While territorially based estimates are necessarily suspect, experts have marginally increased their estimate of rebel-controlled territory from 75 percent of the country (December 1980) to as much as 80 percent (December 1982).[19] It would be more accurate to say that perhaps as much as 80 percent of Afghan territory is neither controlled by the Soviets nor the insurgents on a permanent basis. Soviet forces are free to move in strength into almost any area, but neither they nor their Afghan allies possess the numerical strength to occupy and pacify major areas of the country. The insurgents, of course, depend too much on mobility and concealment for their survival to establish effective control. In any case, the major cities and base areas are only safe for the Soviets during daylight hours. In the countryside, only the narrow strip joining China to Afghanistan, the Wakhan Corridor (which has been occupied by the Soviets), and the thinly populated areas in the extreme northwest and southwest of the country are relatively free of rebel activity.

To date, Soviet strategy appears to have been to hold the major centers of communications, limit infiltration, and destroy local strongholds at minimum costs to their own forces. In essence, the Soviet strategy is one wherein high technology, superior tactical mobility, and firepower are used to make up for an insufficient number of troops and to hold Soviet casualties to a minimum. In effect, Soviet policy continues to be a combination of scorched earth and "migratory genocide." Numerous reports have suggested that Soviet forces, in particular their helicopter gunships, have been deliberately used to burn crops and destroy villages in order to force the population—the main source of resistance logistical support—to flee to Pakistan or Iran. Crops are destroyed by napalm or, more frequently, by white phosphorous bombs while still in the fields or after they have been harvested. Other reports suggest that the Soviets have used a free fire zone approach in areas with strong resistance forces.[20]

One should not believe, however, that the Soviets are intent on winning the war solely by military means. Although military operations increased in frequency and scope in 1983–84, the Soviets and the PDPA are placing great importance on educating a new generation of cadres. In the long run, the Soviets apparently believe that the 20,000 young Afghans who are being educated in the USSR will form the nucleus of a new military and party organization which will rule Afghanistan after the resistance has exhausted itself.

Soviet terror tactics have increased in their ferocity since the invasion. Though few would accuse the Afghans of restrained behavior toward their enemies, the Soviet monopoly on high technology has magnified the destructive aspects of their behavior. One expert testified,

> The International Red Cross and other humanitarian organizations are denied access to Afghanistan. Between last October 26 and November 2 [1981], three hospitals operated by a French humanitarian medical organization, in three separate provinces, were demolished by helicopters that singled them out for bombing and rocketing. Helicopters set the crops aflame just before the harvest; village granaries are emptied and destroyed—all in an effort to starve the people into submission. The planes often bear Afghan markings, but the pilots are Soviet, as they have been since mid-1979—although they reportedly sometimes wear Afghan uniforms. . . .[21]

One of the most blatant terror bombings of the war was directed at the picturesque and historic village of Istalif, only thirty miles north of Kabul. From October 12 to 19, 1983, Soviet planes and artillery pounded the village. According to an eyewitness, the bombardment and the subsequent assault damaged 80 percent of the buildings in the historic town. The inhabitants suffered 500 dead and another 500 wounded in the operation. Close to 80 percent of the survivors were forced to migrate, at least temporarily. The Soviets lost forty soldiers in the attack and another forty in a convoy ambush near the battlefield.[22]

The use of plastic caseless mines, usually dropped from helicopters, is a more passive technique that the Soviets have used to destroy the resistance's morale and their ability to maneuver. One resistance leader noted in 1982 that

> The Soviets also drop small antipersonnel mines by helicopter. These mines are in the form of watches, ballpoint pens, or even books. They have caused enormous damage among the civilian population and livestock and many women and children have lost feet or hands.[23]

U.S. government analysts have stated that the war in Afghanistan has cost the Soviets more than $12 billion up to the end of 1983.[24] Total Soviet casualties (killed and wounded) have been estimated at 53,000 (by December 1984), and some sources would add that the Kremlin may have suffered again as many casualties from sickness and disease. Exact figures on the number of Soviets killed in action (1980–84) are impossible to obtain but responsible analysts have cited estimates up to 13,000.[25] The freedom fighters, up to the end of 1982, may have suffered ten times the total number of Soviet casualties with undoubtedly a higher percentage of deaths as well. In all, despite the costs, the Soviets are preparing for a prolonged stay. Permanent logistics facilities and barracks are being constructed. Airfields are being upgraded and the construction of a permanent bridge across the Amu Darya has been completed. The tour of duty for Soviet soldiers has also been set at two years, with rotations of one-quarter of the force generally taking place on a semi-annual basis.[26]

Operationally, new or untried Soviet equipment and ordnance (for example, the improved BMP infantry fighting vehicle, the AK–74 rifle, the Hind helicopter, scatterable mines, the AGS–17 automatic grenade launcher, fuel-air explosives, liquid pressure-sensitive mines) has been tested, and some technical innovations have been made. For example, the Soviets have experimented with a new main armament on some of their BMP infantry fighting vehicles. Based on their Afghan experience, they have moved to replace some of the slow-firing 73 mm cannon with an automatic 30 mm cannon.[27] This change will enable Soviet forces to achieve a larger volume of anti-personnel suppressive fire. The use of helicopters is also important to operations in Afghanistan. Helicopters are used for resupply, reconnaissance, troop transport, fire support, and command and control. Pilot training in Afghanistan is superb. As one Soviet officer described it,

> Flying in the mountains . . . plus the real possibility of coming under fire by anti-aircraft weapons . . . this is a real training school. . . . No wonder they say that after a month in Afghanistan helicopter pilots can be awarded the top proficiency rating. . . .[28]

This pilot training is also costly, however. The rebels have shot down as many as 600 Soviet aircraft, mostly troop-carrying helicopters, primarily with small arms and anti-tank weapons.

According to two highly detailed U.S. State Department reports, Soviet forces have used chemical weapons in at least fifteen provinces of Afghanistan. Witnesses have made a total of fifty-nine separate incident reports, and the State Department noted that at least thirty-six of the reports were corroborated by additional evidence. The Soviet use of chemical weapons—incapacitants, lethal chemicals, and perhaps even mycotoxin biological weapons—apparently continued throughout 1982 even after the first detailed U.S. report appeared in March 1982. The reports conservatively estimate that the attacks have resulted in 3,000 deaths. One other ominous detail did not go unnoticed: detailed survey and monitoring operations following some of the strikes showed that the Soviets were obviously "interested in studying after-effects, lethality, or some other quasi-experimental aspect of a new chemical weapon."[29]

While the question of mycotoxins, artificially manufactured biological weapons, is still the subject of some controversy, the use of lethal chemicals—blood and nerve agents—in Afghanistan has been proven beyond question. Among the more significant proofs, in addition to the statements of hundreds of eyewitnesses, of lethal agent usage are:

The film of Dutch journalist Bernd de Bruin who himself was wounded in an attack where numerous Afghans perished.

The fact that chemical defense battalions were left in place after extraneous military equipment was withdrawn in June 1980.

The testimony of a Soviet POW who was engaged in post-attack survey and monitoring operations.

The testimony of another Soviet POW who detailed chemical storage sites in Afghanistan and who had seen Soviet soldiers who were contaminated by agents directed at the guerrillas.

Positive test results on three Soviet protective masks taken from dead Soviet soldiers in September and December 1981, and one obtained in February 1982.

In addition to experimental purposes, it is not difficult to understand why the Soviet Union would use chemical agents. These weapons can generate tremendous fear and encourage panic. They can also be used to guard exposed flanks and to clear built-up areas or caves of snipers or ambushes. In other words, while inflicting damage and panic on the enemy, they may enable the user to conserve troop strength and to minimize casualties. In any case, the U.S. State Department noted that verified use of lethal agents apparently dropped to almost zero in 1983, although scattered reports again began to appear in 1984.[30]

There is very little reliable information on the performance of Soviet troops in Afghanistan. A distillation of the scant information that is available reveals three points.

1. The initial complement of regular forces were not trained in counterinsurgency or mountain warfare techniques. In December 1981, one

Soviet source even reported that "it took a while for [an Afghan] soldier to believe that the majority of Soviet servicemen had first seen mountains here—in Afghanistan." Not finding the Chinese or U.S. agents whom they were told were causing the trouble has also been bad for morale. Recent interviews with Soviet POWs indicate widespread discontent among Soviet forces.[31]

2. The pace of operations ranges from frantic offensives or damage-limiting operations to long periods of boredom. Soviet soldiers are apparently not coping very well with this and reports of the use of hashish have surfaced. Numerous separate sources have confirmed the widespread use of hashish and the fact that Soviet soldiers have traded truck parts, uniforms, ammunition, and even rifles for hashish or other local drugs.[32] A Soviet defector early in 1984 noted that discipline in the 40th Army is generally poor and when asked about drug problems, he said,

> Drugs? Nobody can deal with them because a great deal of drugs are being used. . . . For the most part they smoke hashish and cocaine. There are also those who shoot. There are not many of them, of course, but there are some. The soldiers get hold of drugs by means of sale and exchange. They sell literally everything possible: fat, butter, canned goods, soap, hardware, and arms and ammunition.[33]

3. Soviet tactics still tend toward an overreliance on motorized rifle and tank troops employed in sweep or hammer and anvil operations, where one element blocks and the other attempts to push the insurgents into the blocking force. Air assault operations, usually of company or battalion strength, are becoming more important although they are usually conducted in conjunction with movements by motorized rifle units. Tanks are apparently being used mostly in a fire support role. Much of the Soviets operational experience apparently has been in road clearing operations, designed to keep open the ground lines of communication. On the whole, airborne and air assault troops seem to be held in higher esteem by the guerrillas than troops from the motorized divisions.

An Afghan army colonel, who was actually working for the resistance, observed the Soviet forces as both ally and adversary. He characterized them as "oversupervised," "lacking initiative," and addicted to "cookbook warfare," wherein proven "battle recipes" are mechanically applied to new situations. S.B. Majrooh, another close observer, said that Soviet soldiers were "generally undisciplined, isolated, and not motivated."[34]

Ambushes of various sizes have proven to be very effective. An Afghan army major described guerrilla tactics in a conversation with a Soviet reporter. Guerrilla bands of thirty to forty men "prefer to use ambushes by bridges, or in defiles. They destroy the bridge or block the road and then open fire from the commanding heights." If they encounter a stronger unit, they let the security element go by and then attack the main body, using obstacles skillfully covered by fire.³⁵

On a whole, Soviet forces deal very poorly with ambushes. Apparently, Soviet forces have no counter-ambush drills as in Western armies, but they prefer to let the resistance take the vehicles they have disabled and to move the rest of the convoy to safety. A few eyewitnesses have reported that the Soviets will frequently move escorting combat vehicles to a safe distance and then shell the captured vehicles. Also, local villages are routinely bombed by Soviet forces shortly after an ambush.³⁶

A Soviet defector in 1982 evaluated the insurgents' resistance as "strong" and noted: "Pilots as well as all soldiers in the Soviet army respect the courage and tactics of the mujahidin and recognize their successes."³⁷

Censorship within the Soviet military and the media is strictly enforced. Accounts of Soviet soldiers in combat are rare, usually anecdotal, and very heavy in propaganda content. In spite of this fact, some truth has emerged in Soviet sources, perhaps because the leadership wants to squelch rumors which may be worse than reality. Early in 1983, *Krasnaia zvezda* (Red Star) reported that duty in Afghanistan "makes special demands" on Soviet servicemen. Not only is the climate difficult but moving through the mountains also "takes a tremendous and intensive effort." The article also noted that the dushmans (bandits) were continuing their piratical onslaughts."³⁸ The "piratical onslaughts" have also been costly for the Soviets. In addition to nearly 600 aircraft, a French doctor, based on an actual count of burned vehicles in a few provinces, estimated Soviet vehicle losses to the end of 1983 throughout Afghanistan at 3,000–4,000.³⁹

The number of major battles involving multiple battalion-sized units apparently increased in 1982 and 1983. Although there were periodic reports of intraresistance fighting, the Peshawar groups formed two temporary coalitions, both called the "Islamic Unity of Afghan Mujahidin" early in 1981. A year later one alliance fought a coordinated battle in Paktia province in which they defeated two Soviet regiments, destroying twenty-five vehicles and killing sixty Soviet soldiers in the process. Other reports of coordinated multi-battalion operations appeared early in 1983, but they are by far more the exception than the rule.⁴⁰ Local commanders from diverse groups, however, have frequently cooperated in local operations.

There are few accurate accounts of entire battles by which we can judge the state of Soviet military art in Afghanistan. One month-long operation in 1982 was witnessed by *Christian Science Monitor* correspondent Edward Giradet.⁴¹ The battle was apparently designed to eliminate the 3,000 fighters of Ahmed Shah Massoud who had been implicated in numerous raids, including at least one successful penetration of Bagram Airbase. Four previous Soviet forays into the Panjsher Valley had failed to eliminate this resistance unit. While the operation was significant because of its size, it was also important because it appeared to represent an archetypical Soviet battle recipe which has been used time and again in Afghanistan in the past three years.

After an entire week of aerial bombardment, Soviet and Afghan forces were inserted by helicopter into the narrow east-west Panjsher corridor on May 17. The insurgents, having been previously warned of the Soviet battle plan, had escaped down the side valleys or on to the top of the ridge lines. As a *Pravda* military correspondent noted, the first waves of attackers encountered "a multilevel system of fire prepared in advance."⁴² Three days later a tank/motorized-rifle force entered the valley bringing the total of Soviet and Afghan forces to 12–15,000. A series of sharp engagements followed, and within the first ten days fifty Soviet and Afghan vehicles and thirty-five helicopters (by resistance reports) were destroyed in the fighting and the freedom fighters may have netted 100 AK–74 rifles. The Soviets destroyed up to 80 percent of the dwellings in some areas and killed nearly 200 freedom fighters and close to 1,200 civilians, more than 1 percent of the Panjsher's population, but were forced to begin withdrawing on June 13.⁴³ In early September, Soviet fighter planes again began bombing the Panjsher valley. The sixth Soviet offensive against Massoud's forces had begun.

Panjsher VI was a failure also. The Soviets subsequently entered into a truce with Massoud which lasted until April 1984, at which time the Soviets tried again to do away with the charismatic Massoud. Preceded by more than forty Tu–16 strategic bombers, and dozens of Su–24 fighter-bombers—both types being flown from bases inside the USSR—20,000 Soviet troops entered the valley. By November 1984, however, it was again clear that they had failed to capture Massoud or to destroy his forces. The "final solution" to the problem of the Panjsher—Afghan and Soviet propaganda to the contrary—remains in the future.

As a result of the increased fighting in 1981, following a December visit by Marshal Sokolov, a first deputy defense minister, the Soviets added 20,000 additional troops to their complement in Afghanistan. Another 10,000 were added in 1984.

At this point, it is important to point out what the Soviets are not doing in Afghanistan. First, the Soviets have not exploited Baluch separatism by arming irredentist forces. Although there have been scattered reports of Soviet agents in Baluch areas,⁴⁴ there is no significant proof that the Soviets are actively using the Baluchistan lever against Iran or

Pakistan, though they may be keeping their long-term options open in this area.

A number of factors explain Soviet reluctance to exploit the Baluch situation. First, only 90,000 of the 5 million Baluch live in Afghanistan. Secondly, there are significant age and tribal splits among the Baluch. They are far from a single united movement. Third, the Pakistanis have made concerted efforts to garner support among this tribe, although there is apparently far to go in this area. Finally, the Soviets have always been reluctant to vigorously support an independent Baluchistan.[45] Many countries close to the Soviets, like Ethiopia or Iraq, would not support any irredentist movement which might tend to set a negative precedent for their own country. The Baluch problem represents a potential problem of tremendous significance in the region; however, at present, the Soviet policy toward the Baluch provides little proof of larger Soviet designs in the area in the immediate future.

Soviet operations up to the end of 1984 also provide little proof that the Soviets are planning to invade Iran or Pakistan. The size of the Soviet force in Afghanistan is far too small and the relatively balanced geographic distribution does not suggest preparation for any such thrust. Pressure tactics (discussed below) are being applied against Pakistan, but, overall, despite improved opportunities to perform reconnaissance over the Indian Ocean and the closing off of a potential Chinese approach to Afghanistan through the occupied Wakhan corridor, the Soviet invasion has not, to December 1984, brought about any of the disastrous putative consequences predicted by many at the onset of the invasion.

One must add at this point that the end of this war is not in sight. While it is clear that the Soviets do not have sufficient forces in Afghanistan to pacify a country the size of Texas, it is similarly clear that they have not moved toward a withdrawal, nor have they made a decision to attempt to quickly conclude the war on a military level.

Soviet Foreign Policy

Throughout the period in question, the Soviet assessment of the situation in and concerning Afghanistan was—at least for the near-term future—primarily negative. Numerous officials expressed concern over the problem. In March 1981, in response to prodding by American members of a panel in Cincinnati, Ohio, Vitaliy Kobysh, deputy head of the Central Committee International Information Department, characterized the invasion as "a mistake."[46] A month later, Yuri Velikanov, a Soviet diplomat stationed in the strategically important Seychelle Islands called the situation in Afghanistan "an embarrassment" and noted that "there were mistakes when we went in, and we are looking for ways to get out."⁴⁷

Into the spring of 1983, Babrak Karmal still claimed that without Soviet support, "it is unknown what the destiny of the Afghan Revolution would be. . . . We are realists and clearly realize that in store for us yet lie trials and deprivations, losses and difficulties."⁴⁸ Just two weeks before, Prime Minister Keshtmand had admitted that half of the country's schools and three-quarters of its communication lines had been destroyed since 1979.⁴⁹

The Soviet propaganda machinery continued to emphasize the themes it had concentrated on in early 1980. According to Soviet media, the invasion was necessitated by outside interference, most of it from the "Maoist military base" in Pakistan. The U.S. objective, according to A. Petrov, was to "destabilize . . . the entire region from South Asia to the Persian Gulf."⁵⁰ China and Pakistan were U.S. instruments. Claims of outside military aid to the resistance grew, with Soviet "estimates" normally running twice what the U.S. media were reporting as the amount of U.S. aid to the freedom fighters.⁵¹

Pakistan came in for particularly harsh treatment from the Soviet media. Soviet moves were not limited to propaganda. Writing in January 1982, Francis Fukuyama of the U.S. State Department noted,

> Since September, there have been at least ten serious incursions over the Durand Line by Afghan and/or Soviet forces. Most of these involved attacks by MIGs or helicopter gunships against Pakistani border posts or Afghan refugee camps. One, however, consisted of a ground operation by forty Afghan troops against an outpost in Baluchistan. There were, in addition, hundreds of airspace violations, some probably unintentional but many intended to convey a clear political signal to Pakistan. The Soviets also delivered a number of direct and rather bluntly worded warnings to the Pakistani government not to support the Afghan Mujahedeen or to proceed in the security relationship with the United States. The Soviets appear to have given support to (or at least allowed the Afghan government to assist) the al-Zulfiqar terrorist group headed by Murtaza Bhutto, which was responsible for hijacking a Pakistani airliner in March 1981.⁵²

In all, the Pakistanis claimed more than 400 border violations since December 1979. In 1984 alone, Soviet-Afghan air and artillery "errors" killed more than 200 people in Pakistan.

The Reagan administration completed negotiation on a $3.2 billion aid package for Pakistan (1982–88). Although half of this was economic aid, the other half would include 40 F–16 fighters, 100 M–48A5 tanks, 1,005 howitzers and 10 attack helicopters. In return for this aid, Pakistan reportedly assured the United States that it would not develop nuclear weapons.[53]

This package sparked repeated charges in *Pravda* that the U.S. package destabilized the region and threatened India. For its part, the Indian government was particularly concerned about the F–16s which, as Indira Gandhi noted, had an offensive strike capacity three times that of India's Soviet-built MiG–21s.[54] As previously indicated, the Soviets attempted to check this move with a $1.6 million arms transfer to India in late 1980.

India, without disturbing its good relations with the Soviets, sought to close the rift between itself and both China and Pakistan. Speaking about Pakistan, Indira Gandhi pointed out in a 1982 interview that she placed a high degree of importance on regional stability: "Nothing is so dangerous as a weak neighbor."[55] Early in 1983, President Zia ul-Haq travelled to Delhi and secured an agreement with Indira Gandhi to form a commission aimed at improving economic, industrial, and cultural relations. Both sides agreed to consider negotiations on a nonaggression pact.[56]

In other areas, India made a major grain purchase from the United States in 1981 and agreed to mutually acceptable procedures on purchasing fuel for the Tarapur nuclear reactor. In 1981, India also announced that it would broaden its sources of arms and purchased 150 advanced Mirage fighters from France. Discussions began in 1982 to purchase U.S. weapons as well. All of this was not a direct setback for the Soviets but it did appear to rule out any near-term Soviet moves which might include using India against Pakistan. In all, however, Soviet-Indian relations remained excellent and, from the Soviet perspective, represented a major success in their post-invasion damage limitation campaign.

The situation in Soviet-Iranian relation continued its downhill slide. Although, as previously noted, the Soviets greeted the Khomeini-led revolution as a progressive development, as early as mid-1979 it had begun to express its reservations and fears about the Teheran regime. The Khomeini regime, in a fairly consistent fashion, maintained a self-serving "neither East nor West" position. Even though Moscow maintained neutrality at the start of the Iran-Iraq war, even to the point of using its Twenty-sixth Party Congress as a platform to permit the outlawed Iraqi Communist Party to condemn the war, the Soviets were not able to make significant progress in their relations in Iran.

Angered over Soviet spying, the occupation of Afghanistan, and a Soviet tilt toward Iraq in its war with Iran, Iranian authorities began to curtail Soviet activities in Iran. After praising economic cooperation and citing Soviet support for Iran during the hostage crisis, a *Pravda* correspondent noted in March 1981 that the Iranians had reduced the Soviet embassy staff, closed a Soviet consulate, and refused visas for Soviet journalists. The Soviet-Iranian friendship society was closed down and a host of commercial activities were also curtailed. Iran, to the Soviets, chagrin, also began to speak of "two threats," putting the U.S. and the USSR on a nearly equal footing.[57] The source of the problem in Iran, according to repeated Soviet and Tudeh party analyses, was certain "extreme right-wing elements and members of the clergy."[58]

In July 1982, Iran's forces turned their guns on the Tudeh party, but only after Iranian forces had crossed over into Iraq and a Soviet military resupply of Iraq had been initiated. This action was accompanied by the expulsion from Iran of eighteen Soviet diplomats. By February 1983, N. Kianuri, the head of the Tudeh party, was taken into custody, soon to be followed by 1,500 other Tudeh party members.[59] Robert Rand wrote,

> Iran's decision to crack down on the Tudeh Party mirrors the growing deterioration in Tehran's ties with the Soviet Union, a condition in large part attributable to Iran's dissatisfaction with the Kremlin's policy toward the Iran-Iraq war. The Soviet Union, which originally took pains to remain neutral in the conflict despite bilateral treaty obligations with Iran, has since pursued a stance that is sympathetic to Baghdad.
> The change of heart came about last year after Iran refused to heed a Soviet-endorsed United Nations ceasefire resolution and instead expanded the war by invading Iraqi territory. Iranian opposition to the change in Soviet policy, together with Tehran's continued anger over the USSR's presence in Afghanistan, may have convinced the Khomeini government that it no longer has anything to gain by tolerating the continued existence of the pro-Soviet Tudeh Party.[60]

For its part, Soviet patience was also limited. As one Soviet analyst told Karen Dawisha, "there must come a point at which we can no longer support a regime which hurls the people back into the sixteenth century."[61] Although that point has not yet arrived, it may be fast approaching.

On other fronts, condemnations of Soviet activities became pro forma. In addition to condemnation by Islamic foreign ministers in January and May 1980, the United Nations General Assembly continued yearly to condemn the Soviet Union—usually without mentioning it by name—for its activities in Afghanistan. In each of the five UN condemnations, no fewer than 104 nations voted against the Soviets on each occasion. In general, Soviet support was limited to Warsaw Pact nations, regimes with a socialist orientation, or other countries, like Syria and Libya, with close connections to the Soviet Union.

Because of the battlefield situation, international pressure, and other problems described in this chapter, since February 1980 the Soviets have been seeking a diplomatic way to extricate themselves from the Afghan quagmire. Soviet peacemaking attempts have been conducted in the context of continuing to fight in Afghanistan. Moreover, as described above, the Soviets, though not committed to a solely military victory in Afghanistan, have reinforced their limited contingent by more than one-third its original size and have consistently improved their logistical and basing infrastructure in Afghanistan. In short, they have not evidenced any desire for "peace at any price." Although there have been changes in nuance and some rather interesting unofficial statements, the formal Soviet position as described in chapter 6 has changed little since February 1980.

Two significant changes in the Soviet position concern the role of third parties, and the pace of the withdrawal.

Up to the summer of 1981, the Soviets rejected peace plans put forward inter alia by the United States, France, and the European Community. This last initiative, the "Carrington Plan," was rejected in July 1981 because (1) it did not include the Karmal government in early discussions, (2) it did include rebel representation, and (3) it spoke of neutralization, which the Soviets saw as a much more heinous state than nonalignment and which implied that the Karmal government would cease to exist.[62] This last item violated the Soviet pledge that it would not go behind Karmal's back and their assertion that the gains of the revolution were permanent. Brezhnev himself said at the Twenty-sixth Party Congress in 1981,

> We do not object to the questions connected with Afghanistan being discussed together with the questions of Persian Gulf security. Naturally, this applies only to the international aspects of the Afghan problem, and not to internal Afghan affairs. Afghanistan's sovereignty, like its nonaligned status, must be fully protected.[63]

The United Nations, in conjunction with Pakistan and Afghanistan and in accordance with a General Assembly resolution in November 1980, began negotiation on the conduct of trilateral (Afghanistan, Pakistan, and Iran) indirect talks to be held under UN auspices. Pakistan and Afghanistan agreed in principle to the format in January 1981, and the Soviets and Afghans agreed formally to pursue this avenue the following August. Iran has refused to participate but is being kept informed of the talks.[64]

The format of the talks was innovative. UN representatives talked to one side and then the other, obviating the need for the Pakistanis to recognize the Karmal government. The Pakistani position is clear. It wants total Soviet withdrawal; restoration of the nonaligned and independent status of Afghanistan; freedom from outside intervention; and the safe return home of the Afghan refugees. In the UN format, the Pakistanis can at least talk to Afghanistan without recognizing the Karmal government, and thereby admitting the Soviet charge that Pakistani support for the resistance is equivalent to outside interference.

Meetings took place in June 1982 and intermittently thereafter. Although there have been numerous reports of progress, by the end of 1982 little apparent progress had been made. In October 1982, Karmal characterized Iran's and Pakistan's response to Afghan peace initiatives in the following manner: "Iran and Pakistan have so far not adopted concrete and constructive positions."[65] In February 1983, after a subsequent round of talks, Karmal stated that these discussions could bear fruit "whenever the other side shows readiness to conduct talks with the necessary realism and goodwill.[66] The ever-optimistic UN Secretary General Javier Perez de Cuellar noted about the same time, "if you want one to tell you that Mr. Andropov will withdraw Soviet troops tomorrow, I think that you are not as naive as that."[67] In April 1983, after two more rounds of talks, Andropov himself characterized the talks as useful, and "having some prospects," but, he added, the Pakistanis were "still being held by their sleeve by their overseas friends."[68]

There has been some slow movement by the Soviets on the question of the pace of troop withdrawals. Although their initial position stated that they would begin to withdraw *after* all interference had stopped, since 1981 there have been preliminary indications that a Soviet troop withdrawal could be phased into a peace agreement. Brezhnev himself noted that a settlement could generate, "with the concurrence of Afghan side, a time schedule and procedures for the withdrawal of Soviet troops from Afghanistan." He added that withdrawals could begin as the agreements were implemented.[69]

Aside from this glimmer, there have been only rare flashes of hope for a peaceful solution to this problem. When Brezhnev died in November 1982, many thought that Andropov, long rumored to have been against the invasion, would quickly move to end the war. These rumors were supported by some observers, like President Zia, who noted on meeting Andropov that there was a "hint of flexibility" in the Soviet attitude toward Afghanistan.[70] Even the chief editor of *Pravda*, Viktor Afanasyev, who is also a full Central Committee member, went beyond the official line when he told a Japanese newspaper that the USSR wanted a political settlement and that the Afghan government "need not be a Soviet-type socialist government."[71]

The Soviet media soon contradicted Afanasyev and retorted that the Soviet position remained unchanged. Eight months after Brezhnev died,

Andropov indicated how little movement there has really been in the Soviet position:

> Our plans for a political settlement of the Afghan problem are no secret. We have repeatedly stated them publicly. Leonid Ilyich Brezhnev spoke about that. We consider that as soon as outside interference in the affairs of Afghanistan has been terminated and nonresumption of such interference guaranteed, we shall withdraw our troops. Our troops are staying in that country at the request of the lawful Afghan government . . . and they continue staying there at the request of the lawful government headed by Babrak Karmal. We are not after anything for ourselves there. We responded to the request for assistance from a friendly neighboring country. It is, however, far from being a matter of indifference to us what is happening directly on our southern border.[72]

The frequent rumors that the USSR would be willing to sacrifice Karmal and his government for a settlement have not been substantiated. The future of the Karmal government remains a major sticking point in the talks. The Soviets insist on its legitimacy and Pakistan has continued to reiterate Zia's stand of December 1982: "Pakistan will not talk to this man who came to be the head of the Afghan regime by riding on Soviet tanks."[73]

Overall, Soviet efforts to gain a peace in Afghanistan have not progressed very far, and at the end of 1984 both sides were still far apart on a number of issues, including the fate of the Karmal regime, the methods of sealing the border to secure the peace, the scope and speed of the Soviet withdrawal, and the nature of international guarantees of the solution. The Soviets have not put all their effort into making peace. The rigidity of their proposals, when coupled with their military measures inside Afghanistan, suggests that, even though they are pessimistic about the present situation in Afghanistan, they do not perceive the costs of continued operations in Afghanistan to be overwhelmingly excessive. It is quite possible that, as a U.S. diplomat in Moscow told this author, they believe that they have absorbed the worst of the costs (the grain embargo, the Olympic Boycott) and that now it is simply a matter of endurance and fortitude, virtues which their historical experience and highly authoritarian government have given them in great quantities.[74] The Soviets are prepared for peace on their terms or the continuation of warfare at the present level for the foreseeable future.

As Charles Dunbar, the former U.S. chargé d'affaires in Kabul, noted late in 1983,

> Soviet diplomats [in Afghanistan] have been free to admit that the Soviet position in Afghanistan was very poor and that anything other than

a long-term solution was unlikely. They have always said, though, that it was Soviet policy to pursue such a long-term solution.[75]

In light of the previous examination of Soviet motives, it is not difficult to understand why there has been such little change in Soviet peace proposals. The potential for PDPA disintegration is still high and the threat, in Soviet eyes, to its own security is there as well. Indeed, there is even less likelihood that a new, non-PDPA regime could ever—given cultural constraints—behave in a "good neighbor" fashion toward the Soviet Union. The specter of encirclement is still present, and so is the threat of lost prestige. It is one thing to desert an ally, but it is even more damaging to prestige to try very hard to save him and then fail. The Soviets are caught in a trap of their own construction.

Ironically, however, the prognosis for Soviet policy is anything but grim. International pressure on the Soviet Union had subsided, and even with the ritual condemnations of Soviet policy and few thousand casualties per year, the price attached to the war apparently remains, in the eyes of the Soviet leadership, quite manageable. The Soviets know that they are not winning now, but they appear to be quite confident that, in the long term, the resistance will exhaust itself and the 20,000 young Afghans now being trained in the USSR will one day be able to build another communist satellite on the Soviet periphery.

Although a Soviet victory in Afghanistan would not disturb the global balance of power nor provide the Soviets with a convenient base to invade Iran or to strike the Straits of Hormuz, it would be a blow to Western interests and a destabilizing factor in the region. A Soviet victory would improve the Soviet ability to subvert Iran and Pakistan and convince the nations in the region that they will have to come to terms with the USSR by themselves. The West would appear to be, at best, a fair-weather ally, not one to be counted on in the long run or when conflicts arise.

Even more important is the lesson that a communist victory in Afghanistan would hold for the Soviet leadership. Having chosen Afghanistan as the first Third World nation in which to apply the recipe that they used to restore order in Czechoslovakia in 1968, they may come to believe that this tired recipe may be appropriate to other areas of the Third World as well. If history teaches anything, it has taught us that successful acts of aggression breed unhappy repetitions of the same.

Clearly, the West needs to prevent future Afghanistans by insuring that the Afghan freedom fighters are successful in their attempt to remove the Soviets from their homeland. To do this, the West, along with the PRC and Pakistan and other interested nations in the region, must adopt a long-term, coordinated strategy, oriented toward achieving a complete Soviet pullout from Afghanistan. To convince the Soviets that the cost of their occupation of Afghanistan outweighs any future benefits that could be attained there, this strategy might include

> The recognition of an Afghan government-in-exile composed of representatives from the various resistance groups.
>
> The unseating of Kabul's present delegations in international organizations and their replacement with delegations from the government-in-exile.
>
> An increase in economic and military aid (including Western weapons) to the new government-in-exile.
>
> The training of Afghan resistance leaders in regional and Western military schools.
>
> An increase in radar and air defense weapons for Pakistan to help it deal with border violations, coupled with a U.S. condemnation of such incidents and a declaration that we intend to assist Pakistan in this matter.
>
> The insistence by the United States and China that a Soviet withdrawal must be a prelude to any further normalization of economic relations between the parties.

Having taken these actions, the interested parties would be in a good position years hence to propose multilateral negotiations—including representatives from the freedom fighters—to discuss the future of Afghanistan. This could be followed by an internationally supervised plebiscite to decide the shape of a future Afghan government. To answer Soviet security concerns, the new government could declare perpetual nonalignment and abjure both alliances with and military assistance from the superpowers.

None of these measures will come without considerable cost or effort. If taken together, however, they could in the long run dramatically increase political and military pressure on the USSR and form the basis of a strategy to achieve a just and lasting peace in Afghanistan. The alternative is—a decade or two hence—a communist Afghanistan and a destabilized Southwest Asia.

Notes

1. On feuding, see U.S. Dept. of State, *Soviet Dilemmas in Afghanistan;* U.S. Dept. of State, *Afghanistan: Three Years of Occupation,* pp. 1, 6–7; Wafadar, "Afghanistan in 1981: The Struggle Intensifies," pp. 148–150.

2. Wafadar, "Afghanistan in 1981," p. 149. Also, *Afghanistan: Three Years of Occupation,* pp. 6–7.

3. *Afghanistan: Three Years of Occupation,* p. 5. U.S. Dept. of State, *Afghanistan: Four Years of Occupation,* p. 5.

4. Kabul Radio, November 14, 1980 in FBIS–South Asia–VII–223–11/17/80–C4. Cf. U.S. Dept. of State, *Afghanistan: Five Years of Occupation,* pp. 5–6.

5. *New York Times,* August 19, 1981, p. 3.

6. Kabul Radio, November 14, 1980.

7. On aid and trade, see Tass releases in FBIS–Soviet Union–III–176–and 251–9/9/80 and 12/29/80, respectively—p. D1 in both. Also, *Izvestiia,* August 20, 1980, p. 5 in FBIS–Soviet Union–III–166–8/25/80–D4. Also, "Russia in Afghanistan," *Economist,* May 23, 1981, pp. 33–37, and *New York Times,* June 6, 1984, p. 11.

8. *Wall Street Journal,* September 16, 1981, p. 26.

9. On economic relations before the invasion see Tenson, "Soviet View of Soviet-Afghan Relations," pp. 1–4; and CIA, *Communist Aid to Less Developed Countries of the Free World,* pp. 5–6. On trade after the invasion see Bush, "Trade Between USSR and Afghanistan." On the Afghan resource base, see John F. Shroder's input to U.S. Congress, Senate Committee on Foreign Relations, *Hearings on the Situation in Afghanistan,* pp. 59–68.

10. See *New York Times,* January 20, 1982, p. 12; *New York Times,* January 19, 1983, p. 4; U.S. Dept. of State, *Soviet Dilemmas in Afghanistan;* and Wafadar, "Afghanistan in 1981," p. 150. For information on draft measures, in 1984, see *Afghan Information Center Monthly Bulletin* (Peshawar), March 1984, p. 9.

11. Cf. *New York Times,* July 23, 1981, p. 3 and *Christian Science Monitor,* July 23, 1981, p. 1.

12. *New York Times,* June 30, 1982, p. 3; and U.S. Dept. of State, *Afghanistan: Three Years of Occupation,* p. 7; *Afghan Information Center Monthly Bulletin,* September 1984, p. 2.

13. Zalmay Khalilzad's testimony in Senate Committee on Foreign Relations, *Hearings on the Situation in Afghanistan,* p. 81.

14. For the Soviet order of battle, see Isby, "Afghanistan 1982: the War Continues," pp. 1523–26.

15. *New York Times,* December 26, 1980, p. 3; and December 20, 1982, p. 10. See also Agence France Press dispatch (Spanish), November 28, 1980 in FBIS–South Asia–VII–232–2/1/80–C8.

16. On weapons prices, cf. *New York Times,* January 12, 1982, p. 2 and *Christian Science Monitor* series on the Panjsher campaign, noted below. On groups and fronts, see Khalilzad, "Soviet Occupied Afghanistan," pp. 36–8; Gerard Viguie, "Afghanistan: Le Poids du Reel," *Etudes Polemologiques* 27 (April 1983): 39–50; and speeches by Olivier Roy and Jean-Jose Puig at the Institut Francais de Polemologie, Colloque sur Afghanistan, Paris, April 5–6, 1984.

17. On foreign assistance to the freedom fighters, see *New York Times,*

January 22, and April 14, 1981, p. 3 (both editions); *New York Times*, September 23, 1981, p. 15; and Bernstein, "Arms for Afghanistan," pp. 8–10. Also, *New York Times*, May 4, 1983, p. 1, and July 28, 1984, p. 4.

18. Cf. *New York Times*, January 12, 1982, p. 2; and Fukuyama, *The Future of the Soviet Role in Afghanistan*, p. 12. Also, remarks by Bernard Dupaigne, *Colloque sur Afghanistan*. The 80 percent figure was used by the Panjsher commander, A.S. Massoud, in *Washington Post*, October 18, 1983, p. 12, and confirmed by many Western eyewitnesses. In central and western Afghanistan, the amount of foreign-supplied arms is probably much lower than 20 percent.

19. *New York Times*, December 26, 1980, p. 7, and U.S. Department of State, *Afghanistan: Three Years of Occupation*. A Soviet defector in 1984 estimated only 18 percent Soviet control. See *Radio Liberty Research Bulletin*, RL 121/84, March 19, 1984.

20. See Rosanne Klass' statement in *Hearings on the Situation in Afghanistan*, pp. 71–5. Interview with Louis Dupree concerning his trip to the Jalalabad area, New York, April 3, 1984.

21. Klass' statement, p. 72–3.

22. *Les Nouvelles d'Afghanistan* (Paris), March-April 1984, p. 4.

23. *Les Nouvelles d'Afghanistan* (Paris), July-December 1982, pp. 4–16 in JPRS 81812, September 21, 1982, p. 21.

24. Remarks by State Department analyst at the National Forum on Afghanistan, Washington, D.C., December 1983.

25. Some official sources now use 10,000 (through 1983) as the high range estimate of Soviet KIAs. This fact was announced by Ambassador Charles Dunbar at the Harvard–State Department Conference on Afghanistan, October 1983. A State Department estimate of 20–25,000 killed and wounded can be found in *Afghan Resistance and Soviet Occupation*, p. 2.

26. *Soviet Dilemmas in Afghanistan*, p. 3.

27. Mining operations are described in *Washington Post*, July 8, 1980. Photographs of the scatterable mines can be found in *Soldier of Fortune*, April 1981, pp. 23–24. Also see DIA, *Review of Soviet Ground Forces*, May 1980, February 1981, June 1981, for details on AK–74, and AGS–17. On the improved BMP (BMP–2) see DIA, *Review of Soviet Ground Forces*, April 1982, and also *New York Times*, November 8, 1982, p. 1.

28. Colonel V. Stulovskiy, "Stationed in Afghanistan," *Voyennyye znaniya*, March 1981, as cited in Hart, "Low Intensity Conflict in Afghanistan," pp. 66–7.

29. U.S. Department of State, *Chemical Warfare in South Asia and Afghanistan*. The quote is from the former publication, p. 23.

30. Ibid. See also, *Afghanistan: Three Years of Occupation*, p. 5, and the unpublished U.S. State Department collection of media reports, "Reports of the Use of Chemical Weapons in Afghanistan, Laos and Kampuchea, Summer 1980," pp. 4–30. For 1983, see Ambassador Kirkpatrick's submission to U.N. Secretary General in U.S. State Department, *Chemical Weapons Use in Southeast Asia and Afghanistan*, Current Policy 553, February 1984.

31. The quote can be found in *Krasnaia zvezda*, December 31, 1981, p. 2, in FBIS–Soviet Union–III–003–1/6/82–D2–5. An interview with a Soviet officer POW can be found in an Agence France Presse dispatch of April 29, 1982, from Hong Kong. Interview with Soviet enlisted defectors can be found in: *Die*

Welt, October 29, 1982 p. 8, translated in FBIS–Soviet Union–III–212–11/2/82–D1–4; and *Washington Times,* January 23, 1984, p. 2.

32. *Washington Times,* January 23, 1984, p. 2;*Washington Post,* September 28, 1981, p. 15; *Washington Post,* December 27, 1981, p. 1; *New York Times,* January 12, 1982, p. 2; and Agence France Presse dispatch of December 3, 1980, in FBIS–South Asia–VIII–235–12/4/80–C3.

33. See the Radio Liberty interview with a Soviet defector from a Jalalabad-based unit reprinted in "A Soviet Soldier Opts Out in Afghanistan," *Radio Liberty Research Bulletin,* RL 121/84, March 19, 1984, pp. 1–16.

34. On road clearing, see for example, *Komsomolskaia Pravda,* August 7, 1981, p. 2, in FBIS–Soviet Union–III–156–8/13/81–D5–9. The quote on performance is from an interview with Colonel A.A. Jalali, Washington, D.C., April 6, 1983. Majrooh, now Director of the Afghan Information Service, made these remarks at the Harvard–State Department Conference, October 1983.

35. *Pravda,* June 5, 1980 in USAF, *Soviet Press: Selected Translations,* September 1981, p. 273.

36. Interview with Bernard Dupaigne and Tim Cooper, a freelance journalist, both of whom had witnessed Soviet behavior in ambush situations. Paris, April 1984.

37. *Die Welt,* October 29, 1982, p. 8 in FBIS–Soviet Union–III–212–11/2/82–D1–4.

38. *Krasnaia zvezda,* February 26, 1983, p. 1.

39. Speech given by Claude Malhuret, M.D. at the Harvard–State Department Conference on Afghanistan, October 1983.

40. Interview with Colonel A.A. Jalali, former Assistant Chief of the Military Committee of the Islamic Unity of Afghan Mujahiddin, in Washington, D.C., April 6, 1983. See also, *New York Times,* April 21, 1981, p. A11.

41. *Christian Science Monitor,* June 22, 28; July 2, 7, 9, 1982. Also see the description in *Afghanistan: Three Years of Occupation,* pp. 2–4.

42. *Pravda,* August 3, 1982, p. 6. Both the *Pravda* military correspondent, a rear admiral, and Giradet reported that the mujahiddin had at least portions of the Soviet battle plan prior to the start of the battle.

43. Interview with a French doctor who was an eyewitness to Panjsher fighting, Paris, April 1984. For data on Panjsher VII, see *Afghan Information Center Monthly Bulletin,* April 1984; *Les Nouvelles d'Afghanistan,* June–August 1984; and *Newsweek,* June 11, 1984.

44. *New York Times,* April 6, 1980, p. 16. According to Louis Durpee, the Afghan consul in Quetta is funding Baluch youth groups that have a separatist orientation. Interview, New York, April 3, 1984.

45. On the Baluch problem, see Harrison, "Nightmare in Baluchistan," pp. 136–60; Griffith, "The USSR in Pakistan," pp. 38–44; and Fukuyama, *Pakistan Since the Soviet Invasion of Afghanistan,* pp. 9–10. Both Griffith and Harrison do not believe that the Soviets can make good use of the Baluch separatist movement in the near future.

46. This remark was made during the question and answer sessions following Kobysh's address before the Section on Soviet-American Relations, 23d Annual International Studies Association Convention, Cincinnati, Ohio, March 26, 1982.

47. *New York Times,* April 20, 1981, p. 12.

164 • *The Soviet Invasion of Afghanistan*

48. Tass in English, April 28, 1983 in FBIS–Soviet Union–III–89–4/6/83–2.
49. *New York Times,* April 12, 1983, p. 6.
50. *Izvestiia,* January 6, 1981, p. 5; and *Pravda,* August 5, 1981, p. 4.
51. Soviet public estimates varied widely. For one such estimate see, *Pravda,* March 21, 1983, p. 5. For a total estimate over $300 million, see Radio Moscow, Domestic Service, July 13, 1983 in FBIS–Soviet Union–III–137–7/15/83–D23.
52. Fukuyama, "Pakistan Since the Soviet Invasion of Afghanistan," p. 3. On *al-Zulfikar,* see *Business Week,* November 1981, p. 60. *New York Times,* August 23, and October 3, 1984, p. 5 in each.
53. *New York Times,* June 25, 1981, p. 5.
54. Gandhi's remarks can be found in FBIS–South Asia–VIII–133–7/13/81–E2–E3. For the most complete account of Indian reactions to the invasion, see Sen Gupta, *The Afghan Syndrome,* pp. 106–40.
55. *Time,* August 2, 1982, p. 33.
56. For a statement by Indira Gandhi, see *New York Times,* March 10, 1983, p. 2.
57. *Pravda,* March 9, 1981, p. 4.
58. Kianuri, "The Difficult Path of the Iranian Revolution," pp. 31–37 in FBIS–Soviet Union–III–060–3/28/83–3.
59. *New York Times,* May 6, 1983, p. 3.
60. In *Radio Liberty Research Bulletin,* RL202/83, May 83, p. 3.
61. Dawisha, "The USSR in the Middle East," p. 448. On Iranian aid to the Afghan resistance, see *Foreign Report,* September 22, 1983, pp. 1–2.
62. *Pravda,* August 5, 1981, p. 4 in CDSP–33–31–5, 6.
63. *Documents and Resolutions: The 26th Congress of the CPSU,* p. 38.
64. The best sources on these negotiations are Harrison, "Dateline Afghanistan: Exit Through Finland?," pp. 163–87; and "A Breakthrough in Afghanistan?" pp. 3–26. Also, *Far Eastern Economic Review,* April 12, 1984, p. 24.
65. Press release, cited in FBIS–East Europe–II–196–9/8/82–F4.
66. *Patriot* (New Delhi), February 10, 1983, p. 1, 7, in FBIS–South Asia–VIII–41–3/1/83–C3.
67. *New York Times,* March 30, 1983, p. 4.
68. Tass, April 24, 1983 in FBIS–Soviet Union–III–80–4/25/83–AA9.
69. *Pravda,* May 23, 1981, pp. 1–2 in CDSP–33–21–6–8.
70. *New York Times,* November 21, 1982, p. 8.
71. Cited in FBIS–Soviet Union–III–224, Annex 074–12/8/82–cover. For a Soviet rebuttal see *Pravda,* December 16, 1982, p. 4.
72. Tass, April 24, 1983.
73. *New York Times,* December 10, 1982, p. 8.
74. Interview with a U.S. diplomat in Moscow, January 3, 1983.
75. Interview, Cambridge, Mass., October 1983.

10
Conclusions

It is appropriate at this point to return to the questions which have guided this study and to attempt to draw or restate conclusions on the data that have been presented.

What were the Soviet motives for invading Afghanistan? What role was played by conditions internal to Afghanistan, and what role was played by exogenous factors, such as U.S.-Soviet relations?

Single cases rarely, if ever, exert an overriding influence on general theoretical propositions. This examination of Soviet behavior in Afghanistan is no exception. It will not end the debate between those analysts who see the use of force as part of the USSR's grand strategy and those who believe that the Soviets use force "opportunistically" or primarily as a "deterrent" to the West. This analysis of the case of Afghanistan seems more to support the latter views over the former but none of the three perspectives are validated or invalidated by this case. For example, even grand strategies must permit important exceptional cases. In Afghanistan, post-1978, the dominant Soviet perception would have to be characterized as a "need to act," not "exploit an opportunity." Deterrent action is also a less than accurate characterization of Soviet policy post-1978. Preserving a Soviet position of strength against nearly every future eventuality goes far beyond deterrence. The case of Afghanistan suggests that a more complex interpretation, one taking into account rational-actor and organizational-process considerations, and one also strongly influenced by particular sets of Soviet perceptions, should be used to explain Soviet motives in this case.

In light of this, from an analysis of pre-1978 Soviet-Afghan relations, this study determined that there is very little direct and coherent evidence to suggest a long-range Soviet plan to capture or formally control Afghanistan. Rather, pre-1978, Soviet objectives toward Afghanistan included (1) providing incentives for Afghanistan not to join a Northern Tier alliance; (2) developing trade and aid links to encourage dependence on the USSR; (3) conducting mutually beneficial trade relations; (4) using Afghanistan to support the programs of Soviet foreign policy; and (5) using Afghanistan as a model of relations between states system and as a model of "good neighborly" relations between the Soviet Union and a neighboring state. From the mid-1970s on, the Soviets began to burn the candle at both ends, keeping good relations with Daoud while aiding the PDPA.

Post-1978, after Afghanistan had become a state with a "socialist orientation," the Soviets increased their aid and interest in the regime. As the revolt against Taraki and later Amin grew, and instability entered the region, the Soviets began to see a threat to their security growing in an Afghanistan threatened by outside interference and flanked by an unstable Iran and an increasingly hostile China.

The most important factors associated with the invasion were a perceived threat to Soviet security generated by the impending collapse of the Amin regime and other ominous developments in the region, and the serious commitment that the USSR had made to Afghanistan and the subsequent prestige investment. The absence of constraints was a contributory factor. The general deterioration of Sino-Soviet and U.S.-Soviet relations also contributed to a general perception of insecurity and had a negative influence on the decision-making climate in this case.

Soviet civil and military doctrine served as a background factor. Increased Soviet interest in the Third World, attention to states with a socialist orientation, a favorable evaluation of past successes in these states, and an emphasis on the value of Soviet assistance to these states, showed an orientation on the part of Soviet thinkers—and less clearly, the leadership—to assist energetically new states with a socialist orientation, and to view them as inevitably threatened by the combined forces of reaction and imperialism. Although the relationship between doctrine and policy is indirect, Soviet civil and military doctrine showed Soviet policy to be a complex amalgam of ideals and national interests. In the case of Afghanistan, the USSR managed, as usual, to blend Marxist-Leninist doctrine and perceived national interest into a coherent conceptual whole. Soviet security and prestige were aided, abetted, and explained by a policy of proletarian internationalism, a policy which was in turn made credible by the accumulation of Soviet military power. In effect, Soviet policy toward Afghanistan post-1978 was neither realist nor socialist, but both.

How was the invasion conducted and how have subsequent military operations in Afghanistan been prosecuted? What is the relationship between the methods chosen and the Soviet motives for the initial invasion?

The invasion of Afghanistan was designed to unseat Amin and install Babrak Karmal, who, in turn, would stop PDPA infighting, rebuild the army, and restore order. The Soviet invasion force was to be his shield, a temporary army of occupation. In all, the invasion of Czechoslovakia served as a model for the invasion of Afghanistan.

The explanation for this initial miscalculation may already be familiar to historians and political scientists. Scholars have known for some time that decision-makers often apply the lessons of history and their own experience in "cookie cutter" fashion. Drawing on his study of U.S. officials, Ernest R. May concluded that

> Policy-makers ordinarily use history badly. When resorting to an analogy, they tend to seize upon the first that comes to mind. They do not search more widely. Nor do they pause to analyze the case, test its fitness, or even ask in what ways it might be misleading. Seeing a trend running toward the present, they tend to assume that it will continue into the future, not stopping to consider what produced it or why a linear projection might prove to be mistaken.[1]

Soviet theorists, and perhaps Soviet decision-makers as well, downgraded the importance of local conditions in the Third World and tended to draw universally applicable lessons from Vietnam and other cases that overestimated the importance of Soviet military assistance to states with a socialist orientation. The Czech case, as previously mentioned, seems to have exerted an especially strong influence on both the planning and the execution of the Afghan invasion. The Soviet leadership may also have believed that success—as in Angola and Ethiopia—could be bought in Afghanistan with the same currency: military power. Robert Jervis has pointed out that

> When a policy has brought notable success, actors are likely to apply it to a range of later situations. Seeing these cases as resembling the past one, the actor will believe that they are amenable to the policy that worked previously. But when insufficient attention is paid to the reasons why the policy worked in the past, the new situation will not be scrutinized to see if it has the attributes that made the earlier success possible. Because the actor is apt to overestimate the degree to which his policy was responsible for the earlier success, as we discussed above, he will be especially insensitive to variation in the situation.

"Nothing fails like success," as one commentator has noted.[2]

From June 1980 on, the Soviets continued their search for success and slowly began to adapt their policy to a counterinsurgency environment. The Soviets removed some armor and missile troops and began to construct a basing structure to support their forces. The apparent Soviet strategy is relatively modest in scope and long-term in its orientation, aiming at controlling the cities, securing the lines of communication, and destroying at minimum cost the resistance groups that threaten these two objectives. Operationally, the Soviet forces are using their superior mobility and firepower to make up for their low troop strength. Helicopters are important to everyday operations and lethal chemical agents were used in the 1980–82 period. Beginning in February 1980, the Soviets began to search for a political settlement favorable to their interests, and more recently have begun to train great numbers of Afghans in the USSR to run Afghanistan when the war ends.

In the area of military doctrine, Afghanistan appears as a unique case. The Soviets did not expect to fight in Afghanistan, but very soon found themselves embroiled in a full-blown counterinsurgency in the mountains of Asia with an army that had been designed and trained for World War III on the plains of Europe. While the Soviets have in the past shown a strategic appreciation for limited war, they were put in the awkward position of having a force structure and operational and tactical doctrines that did not match the military situation. Moreover, it was a situation that required an independent, decentralized style of command, very much alien to the Soviet experience.

Tactical adaptations, as noted above, have taken place and are in evidence even in Soviet accounts of battles in Afghanistan. The Soviet military press is replete with articles discussing "mountain training," and exhorting leaders to pay more attention to developing the illusive "initiative" and physical fitness among their subordinates. For example, *Voennyi vestnik* (Military Herald), a combined arms and tactical-level journal, showed a steady increase in articles on mountain warfare from zero before 1978, to three in 1979, to fifteen in 1980.[3] A more direct example of Afghanistan's influence on Soviet military doctrine appears in the training guidance given by General V.I. Petrov, commander-in-chief of the Soviet ground forces, after the Twenty-sixth Party Congress in 1981. After praising a guards major for his conduct of a night training exercise over mountainous terrain, Petrov directed his subordinate commanders and inspectors to emphasize, inter alia, physical training, mountain and desert operations, inclement weather training, continuous day-night operations, and operations while "separated from the main forces, on an independent axis, and in the advance guard or flanking detachment."[4] Time and experience may enable to Soviets to turn this evolving body of information into a working doctrine, but, up to December 1984, it does not appear that the Soviet forces have the necessary initiative, motivation, and small-unit expertise to adapt sophisticated counterinsurgency tactics to the fluid Afghan environment.

In the area of weapons development, Afghanistan has been a prize (though a very expensive one) for the Soviet military. Training deficiencies will be detected, and combat experience, though it tends to be fleeting, will ensure a more seasoned Soviet army. Particularly significant here has been the performance of Soviet pilots. We can be assured that the Soviets will hone their fire-support skills to a fine edge in Afghanistan. If nothing else, Soviet command cadres in future conflicts should be better able to control their air and ground firepower.

To date, Soviet operations in Afghanistan do not suggest that the invasion of Afghanistan was oriented toward further expansion in the region. Soviet military efforts have nearly all been directed at prosecuting the war in Afghanistan and not at using Afghanistan as a base for operations outside the country. Rumors of missile bases in the north and new airfields in the southwestern part of Afghanistan have not been confirmed by responsible sources.[5] Although the possession of a secure Afghanistan could provide the Soviet Union with marginal military advantages in an attack on Iran and more significant advantages in a military operation or subversion campaign against Pakistan, there is no evidence from Soviet military operations in Afghanistan to suggest that Iran, Pakistan, or Persian Gulf oil were the ultimate ends and Afghanistan simply a means thereto.

How does the Soviet invasion of Afghanistan fit the commonly accepted theoretical propositions that describe how and under what conditions the Soviets have previously used force in support of their foreign policy? How can one explain the aspects of this case which do not fit the theoretical propositions?

There is a great deal of agreement among experts on the calculation, circumstances, and general methods surrounding the use of force in Soviet foreign policy. On the subject of Soviet calculation prior to using force, observers have long noted the pervasive climate of caution that has cloaked what were sometimes portrayed as decisive and daring moves. Speaking of general crisis behavior, Jan Triska and David Finley have pointed out that "Soviet crisis behavior was found to be conservative rather than radical, cautious rather than reckless, deliberate rather than impulsive, and rational (not willing to lose) rather than nonrational."[6] Stephen Kaplan concluded that the Soviets used military power with "great deliberation," and Hannes Adomeit speaks of "careful preparation" as axiomatic.[7]

There is also wide agreement on the circumstances which normally surrounded the Soviet decision to use force. As Hannes Adomeit has pointed out, "Any Soviet decision for the commitment of forces appears to be based on three calculations or expectations: no resistance (military involvement) of the adversary superpower; low resistance locally; and a high probability that political power can quickly be handed over by the Soviet intervention forces to local political forces."[8]

Stephen Kaplan noted that three other favorable circumstances which attended Soviet operations in the Third World operations were (1) the appearance of support by a principle of international law; (2) the support of a "large number" of Third World nations; and (3) a "large prospect for rapid success."[9]

As for methods, there appeared to be two general cases: one where Soviet security was not directly involved, and the other where it was directly involved. In the former case, Stephen Kaplan noted,

> In the third world, where in contrast to Europe and northern Asia, Soviet security was not directly at stake, Moscow used military power effectively and subtly. . . . In general, Soviet leaders were adept at legitimating their use of force, timed their introduction of military means well, showed good sense in the types of forces called on, and did not gloat over successes. The Kremlin preferred a naval presence, covert tactical air assistance, logistical support, and the use of Cuban combat formations over the open deployment of Soviet military units in third world nations.[10]

Triska and Finley noted that strong concern over an objective and geographical proximity increased the Soviet propensity to take risks. On security-related cases Adomeit has written: "Hence as regards the direct use of force the Soviet leaders act as if they were in full agreement with a principle formulated by the German General Guderian for the use of tank forces in war, namely, that if these forces are to be used, not to use them piecemeal and sporadically, but massively and in concentrated fashion *(Nicht kleckern, sondern klotzen)*."[11]

To summarize, the literature on the use of force in Soviet foreign policy suggests that, in calculating the use of force, the Soviet leadership will prepare carefully and move cautiously. The circumstances for using force will generally be characterized by a low probability of adversary superpower involvement and a high probability of support and success, both of which will be reinforced by the appearance of legitimacy. As for methods, where Soviet security was not involved, the Soviet use of force was incisive, sensitive, and prudent; whereas, when Soviet security was involved, it was massive and concentrated, although not necessarily uncautious or excessive.

The invasion of Afghanistan displayed both congruity and incongruity with the characteristic methods generally associated with previous uses of force in Soviet foreign policy. In calculating their move into Afghanistan, the Soviets repeatedly sent experienced observers to Afghanistan to gather information, and at no time did they move beyond their capabilities. Indeed, one could argue that the movement of Cuban troops into Angola or Ethiopia was a more demanding use of Soviet capabilities. Soviet capabilities are much stronger on the periphery, where the weight of the ground forces can be felt, than outside the periphery, where the Soviets have to depend more on the navy and airlift forces, which are still poor relations to the relatively highly endowed ground forces. The Soviets also displayed caution in their incremental attempt at solving the problem by using the lowest level of force possible, moving from an advisery role to a supervisory role, and then to an invasion only after their previous efforts had proven to be failures. Adherence to the standard pattern was also indicated by the Soviet refusal up to the end of 1983 to widen the war to include Iran or Pakistan.

The circumstances surrounding the invasion also partly fit the pattern. The Soviets faced a low probability of U.S. involvement, and, as previously noted, were partially justified in miscalculating the U.S. reaction. Their apparent attempt at either convincing Amin to accept Soviet troops or removing him suggested that the Soviets wanted the "invitation" to appear more genuine than it did. Throughout their operation in Afghanistan, the Soviets have continued to attempt to wear a rather transparent cloak of international law, citing the "invitation," the friendship treaty, and even the UN Charter as legal justifications. In keeping with the pattern described above, perceiving a security threat on the border, the Soviets, at least at the outset, used massive and concentrated force given their apparent belief that they would essentially be serving as an army of occupation.

On the other hand, certain aspects of Soviet policy in Afghanistan violate the pattern. While the Soviets felt free to use 20,000 air defense troops in Egypt and to station a ground forces brigade in Cuba, the invasion of Afghanistan was the first time that they committed their ground forces to combat—probably at a higher level of intensity than they predicted—outside their accepted sphere of influence in East Europe or the Sino-Soviet border area.

Without substantive details on the process by which the invasion decision was made, we are left with only speculative and inferential explanations for why the Soviets violated some elements of the pattern on the use of force. A number of factors may have been involved. First, the Soviet leadership—in part blinded by the aforementioned limits of its civil and military thinking on the Third World—miscalculated their prospects for success due to their failure to comprehend Afghan culture and the conditions in that country. Second, as mentioned numerous times, the Soviets had reason to have increased confidence in their use of force in the Third World. Third, Amin's genuine unpopularity probably made the Soviets overconfident about Karmal's prospects for success. Fourth, the strong Soviet-Afghan ties made the use of Cuban or East European proxies an irrelevant option in this case. Finally, one must consider the strength of the Soviet need to act. Afghanistan is on the once calm, now turbulent southern border. It was a state with a socialist orientation and one in which the Soviets had made a great investment of both prestige and money. To let a "revolution" on the southern border be reversed (with the perceived interference of the United States *and* China) would be unthinkable, especially at a time when it appeared that the United States might (as it later did) use force against Iran. In a similar vein, the low state of Sino-Soviet and U.S.-Soviet relations, when coupled with deepening cooperation between the United States and China, probably created a climate in which the decision to use force was easier to make.

It is impossible to accurately determine whether the Soviets would have invaded in December if they had accurately predicted the military and political problems attendant on the operation. Although this study has uncovered several apologetic, "we made a mistake" types of statement, they stand alongside a number of more definitive statements from the leadership that suggest strong purpose and perceived righteousness. When added to the tough military policy of the 1980–84 period, the latter set of statements strongly suggest that, even given a perfectly accurate crystal ball in 1979, the Soviets, acting on the strength of the need to act, might have invaded anyway.

What conclusions may be drawn from the Soviet invasion of Afghanistan regarding changing trends in Soviet foreign policy?

Many distinguished scholars saw the invasion of Afghanistan as a watershed event. Seweryn Bialer, for example, noted that the invasion conveyed "a reordering in the Kremlin of priorities and assumptions" that they had "much to gain" and "much to fear" from the United States if they dared to transgress certain implicit behavioral bounds.[12] Others noted that the invasion was a Soviet declaration of an expanded sphere of interest covered by a new Brezhnev Doctrine. As an unsigned editorial in the weekly *New Times* proclaimed, under "extraordinary circumstances," the USSR had to give direct military help to states with a socialist orientation. Not to do so would be evading their "internationalist duty."[13]

These arguments cannot—only five years after the invasion—be refuted with any high degree of certainty. The Soviet Union possesses greater military power and has been steadily developing vastly improved air and naval assets to deliver it far from the Soviet homeland. Power tempts policy, as Zbigniew Brzezinski has reminded us; and its temptation in part produced the invasion of a sovereign, nonaligned state. It may produce others too.

On the other hand, many facts of the Afghan case lead one to question its relevance as a precedent. There are, at present, no nonaligned countries with a socialist orientation on the security-sensitive Soviet periphery. Soviet theoreticians readily admit that socialist orientations may wane or even be reversed. As late as 1977, the Soviets permitted the nonperipheral Somalia to abandon its socialist orientation and to expel Soviet advisers. There is little doubt that the Soviets would engage in covert operations to keep a state with a socialist orientation within the fold, but the dispatch of Soviet or even Cuban troops in such a case may be less likely if the state is nonperipheral.

In a similar vein, the Soviet experience in Afghanistan would seem to make a Soviet invasion of Iran only a remote possibility in the near future. The conditions that led up to the Soviet move in Afghanistan—a pro-Soviet government, a long history of direct involvement, the friendship treaty, a low probability of direct U.S. response—are all, at least for the present, absent from Iran. The recent fortunes of the Tudeh party also seem to diminish the chance that anyone in Iran would ever offer the Soviets an invitation to come into the country. Moreover, the bloody and frustrating Soviet experience in Afghanistan may cause the lessons learned, unlike those in Angola and Ethiopia, to be largely recorded on the debit side of the ledger. The Soviets looked favorably on their experience in Czechoslovakia in 1968 and attempted to use the Czech recipe in Afghanistan. It is highly unlikely in the near term that they will attempt to apply the Afghan recipe to any other country. Finally, Iran is a difficult objective.[14] The Soviets know this, and Afghan bases would be of only limited assistance in invading Iran. While it is clear that the Soviets will benefit at least marginally from being able to move their air assets closer to the Indian Ocean, it is not similarly clear that this or any other asset secured in Afghanistan would greatly assist them in an invasion of Iran, an act which the United States has sworn to deter or defeat.

As for a "reordering of the Kremlin's priorities," examination of the case of Afghanistan and collateral Soviet policy does not, five years afterward, prove this to be the case. Although U.S.-Soviet relations have been poor since the invasion (and indeed for nearly a year before the invasion as well), there is no evidence to suggest that the Soviets have discarded the policy of detente or that they have abandoned the search for a modus vivendi with the United States. The fruits of detente—trade, technology transfer, and arms control—are still high on the Kremlin's priority list. Even in the Third World, since 1979, the Soviets have maintained a fairly low profile, even if their support for Nicaragua and their military aid to Syria are included in the calculation. Perhaps the transport of new Cuban expeditionary forces simply awaits new opportunities as compelling as the disintegration of the Portuguese colonial empire or the downfall of Haile Selassie. Perhaps the Soviets today are simply consolidating the gains—Angola, Ethiopia, Yemen—of the mid-1970s before moving on to other areas. The fact remains, however: the years 1980–84 have not been nearly so full of Soviet Third World adventures as the years 1975–1979 were.

All of this is not meant to imply that the invasion of Afghanistan was an unimportant, exceptional event with no relevance for the future. To the contrary, it is an important, even if unusual, event for three reasons. First, it clearly demonstrates, if we needed a reminder, that superpowers can seriously misinterpret situations in the Third World, and that both unfortunately now possess the capability (and occasionally the will) to use force to pursue their interests outside their core security areas. In Afghanistan there was little chance of a superpower collision, but a dash of misadventure or misestimate could bring about a confrontation where neither side believed it could back down. If nothing else, the invasion of Afghanistan and the attendant crisis in Iran have highlighted the need for an improved superpower management mechanism for Third World conflict situations.

Second, the Soviet-Afghan war is now the longest Soviet military conflict. While its scope will prevent it from achieving the importance of the Great Patriotic War, it has become a laboratory for Soviet military experiments and a test—although one under peculiar conditions—for Soviet arms. Thus, the war demands the close attention of the same Western analysts who talk of "the threat," the strategic balance, and NATO-Warsaw Pact issues. As the lessons of Spain were applied in Poland, so too the Soviet lessons from Afghanistan may appear in different wars, in different regions, under vastly different circumstances.

Finally, one should not lose sight of the fact that the Soviet lessons from the war have not yet been recorded. If, ten years hence, the Soviets muddle through to a victory, Soviet analysts may well put their activities in a more favorable light. Unfortunately, the Soviets are pursuing such a long-range solution and the high price imposed by the international community has long since been paid. In a decade from now, one could readily imagine an exhausted Afghanistan securely under a Soviet puppet regime. The Soviet political system is the mujahidin's greatest enemy in this regard. It does not require an immediate solution or even one in the near term. As a valiant French doctor, himself a veteran of the Soviet-Afghan war, noted,

> The Russians do not need smashing victories to announce to their citizenry, as Soviet public opinion does not influence Soviet policy. Catastrophes . . . do not incite an outcry in Moscow for Soviet "boys"

to come home. The Soviet army can wait it out as long as it did for the Basmachi revolt to end—and it waited for that for twenty years. It can wait even longer if necessary.¹⁵

Notes

1. May, *Lessons of the Past: The Use and Misuse of History in American Foreign Policy,* p. xi.
2. Jervis, *Perception and Misperception in International Politics,* p. 278.
3. Defense Intelligence Agency, *Review of Soviet Ground Forces,* July 1982, pp. 13–16.
4. Petrov's article, "The Main Concern Is Combat Training," appeared as the lead article in *Voennyi vestnik (Military Herald),* no. 3 (March 1981). For a pessimistic Soviet account of progress in mountain training, see the unsigned editorial, "Gornaya Podgotovka Voisk" (The Mountain Training of Troops), *Voennyi vestnik,* no. 5 (May 1983), pp. 3–5.
5. For an interesting account of missile and strategic airbase rumors, see the interview with Karen McKay of the Committee for a Free Afghanistan in *Washington Times,* March 21, 1984, p. 3C. These rumors were denied by responsible intelligence and State Department officials in a telephone interview with the author, April 10, 1984, and again by State Department officials in Undersecretary of State Michael Armacost's press briefing on the Soviet occupation of Afghanistan, December 20, 1984, Washington, D.C.
6. Triska and Finley, *Soviet Foreign Policy,* p. 346.
7. Kaplan, *Diplomacy of Power,* p. 667; Adomeit, *Soviet Risk-Taking and Crisis Behavior,* p. 319.
8. Adomeit, *Soviet Risk-Taking and Crisis Behavior,* p. 322. See also Hosmer and Wolfe, *Soviet Policy and Practice Toward Third World Conflicts,* p. 135.
9. Kaplan, *Diplomacy of Power,* pp. 668–69.
10. Ibid. See also Hosmer and Wolfe, *Soviet Policy Toward Third World Conflicts,* p. 135.
11. Adomeit, *Soviet Risk-Taking and Crisis Behavior,* p. 322. The origin of the German term is obscure, but Guderian translated it as "boot them, don't spatter them." See Guderian, *Panzer Leader,* p. 255. Also, Triska and Finley, *Soviet Foreign Policy,* p. 347.
12. Bialer, *Stalin's Successors,* p. 2.
13. *New Times* (Moscow), no. 3, January 1980, p. 10.
14. For some dated though rigorous Soviet military thinking concerning Iran, see *Soviet Intelligence Estimate—Iran,* an unpublished mimeographed translation, 1941, especially the "Conclusions and Summary." In the summary, the author accurately described the weather and terrain conditions present in Iran and concluded that, even though an invasion was possible, "these difficulties . . . ought not be underestimated."
15. Claude Malhuret, "Report from Afghanistan," *Foreign Affairs* 62 (Winter 1983–84), p. 435.

References

Books and Articles

Adamec, Ludwig W. *Afghanistan's Foreign Affairs to the Mid-Twentieth Century: Relations with the USSR, Germany and Britain.* Tucson: University of Arizona Press, 1974.

Adomeit, Hannes. *Soviet Risk-Taking and Crisis Behavior: A Theoretical and Empirical Analysis.* Studies of the Russian Institute of Columbia University. London: George Allen and Unwin, 1982.

Alexeyev, A. and Fialkovsky, A. "Peace and Security for the Indian Ocean." *International Affairs* (Moscow), no. 9 (September 1979): 51–55.

Allard, Kenneth. "Soviet Airborne Forces and Preemptive Power Projection." *Parameters: Journal of the U.S. Army War College* 10 (December 1980): 42–51.

Allison, Graham. *Essence of Decision: Explaining the Cuban Missile Crisis.* Boston: Little, Brown and Co., 1971.

Anderson, Richard D., Jr. "Soviet Decision-Making and Poland." *Problems of Communism* 31 (March-April 1982): 22–27.

Arbatov, Georgiy. "On Soviet-American Relations." *Kommunist,* no. 3 (February 1973): 101–13.

Arnold, Anthony. *Afghanistan: The Soviet Invasion in Perspective.* Stanford, California: Hoover Press, 1981.

Aspaturian, Vernon. "Soviet Global Power and the Correlation of Forces." *Problems of Communism* 29 (May-June 1980): 1–18.

Azrael, Jeremy. "The 'Nationality Problem' in the USSR." In Bialer, Seweryn, ed. *The Domestic Context of Soviet Foreign Policy.* Boulder, Colorado: Westview Press, 1981, pp. 139–54.

Bennigsen, Alexandre, "Soviet Muslims and the World of Islam." *Problems of Communism* 29 (March 1980): 38–51.

———. *The Soviet Union and Muslim Guerrilla Wars* (Draft), Rand Research Note WD1129RC/NA. Santa Monica, California: Rand, 1981.

Berman, Robert R. *Soviet Air Power in Transition.* Washington, D.C.: Brookings Institution, 1978.

Bernstein, Carl. "Arms for Afghanistan." *New Republic,* July 18, 1982, pp. 8–10.

Bialer, Seweryn. *Stalin's Successors: Leadership, Stability and Change in the Soviet Union.* New York: Cambridge University Press, 1980.

Blechman, Barry M. and Kaplan, Stephen S. *Force Without War: U.S. Armed*

Forces as a Political Instrument. Washington, D.C.: Brookings Institution, 1978.

Bort, Roger E. "Air Assault Brigades: New Element in the Soviet *Desant* Force Structure." *Military Review* 63 (October 1983): 21–39.

Bradsher, Henry S. *Afghanistan and the Soviet Union.* Durham, North Carolina: Duke University Press, 1983.

Brzezinski, Zbigniew. *Power and Principle: Memoirs of the National Security Adviser 1977–81.* New York: Farrar, Straus, Giroux, 1983.

Bunce, Peter L. "Soviet Airborne: The Quiet Revolution." *Military Intelligence,* October-December 1983, pp. 4–9.

Bush, Keith. "Trade Between USSR and Afghanistan." An unpublished report from Radio Liberty, October 1983.

Byely, B., ed. *Marxism-Leninism On War and Army.* Moscow: Progress Publishers, 1972.

Castaneq, Joseph. "Soviet Imperialism in Afghanistan." *Foreign Affairs* 13 (April 1935): 698–703.

Chaffetz, David. "Afghanistan in Turmoil." *International Affairs* (London) (January 1980): 15–36.

Charters, David. "Afghanistan: Coup and Consolidation." *Conflict Quarterly* (Spring 1981): 41–48.

Cobb, Tyrus W. "From Russia With Doves." An unpublished IREX trip report, January 1981.

Collins, Joseph. "Afghanistan: The Empire Strikes Out." *Parameters: Journal of the U.S. Army War College* 12 (March 1982): 32–41.

———. "The Soviet Invasion of Afghanistan: Methods, Motives and Ramifications." *Naval War College Review* 33 (November-December 1980): 53–62.

———. "Soviet Military Performance in Afghanistan: A Preliminary Assessment." *Comparative Strategy* 4 (Spring 1983): 147–68.

———. "Use of Force in Soviet Foreign Policy: The Case of Afghanistan." *Conflict Quarterly* 3 (Spring 1983): 20–44.

Corcoran, Edward. *Soviet Muslim Policy.* Strategic Issues Research Memo. ACN 80042. Carlisle, Pennsylvania: U.S. Army War College, 1980.

Dawisha, Karen. "The USSR in the Middle East." *Foreign Affairs* 61 (Winter 1982–83): 438–52.

d'Encausse, Helene Carrere. *Decline of an Empire: The Soviet Socialist Republics in Revolt.* Translated by Martin Sokolinsky and Henry LaFarge. New York: Harper Colophon Books, 1979.

Degras, Jane, ed. *Soviet Documents on Foreign Policy,* vol. 1. New York: Oxford University Press, 1951.

Dinerstein, Herbert S. *The Making of a Missile Crisis: October 1962.* Baltimore: Johns Hopkins University Press, 1979.

Donaldson, Robert, ed. *The Soviet Union in the Third World: Successors and Failures.* Boulder, Colorado: Westview Press, 1981.

Dunn, Keith A. *Soviet Constraints in Southwest Asia.* Strategic Issues Research

Memo. ACN 81066. Carlisle, Pennsylvania: U.S. Army War College, December 1981.

Dupree, Louis. *Afghanistan*. Princeton, New Jersey: Princeton University Press, 1973.

———. "Afghanistan Under the Khalq." *Problems of Communism* 28 (July-August 1979): 34–43.

———. "The Democratic Republic of Afghanistan, 1979." *American Universities Field Staff Reports (AUFSR)*, Asia Series, no. 32, September 1979.

———. *New Republic of Afghanistan: The First Twenty-one Months*. Special Paper of the Afghanistan Council of the Asia Society, Spring 1976.

———. "A Note on Afghanistan, 1974." *AUFSR*. South Asia Series, no. 18, September 1974.

———. "Red Flag Over the Hindu Kush, Part I: Leftist Movements in Afghanistan." *AUFSR*. Asia Series, no. 44, September 1979.

———. "Red Flag Over the Hindu Kush, Part II: The Accidental Coup or Taraki in Blunderland." *AUFSR*, Asia Series, no. 45, September 1979.

———. "Red Flag Over the Hindu Kush, Part III: Rhetoric and Reforms, or Promises! Promises!" *AUFSR*, Asia Series, no. 23, March 1980.

———. "Red Flag Over the Hindu Kush, Part IV: Foreign Policy and Economy." *AUFSR*, Asia Series, no. 27, June 1980.

———. "Red Flag Over the Hindu Kush, Part V: Repressions, or Security Through Terror—Purges I–IV. *AUFSR*, Asia Series, no. 28, June 1980.

———. "Red Flag Over the Hindu Kush, Part VI: Repressions, or Security Through Terror." *AUFSR*, Asia Series, no. 29, June 1980.

———. "Toward Representative Government in Afghanistan," Part 1: The First Five Steps." *AUFSR*, Asia Series, no. 1, February 1978.

Eliot, Theodore L. "Afghanistan After the 1978 Revolution." *Strategic Review* 7 (Spring 1979): 57–62.

Epstein, Joshua M. "Soviet Vulnerabilities in Iran and the RDF Deterrent." *International Security* 6 (Fall 1981): 126–58.

Fischer, Louis. *The Soviets in World Affairs*, Vol. 1. Princeton, New Jersey: Princeton University Press, 1951.

Fletcher, Arnold. *Afghanistan: Highway of Conquest*. Ithaca, New York: Cornell University Press, 1965.

Fraser-Tytler, W.K. *Afghanistan: A Study of Political Developments in Central and Southern Asia*, 3d ed. New York: Oxford University Press, 1967.

Freistetter, Fritz. "The Battle in Afghanistan." *Strategic Review* (Winter 1981): 37ff.

Fromkin, David. "The Great Game in Asia." *Foreign Affairs* 58 (Spring 1980): 936–51.

Fukuyama, Frank. *The Future of the Soviet Role in Afghanistan*. Rand Research Note N–1579–RC. Santa Monica, California: Rand, 1980.

———. *Pakistan Since the Soviet Invasion of Afghanistan*. Strategic Issues Research Memo. ACN 82002. Carlisle, Pennsylvania: U.S. Army War College, January 1982.

———. *The Soviet Threat to the Persian Gulf.* Rand/P–6596. Santa Monica, California: Rand, March 1981.

Garrity, Patrick. "The Soviet Military Stake in Afghanistan: 1956–79." *RUSI: Journal of the Royal United Services Institute For Defence Studies* (September 1980): 31–36.

Garthoff, Raymond. "Mutual Deterrence and Strategic Arms Limitation in Soviet Policy." *Strategic Review* 10 (Fall 1982): 36–63.

Goldman, Marshall I. *USSR in Crisis: The Failure of an Economic System.* New York: W.W. Norton, 1983.

Gorshkov, Sergei. *Sea Power of the State.* New York: Pergamon, 1979.

Grachev, A.S., ed. *The Undeclared War: Imperialism vs. Afghanistan.* Moscow: Progress Publishers, 1980.

Gray, Colin S. *The Geopolitics of the Nuclear Era: Heartland, Rimlands, and the Technological Revolution.* New York: Crane, Russak and Co., 1977.

Griffith, William E. "USSR and Pakistan." *Problems of Communism* 31 (January-February 1982): 38–44.

Griffiths, John. *Afghanistan: Key to a Continent.* Boulder, Colorado: Westview Press, 1981.

Grechko, A.A. *Armed Forces of the Soviet State.* Moscow: Voyennizdat, 1975.

———. *On Guard for Peace and the Building of Communism.* Moscow: Voyennizdat, 1971.

Guderian, Heinz. *Panzer Leader*, abridged edition. New York: Ballantine Books, 1951.

Gurevich, N.M. "Socioeconomic Preconditions of the 1978 Revolution in Afghanistan." *Voprosy istorii (Questions of History)*, no. 7 (July 1982): 55–70 in JPRS 410807, September 1982.

Hajda, Joseph. "The Soviet Grain Embargo." *Survival* 22 (November-December 1980): 353–58.

Hammond, Thomas T. *Red Flag Over Afghanistan: The Communist Coup, The Soviet Invasion, and the Consequences.* Boulder, Colorado: Westview Press, 1984.

Hansen, James. "Afghanistan: The Soviet Experience." *National Defense*, January 1982, pp. 20–24ff.

Harrison, Selig. *In Afghanistan's Shadow: Baluch Nationalism and Soviet Temptations,* Washington, D.C.: Carnegie Endowment for International Peace, 1981.

———. "A Breakthrough in Afghanistan?" *Foreign Policy* 51 (Summer 1983): 3–26.

———. "Dateline Afghanistan: Exit Through Finland?" *Foreign Policy* 41 (Winter 1980–81): 163–87.

———. "Did Moscow Fear an Afghan Tito?" *New York Times,* January 13, 1980, p. 23.

———. "Nightmare in Baluchistan." *Foreign Policy* 32 (Fall 1978): 136–60.

———. "The Shah, Not the Kremlin, Touched Off Afghan Coup." *Washington Post,* February 13, 1979, pp. C1, 5.

Hart, Douglas. "Low-Intensity Conflict in Afghanistan." *Survival* 24 (March-April 1982): 61–67.
Haselkorn, Avigdor. *Analysis of Soviet Casualties in Afghanistan*. An unpublished paper from the Analytical Assessments Corporation, prepared for the Office of the Deputy Under Secretary of Defense (Policy Review), February 1981.
Hoffmann, Erik and Fleron, Frederic, eds. *The Conduct of Soviet Foreign Policy*, 2d ed. New York: Aldine, 1980.
Horelick, Arnold L.; Johnson, A. Ross; and Steinbruner, John D. *The Study of Soviet Foreign Policy: A Review of Decision-Theory-Related Approaches*. R–1334. Santa Monica, California: Rand, 1973.
Hosmer, Stephen T. and Wolfe, Thomas W. *Soviet Policy and Practice Toward Third World Conflicts*. Lexington, Massachusetts: D.C. Heath and Co., 1983.
Hough, Jerry. "Why the Russians Invaded." *Nation*, March 1, 1980, p. 232.
Hurewitz, J.C. *Middle East Politics: The Military Dimension*. New York: Praeger for the Council on Foreign Relations, 1969.
Hyland, William. "The Sino-Soviet Conflict: Dilemmas of the Strategic Triangle." Unpublished paper presented at the American Assembly Conference on "The China Factor," Harriman, New York, March 1981.
Isby, David. "Afghanistan 1982: The War Continues." *International Defense Review* 11 (November 1982): 1523–26.
Jervis, Robert. *Perception and Misperception in International Relations*. Limited paperback edition. Princeton, New Jersey: Princeton University Press, 1976.
Kanet, Roger E., ed. *The Soviet Union and the Developing Nations*. Baltimore: Johns Hopkins University Press, 1974.
Kaplan, Stephen, et. al. *Diplomacy of Power: Soviet Armed Forces as a Political Instrument*. Washington, D.C.: Brookings Institution, 1981.
Katz, Mark N. *The Third World In Soviet Military Thought*. Baltimore: Johns Hopkins University Press, 1983.
Kennan, George. "America's Unstable Soviet Policy." *Atlantic Monthly*, November 1982, pp. 78–80.
———. *Soviet Foreign Policy, 1917–1941*. Princeton, New Jersey: D. Van Nostrand Co., 1960.
———. "Washington's Reactions to the Afghan Crisis: Was This Mature Statesmanship?" *New York Times*, February 1, 1980, p. 28.
Khalilzad, Zalmay. "Soviet-Occupied Afghanistan." *Problems of Communism* 30 (November-December): 23–40.
———. "The Strategic Significance of South Asia." *Current History* 81 (May 1982): 193–96ff.
———. "The Superpowers and the Northern Tier." *International Security* 4 (Winter 1979–80): 6–30.
Khrushchev, Nikita. *Khrushchev Remembers*. Strobe Talbott, trans. and ed. London: Andre Deutsch, 1971.
———. *Khrushchev Remembers: The Last Testament*. Strobe Talbott, trans. and ed. Boston: Little, Brown and Co., 1974.

Kianuri, N. "The Difficult Path of the Iranian Revolution." *Problemy mira i sotsializma,* no. 3 (March 1983): pp. 31–37.

Kim, G. "The Soviet Union and the National Liberation Movement." *Mirovaya ekonomika i mezhdunarodniye otnosheniia (World Economy and International Relations),* no. 9 (September 1982): 19–33.

Kissinger, Henry. *White House Years.* Boston: Little, Brown and Co., 1979.

———. *Years of Upheaval.* Boston: Little, Brown and Co., 1982.

Klass, Rosanne T. "The Great Game Revisited." *National Review,* October 26, 1979, pp. 1366–70.

Knorr, Klaus E. *On the Uses of Military Power in the Nuclear Age.* Princeton, New Jersey: Princeton University Press, 1966.

Krasin, Y. "The Immutable Principles of Soviet Foreign Policy." *International Affairs* (Moscow), no. 4 (April 1977): 78–84.

Kruzhin, Peter. "The Ethnic Composition of Soviet Forces in Afghanistan." *Radio Liberty Research Bulletin.* RL 20/80, January 11, 1980.

Kulish, V.M., et. al. *Military Force and International Relations.* Moscow: International Relations Publishing House, 1972. Translated by the Joint Publications Research Service, JPRS 58947, 1973.

Kunov, A. "Developing Good Neighborly Relations." *International Affairs* (Moscow), no. 5 (May 1977): 201–05.

Kuznin, V. "China in the West's Aggressive Policy." *International Affairs* (Moscow), no. 4 (April 1980): 28–37.

Legvold, Robert. "Containment Without Confrontation." *Foreign Policy* 40 (Fall 1980): 74–98.

———. "The Nature of Soviet Power." *Foreign Affairs* 56 (October 1977): 49–71.

Leites, Nathan. *The Operational Code of the Politburo.* New York: McGraw-Hill, 1951.

Lenin, V.I. "Theses on the National and Colonial Question." In Robert C. Tucker, ed. *Lenin Anthology.* New York: Norton and Co., 1975, pp. 622–25.

Lodozhsky, A. "The USSR's Efforts to Turn the Indian Ocean into a Zone of Peace." *International Affairs* (Moscow), no. 8 (August 1981): 40–46.

Lowenthal, Richard. "Dealing with Soviet Global Power." *Encounter* 50 (June 1978): 90ff.

Luttwak, Edward. "After Afghanistan, What?" *Commentary,* April 1980, pp. 46–47.

Malhuret, Claude. "Report from Afghanistan." *Foreign Affairs* 62 (Winter 1983–84): 426–35.

Malinovskiy, G. "National-Liberation Movement at the Present Stage." *Kommunist vooruzhennykh sil (Communist of the Armed Forces),* no. 24 (December 1979): 25–36 in JPRS 75264, March 1980.

Matsulenko, V. "Lessons of Imperialist Local Wars." *Soviet Military Review* (Moscow), no. 1 (January 1982): 44–46.

May, Ernest R. *Lessons of the Past: Use and Misuse of History of American Foreign Policy.* New York: Oxford University Press, 1973.

Mikhailov, K. "Provocatory Campaign over Afghanistan." *International Affairs* (Moscow), no. 3 (March 1980): 97–100.
Mironov, L. and Polyakov, G. "Afghanistan: Beginning of a New Life." *International Affairs* (Moscow), no. 3 (March 1979): 46–54.
Misra, K.P., ed. *Afghanistan In Crisis*. New York: Advent Books, 1981.
Monks, Alfred. *The Soviet Invasion of Afghanistan*. Washington, D.C.: American Enterprise Institute, 1981.
Murphy, Paul. *Brezhnev: Soviet Politician*. Jefferson, North Carolina: McFarland and Co., 1981.
"Nearby Observer." "The Afghan-Soviet War: Stalemate or Evolution." *Middle East Journal* 36 (Spring 1982): 151–64.
Neely, Theodore A., ed. *Red Star Rising at Sea*. Washington, D.C.: U.S. Naval Institute, 1974.
Negaran, Hannah (pseudonym). "Afghan Coup of 1978: Revolution and International Security." *Orbis* 23 (Spring 1979).
Newell, Nancy and Newell, Richard. *The Struggle for Afghanistan*, Ithaca, New York: Cornell University Press, 1981.
Newell, Richard S. *The Politics of Afghanistan*. Ithaca, New York: Cornell University Press, 1972.
Nikolayev, B. "Third World: Choice of Path." *International Affairs*, no. 7 (July 1970): 31–36.
Nollau, Gunther and Wiche, Hans J. *Russia's South Flank*. New York: Praeger, 1963.
Olcott, Martha Brill. "Soviet Islam and World Revolution." *World Politics* 34 (July 1982): 487–504.
Ovsyany, I.D., ed. *A Study of Soviet Foreign Policy*. Moscow: Progress Publishers, 1975.
Paarlberg, Robert. "Lessons of the Grain Embargo." *Foreign Affairs* 59 (Fall 1980): 144–62.
Penkovskiy, Oleg. *The Penkovskiy Papers*. New York: Ballantine Books, 1965.
Petukhov, V. "PRC–USA: A Threat to Peace and Security." *Far Eastern Affairs* (Moscow), no. 3 (March 1980): 55–68.
Phillips, James. "Afghanistan: The Soviet Quagmire." *The Heritage Foundation Backgrounder*, no. 101 (October 1979).
Pipes, Richard. *The Foundation of the Soviet Union: Communism and Nationalism, 1917–23*, revised ed. Cambridge, Massachusetts: Harvard University Press, 1964.
———. "Soviet Global Strategy." *Commentary*, April 1980, p. 31–9.
Ponomarev, B.N. "Joint Struggle of the Workers and National-Liberation Movements Against Imperialism and for Social Progress." *Kommunist*, no. 16 (November 1980): 30–44.
Poullada, Leon B. "Afghanistan and the United States: The Crucial Years." *Middle East Journal* 35 (Spring 1981): 178–90.
Rader, Ronald R. "The Russian Military and Afghanistan: An Historical Perspective." In Jones, David, ed. *Soviet Armed Forces Review Annual*, vol. 4. Gulf Breeze, Florida: Academic International Press, 1981, pp. 308–28.

Rand, Robert. "Cuba Continues to Take an Ambiguous Stand on Soviet Actions in Afghanistan." *Radio Liberty Research Bulletin*. RL 56–80, February 6, 1980.

Ross, Dennis. "Considering Soviet Threats to the Persian Gulf." *International Security* 6 (Fall 1981): 159–80.

Rubin, Barry. *Paved With Good Intentions: The American Experience and Iran.* New York: Oxford University Press, 1980.

Rubinstein, Alvin. *Soviet Policy Toward Turkey, Iran, and Afghanistan: The Dynamics of Influence.* New York: Praeger, 1982.

"Russia in Afghanistan." *Economist*, May 23, 1981, pp. 33–37.

Rybkin, Ye. "The 25th CPSU Congress and Wars of Liberation of the Contemporary Era." *Voyenno-istoricheskiy zhurnal (Military-Historical Journal),* no. 11 (November 1978): 10–17.

Rywkin, Michael. *Russia in Central Asia.* New York: Collier Books, 1963.

Saint Brides, Lord. "Afghanistan: The Empire Plays to Win." *Orbis* 24 (Fall 1980): 533–40.

Schwab, George, ed. *Ideology and Foreign Policy: A Global Perspective.* New York: Cyrco Press, 1977.

Sen Gupta, Bhabani. *The Afghan Syndrome: How to Live with Soviet Power.* Delhi: Vikas Publishing, 1982.

Shavrov, I. "Local Wars and Their Place in the Global Strategy of Imperialism" *Voyenno-istoricheskiy zhurnal* (Moscow), no. 3 (March 1975). Translated in USAF, *Soviet Press: Selected Translations* nos. 75–8, 75–9 (August and September 1975): 1–38ff.

Sidenko, Victor. "Two Years of the Afghan Revolution." *New Times,* no. 17, April 1980, pp. 18–25.

Sivachev, N. and Yakovlev, N. *Russia and the United States: U.S.-Soviet Relations from the Soviet Point of View.* Chicago: University of Chicago Press, 1979.

Sokolovskiy, V.D. *Soviet Military Strategy,* 3d ed. Harriet Fast Scott, ed. and trans. New York: Crane Russak and Co., 1975.

Soviet Human Rights Violations in Afghanistan. An unedited transcript of a presentation by five Afghans on the massacre at Padkahwab-e-Shana, Georgetown Center for Strategic and International Studies, February 1983.

Spector, Ivar. *The Soviet Union and the Muslim World, 1917–58.* An unpublished manuscript distributed by the University of Washington Press, 1958.

Tenson, Andreas. "Soviet View of Soviet-Afghan Relations." *Radio Liberty Research Bulletin,* RL 84/180.

Teplinskiy, L.B. *SSSR i Afghanistan.* Moscow: Izdatel'stvo "NAUKA," 1982.

Triska, Jan F. and Finley, David D. *Soviet Foreign Policy.* London: Macmillan Co., 1968.

Trofimenko, Genrikh. "The Third World In U.S.-Soviet Competition: A Soviet View." *Foreign Affairs* 59 (Summer 1981): 1021–40.

The Truth About Afghanistan—Documents, Facts, Eyewitness Reports. Moscow: Novosti Press Agency, 1980.
Tucker, Robert C., ed. *The Lenin Anthology.* New York: W. W. Norton and Co., 1975.
Ulam, Adam. *Expansion and Coexistence: Soviet Foreign Policy 1917–73*, 2d ed. New York: Praeger, 1974.
Ul'yanovskiy, R.A. "The Afghan Revolution at the Current Stage." *Voprosy istorii KPSS (Questions of History of the Communist Party of the Soviet Union)*, no. 4 (April 1982): 84–95, in JPRS 81313, July 1982.
———. *National Liberation.* Moscow: Progress Publishers, 1978.
———. *Present-Day Problems in Asia and Africa: Theory, Politics, Personalities.* Moscow: Progress Publishers, 1980.
———. "The 'Third World'—Problems of Socialist Orientation." *International Affairs* (Moscow), no. 9 (October 1971): 26–35.
Valenta, Jiri. "From Prague to Kabul: The Soviet Style of Invasion." *International Security* 5 (Fall 1980): 114–40.
———. "The Soviet Invasion of Afghanistan: The Difficulty in Knowing Where to Stop." *Orbis* 24 (Summer 1980): 201–18.
———. "Czechoslovakia and Afghanistan: Comparative Comments." *Studies in Comparative Communism* (Winter 1980): 332–43.
Vance, Cyrus. *Hard Choices: Critical Years in America's Foreign Policy.* New York: Simon and Schuster, 1983.
Vigor, Peter H. *Soviet Blitzkrieg Theory.* New York: St. Martin's Press, 1983.
———. *The Soviet View of War, Peace and Neutrality.* London: Routledge and Keegan Paul, 1975.
Volsky, D. "A Strategy Without A Future." *New Times* (Moscow), no. 33, August 1975, pp. 4–5.
Von Clausewitz, Karl. *On War.* Anatol Rapoport, ed. Baltimore, Maryland: Penguin, 1968.
Wade, Nicholas. "Afghanistan: The Politics of Tragicomedy." *Science*, May 1981, pp. 521–23.
Wafadar, K. "Afghanistan in 1981: The Struggle Intensifies." *Asian Survey* 22 (February 1982): 147–54.
Waltz, Kenneth. *Theory of International Politics.* Reading, Massachusetts: Addison-Wesley, 1979.
Warhurst, Geoffrey. "Afghanistan: A Dissenting Appraisal." *RUSI: Journal of the Royal United Services Institute for Defense Studies* (September 1980): 26–36.
Weinland, Robert. *An (The?) Explanation of the Soviet Invasion of Afghanistan*, CNA Memo. 81-0366.09. Alexandria, Virginia: Center for Naval Analysis, 1981.
Whitney, Craig R. "The View From the Kremlin." *New York Times Magazine*, April 20, 1980, pp. 30–33ff.

Wilber, Donald N. "Afghanistan: Independent and Encircled." *Foreign Affairs* 31 (April 1955): 486–94.
Wimbush, S. Enders and Alexiev, Alex. *The Ethnic Factor in the Soviet Armed Forces*, R–278771. Santa Monica, California: Rand, 1982.
———. *Soviet Central Asian Soldiers in Afghanistan,* Rand Research Note N–1634–NA. Santa Monica, California: Rand, 1981.
Wolpert, Stanley. *Roots of Confrontation in South Asia.* New York: Oxford University Press, 1982.
"World Communist Solidarity with the Afghan Revolution." *New Times*, no. 3, pp. 8–10.
Yurlov, V. "USSR-Afghanistan: Good Neighborly Relations." *International Affairs* (Moscow), no. 7 (July 1976): 137–8.
Zagladin, V. "Revolutionary Forces and Their Ideological and Political Unity." *International Affairs* (Moscow), no. 4 (April 1977): 65–70.
Zimmerman, William and Axelrod, Robert. "The 'Lessons' of Vietnam and Soviet Foreign Policy." *World Politics* 34 (October 1981): 1–24.

Selected Government Documents

Afghanistan

Government of Afghanistan. *Afghanistan's Foreign Trade, 1335 Through 1342* (March 1956–March 1964), 1965.
Political Department of the Armed Forces of the People's Democratic Republic of Afghanistan. *On the Saur (April) Revolution.* May 22, 1978.
People's Democratic Party of Afghanistan. *The Establishment of the Marxist Leninist Party of Afghanistan.* Unpublished mimeograph translation, July 1976.
———. *Constitution of the People's Democratic Party of the Working Class of Afghanistan,* June 1978.

Union of Soviet Socialist Republics

Communist International. *A Manifesto to the Peoples of the East,* 1920.
Current Soviet Policies: The Documentary Record of the 19th Party Congress and the Reorganization After Stalin's Death. New York: Praeger for the AAASS, 1953.
Documents and Resolutions: The 26th Congress of the Communist Party of the Soviet Union. Moscow: Novosti, 1981.
Treaty of Friendship, Good Neighborliness and Cooperation Between the Union of Soviet Socialist Republics and the Democratic Republic of Afghanistan. Reprinted in *Pravda,* December 6, 1978, p. 1.
USSR. *Appeal of the Council of People's Commissars to the Moslems of Russia and the East.* December 1917.

USSR. *Intelligence Estimate—Iran,* 1941. Unpublished mimeograph translation.
USSR. Ministry of Foreign Affairs and Ministry of Foreign Affairs of Afghanistan. *Sovetsko-Afghanskie Otnosheniia, 1919–1969 gg. (Soviet-Afghan Relations, 1919–69).* Moscow: Politizdat, 1971.
USSR. *Constitution (Fundamental Law) of the Union of Soviet Socialist Republics.* Moscow: Novosti Press, 1977.

United Kingdom.

House of Commons. Foreign Affairs Committee. *Afghanistan: The Soviet Invasion and Its Consequences for British Policy.* Session 1978–1979. July 1980.

United States of America: Legislative Branch

U.S. Congress. House Committee on Foreign Affairs. *An Assessment of the Afghanistan Sanctions: Implications for Trade and Diplomacy in the 1980's.* 97th Congress, 1st session, April 1981.
———. *East-West Relations in the Aftermath of the Soviet Invasion of Afghanistan.* Hearings before Subcommittee on Europe and the Middle East. 96th Congress, 2d Session, January 1980.
U.S. Congress. Joint Economic Committee (JEC). *Selected Papers Submitted to the JEC on the Soviet Economy in the 1980's.* Part 2, 97th Congress, 2d Session, December 1982.
U.S. Congress. Library of Congress, Congressional Research Service. *Afghanistan: Soviet Invasion and U.S. Response.* Issue Brief IB80006. Originated January 1980; updated February 1982.
U.S. Congress. Senate Committee on Foreign Relations. *Hearings on the Situation in Afghanistan.* 97th Congress, 2d session, March 1982.
U.S. Congress. Senate Committee on Banking, Housing and Urban Affairs. *Hearings on the Suspensions of United States Exports of High Technology and Grain to the Soviet Union.* 96th Congress, 2d session, August 1980.

United States of America: Executive Branch.

U.S. Arms Control and Disarmament Agency. *World Military Expenditures and Arms Transfers 1971–1980.* March 1983.
U.S. Central Intelligence Agency. *Communist Aid to Less Developed Countries of the Free World, 1977.* ER 78–10478U. November 1978.
U.S. Department of the Air Force. *Selected Soviet Military Writings, 1970–1975.* Washington, D.C.: U.S. Government Printing Office, 1977.
U.S. Department of the Army. *Area Handbook for Afghanistan.* Pamphlet 550–65, 4th ed. 1973.

U.S. Department of the Army. *Historical Study: Russian Combat Methods in World War II*. Pamphlet no. 20–230. November 1950, reprinted 1983.
U.S. Department of Defense, Joint Special Operations Command. *Special Operations: Military Lessons from Six Selected Case Studies*. Fall 1982.
U.S. Department of State. *Afghan Resistance and Soviet Occupation*. Special Report 118, December 1984.
Afghanistan. Background Notes Series, April 1983.
———. *Afghanistan: Eighteen Months of Occupation*, Special Report 87, August 1981.
———. *Afghanistan: Five Years of Occupation*. Special Report 120, December 1984.
———. *Afghanistan: Four Years of Occupation*. Special Report 112, December 1983.
———. *Afghanistan: Three Years of Occupation*. Special Report 106, December 1982.
———. *Afghanistan: Two Years of Occupation*, Special Report 91, December 1981.
———. *Afghanistan: A Year of Occupation*, Special Report 79, February 1981.
———. *Chemical Warfare in Southeast Asia and Afghanistan*, Special Report 98, and 104, March and November 1982.
———. *Further Comments . . . About Soviet Efforts to Alter Afghan Regime*. Cable 199533. August 1, 1979.
———. *Glossary of Soviet Military Terms*, 1982.
———. *Reports of the Use of Chemical Weapons in Afghanistan, Laos and Kampuchea*, Summer 1980.
———. *Soviet Dilemmas in Afghanistan*, Special Report 72, June 1980.
———. *Soviet Invasion of Afghanistan*. Special Report 70, April 1980.
———. *Tales of Afghanistan: Moscow Style*, Current Policy 143, March 1980.
———. Bureaus of Intelligence and Research, and Near East Affairs. *The Coup in Afghanistan*. April 27, 1978.
———. Bureau of Intelligence and Research. *Political Feuding in Afghanistan*. I and R Report 1387, June 1980.
———. Bureau of Near East Affairs. *The Afghan Coup*. April 28, 1978.
———. Bureau of Near East Affairs. *Long-Term Commitment to Afghanistan Economic Development Program*. March 1962.
———. Bureau of Near East Affairs. *Situation in Afghanistan*. April 30, 1978.
———. Bureau of Near East Affairs. *Soviet-Afghan Relations: Is Moscow's Patience Wearing Thin?* May 24, 1979.
———. Office of Intelligence and Research. *The Future of Soviet-Afghan Relations*. Intelligence Report no. 7528, May 1956.
U.S. Embassy. Kabul. *Afghan Communist Leader Becomes Ruler of Afghanistan*. Telegram 03372, April 30, 1978.
———. *Afghan Leadership Underscores Ties to USSR*. Cable 09163. November 16, 1978.
———. *Afghanistan's Khalqi Regime at 18 Months: Still In Power but Facing Long-term Instability*. Cable 8073, November 20, 1979.

---. *Amin Publicly Acknowledges That Soviet Support is Essential for Khalqis' Survival.* Cable 08117, November 21, 1979.
---. *Annual Policy Assessment 1977.* Telegram 00468, January 19, 1977.
---. *DRA Decisions Come to Light Respecting Taraki and Others.* Telegram 07428. October 11, 1979.
---. *History of Khalqi-Parchami Infighting Before the Afghan Revolution.* Airgram A–79, October 15, 1978.
---. *Meeting with President Amin.* Telegram 07726, October 28, 1979.
---. *Military Conflict in Kabul.* Telegram 03234, April 25, 1978.
---. *Policy Review: A U.S. Strategy for the '70's.* Airgram 71, June 26, 1971.
---. *President Amin's Desire for Better Relations.* Telegram 07645, October 2, 1979.
---. *A Second Underground Night Letter Blasts Prime Minister Amin for Creating Domestic Trouble* Telegram 06605, September 2, 1979.
---. *Signs Continue of Strained Relations Between President Hafizullah Amin and the Soviets.* Cable 07444, October 11, 1979.
---. *Tension Lessens in Kabul as President Amin Digests His Recent Political Gains.* Telegram 06936, September 17, 1979.
---. *USSR Recognizes New Regime in Kabul.* Telegram 03381, April 30, 1978.
U.S. Embassy. Moscow. *Churbanov and Paputin—Recent Gossip.* Cable 03195, January 25, 1980.
---. *USSR First Deputy Interior Minister (MVD) Paputin Dies—In Afghanistan?* Cable 00094, January 3, 1980.
U.S. Embassy. Teheran. *Military Conflict in Kabul.* Telegram 04062, April 30, 1978.
U.S. International Communications Agency. *Soviet Elites: World View and Perceptions of the United States,* R–18–81. September 1981.
U.S. National Security Council. *Expansion of Soviet Influence in Afghanistan and U.S. Countermeasures,* May 1956.
U.S. President. *State of the Union Address.* Reprinted in U.S. Department of State, Current Policy, 132 (January 1980).

Newspapers, Serials, and Miscellaneous Publications

Afghanistan Information Center Monthly Bulletin
American University Field Staff Reports
Christian Science Monitor
Current Digest of the Soviet Press (CDSP)
Daily Report—South Asia (FBIS)
Daily Report—Soviet Union (FBIS)
Izvestiia
Kabul Times
Kabul New Times

Kommunist
Komsomol pravda (Pravda of the Young Communist League)
Krasnaia zvezda (Red Star)
Les Nouvelles d'Afghanistan (News of Afghanistan) (Paris)
Literaturnaya gazeta (Literary Gazette)
New York Times
Newsweek
Pravda
Radio Liberty Research Bulletin
Review of the Soviet Ground Forces (U.S. Defense Intelligence Agency)
Soviet World Outlook
Time
U.S. News and World Report
Washington Post
Washington Times

Index

Note: Afghan and Central Asian names in this index have been alphabetized as if they were English language names. The spelling of Afghan and Central Asian names is the most-commonly found version, without reference to any single system of transliteration.

Adomeit, Hannes, 169
Afanasyev, Viktor, 157
Afghan Air Force, 11, 12, 49–52, 69, 71, 144, 146–47
Afghan Army, 49–50, 59–60, 65, 68–71, 77, 79, 85, 140, 144, 146. See also Anglo-Afghan War, Soviet Armed Forces, Basmachi
Afghan culture, 2–4
Afghan demography, 2
Afghan domestic politics, 2, 4; under the monarchy, 8, 11–13, 20, 23–24, 27–28; under the republic, 30, 33–35, 37–38. See also People's Democratic Republic of Afghanistan
Afghan economy, 1–2, 25, 40, 54–55, 70, 141–142, 153. See also Afghan-Soviet economic/aid relations
Afghan foreign policy: with Iran (Persia), 5–8, 25, 36–38, 57–58, 60, 154–155; with Pakistan, 18, 22–24, 27, 37–38, 100, 106–107, 156–158; with United Kingdom, 6–9, 156; with United States, 18–20, 56–59, 63n.44, 100, 156–159; with USSR (friendship treaties) 11, 12, 127, 129–130
Afghan geography, 1–3
Afghan resistance groups, 144–45, 150; foreign assistance to, 92–93, 145
Afghan-Soviet economic/aid relations, 21, 24, 26, 36, 40, 51, 54, 141–142, 146, 161 n.9
Ali, Sher, 6
Alim Khan, Amir Said, 9
Aliyev, Geidar A., 127
Amin, Hafizullah, 41, 48, 49, 53–54, 60–61, 65, 72, 78, 82, 100, 166, 171
Amstutz, Bruce, 70
Andropov, General Secretary Yuri V., 101, 109, 124, 158
Anglo-Afghan wars, 6–10, 14n.12
Anglo-Russian Convention (1907), 7
Angola, xiii, 35, 111, 129, 132, 171, 174
April 1978 coup. See Saur Revolution
Arab-Israeli dispute, 27
Arbatov, Georgiy, 101, 124, 132–33
Arg Palace, 49, 66, 79
Arnold, Anthony, 34, 51
Ataturk, Mustafa Kemal, 10, 11

Bacha Saqqao (Habibullah), 11
Baghdad Pact, 19
Bagram airbase, 71, 80, 151
Bakhtary, Ghulam Jilani, 35
Baluch(istan), 2, 151–152, 163 n.44, 45
Barialay, Mahmud, 55
Basmachi, 9–10, 12, 125, 136n.4, 175
Beg, Ibrahim, 10, 12
Bhutto, Zulfikar Ali, 36–38
Bialer, Seweryn, 110, 172
Blood, Archer, 74, 100

Bradsher, Henry S., 28, 39
Brezhnev, General Secretary Leonid I., 25, 34, 39, 41, 53, 55, 56, 66, 68, 72, 74, 101, 104, 124, 126, 131, 156–157
Brezhnev Doctrine, 108, 172
Brown, Harold, 57, 131
Brzezinski, Zbigniew, 57, 64n.56, 65, 129, 172
Bukhara, 5, 9–10
Bulganin, Chairman Nikolai A., 21, 22
Bush, George H.W., 57

Camp David Accords, 156
Carrington Plan, 156
Carter, President Jimmy, 88–89, 103
Carter Doctrine, 89
Castro, Fidel, 51, 86
Central Treaty Organization (CENTO), 20, 22, 127
Chaffetz, David, 51–52
Charkhi, Ghulam Nabi, 12
Chile, 35, 110, 130
Churbanov, Lieutenant General Yuri, 82
Clausewitz, General Karl von, 81–82
Committee of Afghan Communists Abroad, 43
Communist Party of India (CPI), 39, 41
Congress of the Peoples of the East, 8
Crawford, William R., 61
Cuba, 38, 115
Czechoslovakia, 23, 25; invasion of, 77, 81, 99, 102, 113, 134, 159, 167

Daoud, Mohammed, 12, 19, 23, 25–27; as ruler of Afghanistan, 33, 37–41, 43, 48, 49, 50, 53, 56–57
Deception, military. *See* Maskirovka
Decrees of the PDRA, 54–56
Denmark, 7
Dost, Foreign Minister Shah Mohammed, 83
Dobrynin, Ambassador Anatoliy, 73, 82
Dubs, Ambassador Adolph ("Spike"), 58–59, 63n.44
Dunbar, Charles, 158
Dunn, Keith, 104
Dupree, Louis, 2, 17, 43, 52

Durand Line, 7

Egypt, 35, 38, 92, 135, 171
Eliot, Ambassador Theodore L. Jr., 51, 61n.2
Enver Pasha, 10
Ethiopia, xiii, 110–111, 129, 171, 174

Faqir, Faqir Mohammed, 72
Finland, 25
Finley, David D., 169–170
Friendship treaties. *See* Afghan foreign policy
Fromkin, David, 5

Garrity, Patrick, 59
Gandhi, Prime Minister Indira, 154
Garthoff, Raymond, xiv
Gentlemen's Agreement (1873), 7
Germany, 11, 13
Gorchakov, Prince Alexandre M., 4–5, 7
Gorshkov, Admiral of the Fleet Sergei, 115
"Great game," 5, 7, 14n.11
Great October Revolution (1917), 28, 53
Grechko, Marshal Andrei A., 26, 115
Gromyko, Foreign Minister Andrei A., 53, 56, 66, 101, 124, 131–132
Guderian, General Heinz, 170
Gul Wafadar, Pacha, 35
Gulabzoy, Said Mohammed, 34, 66

Habibullah Khan, Amir, 7–8
Herat massacre, 59–60

Imperial Russia. *See* Soviet Union
Inayatullah, 11
India, 7–9, 18, 27, 36, 38, 85, 91, 154
Indo-Pakistani War, 27
Invasion of Afghanistan, xiii, 71, 77–82, 100; international reaction: 85–91, 152–153, 156–160
Iran (Persia), 7–8, 36, 38–39, 47, 56–57, 77, 85, 91, 103, 105–106, 125–127, 134
Iraq, 57, 86
Ireland, unrest in (1919), 9

Islam, 4, 8–9; in USSR, 14n.20, 80–81, 125–127. *See also* Soviet motives for invasion; Soviet Muslims
Istalif, 146

Jervis, Robert, 167

Kampuchea (Cambodia), 36, 110, 130
Kaplan, Stephen S., 169–170
Karmal, Babrak, 28, 54, 55, 153, 171; as ruler in Afghanistan, 78, 81, 83–85, 100, 139–144, 153, 166
Kennan, George, 101
Kerala massacre, 60
Keshtmand, Prime Minister Sultan Ali, 55, 68, 78, 85, 140, 153
Khalq faction of the PDPA: under the constitutional monarchy, 28–29; under the PDRA, 49–52, 54–56, 61, 62n.3, 65–66, 70, 83–85, 140; under the republic, 38, 39, 41–43, 45n.35, 48
Khiva, 6, 9
Khost, 11
Khrushchev, Chairman Nikita S., 21, 22, 25
Khyber, Mir Akbar, 48
Kissinger, Secretary of State Henry A., 38, 107
Kobysh, Vitaliy, 152
Kokand, 6
Korean War, 17
Kosygin, Premier Alexei N., 26, 34, 68, 101, 124
Kulish, V.M., 113–115
Kunar Valley, 56, 85

Legvold, Robert, xiii, xiv, 101
Lenin, Vladimir I., 9, 14n.20, 126
Libya, 85
Loya Jirga, 11, 23, 141

Macnaghten, Sir William, 6
Maiwandwal, Prime Minister Mohammed Hashim, 34
Majrooh, Sayed, 149
Manifesto to the Peoples of the East, 8, 14n.20
Maskirovka (deception), 72, 79–80
Massoud, Ahmed Shah, 150–151
May, Ernest R., 167

May 14th Proposals, 93
Mazar-i-Sharif, 12
Mazdooryar, Sher Jan, 34, 66
Miraki, Lieutenant General G.S., 107–108
Mohammed, Amir Dost, 6
Mohammed Khan, Prime Minister Shah, 18
Mohtat, Abdul Hamid, 35
Mondale, Vice President Walter, 131
Mongolia, 115
Monks, Alfred, 101
Moslem Brotherhood, 56
Murray, Wallace Smith, 18
Mustafa, Ghulam, 72

Nabi, Ghulam. *See* Charkhi, Ghulam Nabi
Nadir Khan, Mohammed, 10, 12–13, 34
Nadir Shah. *See* Nadir Khan
Naim Khan, Mohammed, 43, 49
National Revolutionary Party, 35
Nazi-Soviet Non-Aggression Pact, 13, 105
Newell, Nancy, 23
Newell, Richard, 23
Newsom, David D., 58
Nicaragua, 110
"Night Letters," 61
North Atlantic Treaty Organization (NATO), 91, 128, 132, 174

Ogarkov, Marshal Nikolai V., 83, 114
Olcott, Martha B., 125

Pahlavi, Reza (Shah of Iran), 25, 38, 57–58
Pakistan, 131, 134; relations with Afghanistan, 18, 22–24, 27, 37–38, 100, 106–107, 156–158; relations with USSR, 22, 27, 36, 38, 91, 153, 157–160; relations with United States, 19–20, 92, 134, 153–154, 160. See also Refugees; Peace process
Paktia Province, 69, 85
Panjdeh Incident, 7
Paputin, Lieutenant General Viktor S., 66, 72–73, 82
Parcham faction of the PDPA: under Daoud (1973–78), 33–35, 38–39, 41–43, 45n.35, 48; under

Karmal (1980–), 83–85, 140; under the monarchy, 28–29; under Taraki and Amin, 49–52, 54–56, 58, 62n.3, 65, 70, 123
Paris Peace Conference (1919), 8
Pavlovskiy, General Ivan G., 66, 77, 83, 103
Pazhwak, Nehmatullah, 35
Peace Corps, 59
Peace process (post-1980), 93, 139, 156–158
Penkovskiy, Colonel Oleg, 23
People's Democratic Party of Afghanistan (PDPA). *See* Khalq; Parcham; People's Democratic Republic of Afghanistan
People's Democratic Republic of Afghanistan (PDRA): Amin regime, 67–74, 78; defections from PDRA, 85; Karmal regime, 77–78, 83–85, 139–144; Taraki regime, 51–56, 58–61, 65–66. *See also* Saur Revolution; Invasion of Afghanistan
People's Republic of China, 35, 38, 56, 87, 116–117, 128, 130–133. *See also* Invasion of Afghanistan; Soviet foreign policy
People's Republic of Khorezm, 9
Perez de Cuellar, Secretary General Javier, 157
Persia. *See* Iran
Petrov, General Vasiliy I., 83, 168, 175n.4
Pipes, Richard, xiv, 10
Podgorny, Chairman Nikolai S., 26, 34
Ponomarev, Boris N., 110
Poullada, Leon, 18
Pushtunistan, 7, 13, 17–18, 20–22, 23, 27, 36, 38
Pushtuns, 2, 7, 28, 80
Pushtunwali, 4
Puzanov, Ambassador Alexander M., 66, 68, 101

Qader, General Abdul, 34, 50, 55, 68, 78, 140
Qom (Iran), 47

Rafie, Mohammed, 140
Rahman, Abdur (son of Hafizullah Amin), 49
Rahman Khan, Amir Abdur, 4, 6

Rapid Deployment Force, 132
Refugees from Afghanistan, 85, 142–144, 159–160
Republican Guard, 49
Revolution of 1905, 7
Rostovskii, S.N., 20–21
Rubinstein, Alvin Z., 63n.44
Russo-Japanese War, 7

Safronchuk, Vasiliy S., 60, 68
Salang Tunnel, 2, 69
SALT II Treaty, 89, 132–133
Sarwari, Assadullah, 84–85
Saudi Arabia, 56, 92
Saunders, Harold, 57
Saur Revolution (April 1978 coup), 38, 47–52
Selassie, Emperor Haile, 35
Seven Year Plan, 40
Shah Shura, 6
Shindand airbase, 50, 104, 144
Shulman, Ambassador Marshall, 100
Sino-Vietnamese War, 131
Socialist orientation in Third World, 47, 53, 99, 109–111, 166
Sokolov, Marshal Sergei L., 151
Sokolovskiy, Marshal V.D., 22–23, 113–114
Somalia, 35, 135, 173
Southeast Asia Treaty Organization (SEATO), 20, 127
Soviet armed forces in Afghanistan: advisers/military assistance, 11, 23, 26, 36, 40, 52, 59–60, 66, 71; casualties, 90, 147, 150; chemical weapons, 147–148; equipment, 79, 90, 144, 146–147, 150–151, 168; major battles, 150–151, 161n.16; reservists, 71, 79–81, 94n.6; size/formations, 71, 79, 144, 151; spetsnaz, airborne troops, 78, 81, 144; strategy and deployments, 79–80, 90, 104–105, 139, 144–145, 149, 151, 169; tactics, performance, and troop behavior, xiii, 145–146, 149–151, 153; training, 147–149, 168, 175n.4
Soviet motives for invasion, xiii; annexation, 107–108; assessment of situation (1979), 69–71; commitment to Afghan government, 129–131; explanations by USSR, 99–100;

politico-military theory in USSR, 108–111, 113–118; security concerns, 123–133, 159; Western explanations of motives, 101–107
Soviet muslims, 79–81, 94n.6, 125–127
Soviet/Russian foreign policy, xiii, 1, 101–102, 107, 119n.5, 135, 169–172; with India, 7, 27, 36, 154; with Iran, 38, 126–129, 154–155, 157; with Pakistan, 22, 27, 36, 38, 91, 128, 153, 157–160; with PRC, 27, 35–36, 130–131, 134; with United States, 35, 129–133, 159–160, 172. *See also* Invasion of Afghanistan; Soviet armed forces; Soviet motives for invasion
Soviet/Russian military capabilities, 104–105, 111–112
Special Unit Palace Guard, 33
Stalin, Premier Josif V., 20, 101
Sullivan, Ambassador William, 57
Suslov, Mikhail, 101, 124

Tabeyev, Ambassador Fikryat A., 72
Tabriz (Iran), 47
Tajiks, 2, 80
Talizin, Nikolai V., 72
Taraki, Nur Mohammed, 12, 28, 34, 41, 43, 48–49, 53–54, 60, 66, 67. *See also* People's Democratic Republic of Afghanistan; Khalq
Taroon, Sayed Daoud, 59, 67
Teng Hsiao-ping, 130
Tikhonov, Premier Nikolai A., 102
Treaty of Gandamak, 6
Triska, Jan F., 169–170
Turkey, 6, 128
Twenty-fifth Party Congress (USSR), 110, 116
Twenty-sixth Party Congress (USSR), 83, 85, 126, 154
Twenty-third Party Congress (USSR), 25
Two-camp theory, 17, 30n.12

Ul'yanovskiy, Rostislav A., 60–61, 70, 78
Ulam, Adam, 20
United Nations, 19, 56, 124, 155. *See also* Peace process
U.S. Defense Intelligence Agency, 88
U.S. Department of Agriculture, 88–89
U.S. foreign policy: with Afghanistan, 18–20, 56–59, 63n.44, 100, 156–159; with Pakistan, 19–20, 92, 134, 153–154, 160; with USSR, 35, 87–89, 129–133, 159–160, 172. *See also* Dubs, Adolph; Invasion of Afghanistan
U.S. National Security Council, 20. *See also* Brzezinski, Zbigniew
USSR Academy of Sciences Institute for the Study of the USA and Canada, 101
Uzbeks, 2, 80

Valenta, Jiri, 101
Vance, Secretary of State Cyrus R., 57–58, 73
Vietnam, 110, 115, 116, 130

Wali, Major General Abdul, 34
Wali, Shah, 68, 72, 100
Ward, Angus, 19
Watanjar, Mohammed Aslam, 34, 60, 66
Watson, Ambassador Thomas, 73
Weisner, Admiral Maurice, 38
World War I, 7–8
World War II, 13

Yaqub Khan, Amir, 6
Yepishev, General Alexei A., 60, 77, 101
Young Bukharans, 9
Yugoslavia, 38, 86
Yusif-Zade, Ziya M., 126

Zahir Shah, King Mohammed, 13, 24, 26, 33, 53
Zamyatin, Leonid, 91
Zhou Enlai, 38
Zhukov, E., 21
Zia-ul-Haq, Mohammed, 38, 89, 157–158
Zinoviev, Gregoriy, 9

About the Author

Joseph J. Collins is a major in the U.S. Army who has commanded infantry units in West Germany and South Korea and has served as an associate professor of international studies, Department of Social Sciences, U.S. Military Academy. He holds two master's degrees and a doctorate from Columbia University and is a graduate of the U.S. Army Command and General Staff College. He has contributed to *American National Security: Policy and Process* (Johns Hopkins) and to *The Lessons of Recent Wars in the Third World, Volume I: Approaches and Case Studies* (Lexington Books). His articles on Soviet policy towards Afghanistan have appeared in the *Naval War College Review; Parameters: The Journal of the U.S. Army War College; Comparative Strategy; Conflict Quarterly;* and *Military Review*. Major Collins is currently serving as a staff officer in the Strategic Plans and Policy Division of the Army's Office of the Deputy Chief of Staff for Operations and Plans in the Pentagon.